Faye Levy

SENSATIONAL
PASTA

DEDICATION: For my mother, Pauline Kahn Luria

ACKNOWLEDGEMENTS: I would like to express my gratitude to the friendly cooks in France and Italy who invited me into their kitchens and shared their passion for their métier with me. I owe a million thanks to the great chefs who taught me the art of fine cooking, especially my mentor, chef par excellence Fernand Chambrette of Paris. For an inspiring introduction to Oriental cuisine, I am grateful to two gifted teachers: Chinese cooking authority Nina Simonds of Boston, and Thai chef Somchit Singchalee of Bangkok.

I was fortunate to have dedicated assistants—Annie Horenn, Patsy Allen, and Leona Fitzgerald—testing and retesting the recipes with me, and I sincerely appreciate their help.

I am deeply grateful to Veronica Durie, a world-class cookbook editor, not only for her fine editing but also for her patience, concern for high quality and for coordinating the whole project and making sure everything came together in the best possible way.

Special thanks to Elaine Woodard, Jeanette Egan, Linda Johns, Nick Clemente, John Beach, Leslie Sinclair, Jan Thiesen, Rick Bailey, Michael Taylor and to the other first-rate professionals at HPBooks and Price Stern Sloan for their important contributions to the book and their enthusiastic support.

I love the imaginative work of photographers Tommy Miyasaki, Dennis Skinner and David Wong of deGennaro Associates, food stylist Mable Hoffman, and assistant food stylist Annie Horenn. I truly enjoyed working with them.

Thanks to Gary Ciminello of De Cio Pasta Primo in Cave Creek, Arizona, for coming to my home bearing delicious flavored pasta and for providing me with fascinating information. Thanks also to Emmanuel Roux of Gaston Dupré pasta in Tampa, Florida, to JoEllen Helmlinger of The President's Silver Award pasta in Lowell, Massachusetts and to Elena Quistini of European Noodles in North York, Ontario, Canada for the samples of their excellent pastas.

And to my husband Yakir, who is practically the co-author of this book, thanks for everything.

ANOTHER BEST SELLING
VOLUME FROM HPBOOKS
HPBooks
A division of Price Stern Sloan, Inc.
360 North La Cienega Boulevard
Los Angeles, California 90048

© 1989 HPBooks
Printed in U.S.A.
10 9 8 7 6 5 4 3 2

PHOTOGRAPHY: deGennaro Associates
FOOD STYLING: Mable Hoffman
COVER PHOTO: Lemon Fettuccine with Asparagus, Smoked Salmon & Herb Butter, page 47.

Library of Congress Cataloging-in-Publication Data

Levy, Faye.
    Sensational pasta / by Faye Levy.
        p.   cm.
    Includes index.
    ISBN 0-89586-631-5
    1. Cookery (Pasta)   I. Title.
TX809.M17L48   1989
641.8'22—dc19

89-1662
CIP

CONTENTS

PASTA WITH POULTRY 82

PASTA WITH CHICKEN 84 * Tomato Noodles with Chicken & 40 Cloves of Garlic * Pasta Paella * Noodles with Mustard-Grilled Chicken & Gruyère Cheese * Spaghetti with Chicken & Zucchini in Curry Cream * Tri-Colored Pasta-Pepper Medley with Chicken * Pasta Spirals with Chicken Livers & Onions * Vermicelli with Chicken in Peanut Sauce * Chicken with Raspberries, Fettuccine & Raspberry Butter Sauce * Fusilli with Citrus-Barbecued Chicken * Pasta with Creamy Tomato Sauce, Chicken & Provençal Herbs * Butter-Baked Chicken with Pasta & Leeks

PASTA WITH OTHER POULTRY 94 * Spicy Southwestern Turkey with Cocoa Pasta * Chili Pasta with Smoked Turkey * Vermicelli with Turkey, Tomatoes & Tarragon * Tortellini with Walnut Sauce, Smoked Turkey & Spinach * Stuffed Cornish Hens with Orzo, Raisins & Pecans

PASTA WITH MEAT 100

PASTA WITH BEEF 102 * Pasta Shells with Tunisian Beef & Artichoke Sauce * Chili-Topped Spaghetti * Aromatic Macaroni & Beef Stew with Fennel, Marjoram & Mint * Linguine with Steak & Double-Mushroom Madeira Sauce * Pasta with Bolognese Sauce & Sautéed Squash * Fettuccine with Old-Fashioned Italian Meat Sauce

PASTA WITH VEAL 108 * Veal with Couscous & Dill * Vermicelli with Veal & Lemon Sauce * Ligurian Veal with Zucchini & Fusilli * Ruffled Pasta with Veal, Saffron & Ginger * Green & White Fettuccine with Veal, Spinach & Morel Sauce * Veal Dijonnaise with Green Peppercorns & Tri-Colored Noodles

PASTA WITH OTHER MEATS 114 * Linguine with Lamb, Pine Nuts & Pistachios * Rigatoni with Lamb & Peas * Pasta Corkscrews with Bacon, Avocado & Tomato * Pasta Shells with Mortadella, Dill Butter & Vegetables * Lazy-Day Pasta with Smoked Sausage, Tomato Sauce & Corn

STUFFED & BAKED PASTA 118

STUFFED PASTA 121 * Basic Ravioli * Fillings for Ravioli * Herb Butter * Easy Spinach-Filled Ravioli Made with Won-Ton Wrappers * Shrimp & Swiss-Chard Ravioli with Basil Butter Sauce * Ravioli with Mushroom Sauce & Chives * Ravioli with Sun-Dried Tomato Cream Sauce * Tortellini with Spicy Meat Filling * Chili Tortelloni with Cheese Filling * Eggplant & Feta-Filled Cannelloni * Creamy Seafood Cannelloni

BAKED PASTA 134 * Macaroni Moussaka * Layered Spinach, Pasta & Parmesan Soufflé * Pasta Gratin with Porcini Mushrooms * Pasta "Cassoulet" * Lasagne with Rich Meat Sauce & Fontina Cheese * Creamy Macaroni with Four Cheeses * Mediterranean Vegetable Lasagne * Noodle Kugel with Sautéed Mushrooms * Pasta & Cheese Timbales with Roasted-Pepper Sauce

Faye Levy

In developing recipes for this book, Faye Levy has been able to draw on her culinary experiences in three continents.

She was born and brought up in Washington, D.C., then went to Israel to attend university where she graduated with honors in sociology and anthropology. It was only after her marriage that Faye decided that she should learn to cook—up until then she knew nothing about the art, let

alone the basics required to sustain a husband! From an eager beginning using the one cookbook in the university library, Faye discovered a fascinating new world. Applying the same enthusiastic dedication to this interest as she had so successfully to her academic studies, Faye soon had a job as assistant to Ruth Sirkis, Israel's leading cooking expert.

It was only natural that Faye's quest for more knowledge should lead her to France. Once there, she spent five years at the famous Parisian cooking school, La Varenne, first earning her Grand Diplôme, then working as head of the editorial department. This position involved revising and adding to the school's vast recipe collection and overseeing several award-winning publishing projects.

Since her return to the United States, Faye's reputation has soared. As a regular contributor to *Gourmet,* Faye has been praised by the food editor of that magazine as "one of the finest cooks in the country." Her *Bon Appétit* column, "The Basics," which she wrote for six years, is a comprehensive and concise cooking course and reflects Faye's talent as a teacher. Faye writes frequently for newspapers across the country, including the *Washington Post,* the *Chicago Tribune,* the *Boston Globe,* the *New York Post,* the *Philadelphia Inquirer,* the *San Francisco Chronicle* and the *Los Angeles Herald Examiner.*

Faye scored a culinary coup in 1986 when two of her books won prestigious Tastemaker awards, the "Oscars" for cookbooks, and she became the only author in the history of the awards to have won top prizes for two books in a single year. *Chocolate Sensations* was voted the

Best Dessert and Baking Book of the year by the International Association of Cooking Professionals/Seagram Awards; and *Classic Cooking Techniques* won as the Best General Cookbook. A year later, her *Fresh From France: Vegetable Creations* also won an IACP/Seagram award and was chosen by *Publishers Weekly,* the book-trade bible, for their honor list of "The Best Books of the Year."

In the international culinary scene, Faye's achievements have been outstanding. She is the first American to have written a cookbook on French cooking for the French. Co-authored by Chef Fernand Chambrette, *La Cuisine du Poisson* was published in Paris by Flammarion, the most distinguished cookbook publisher in France. Faye is the first woman to be included in Flammarion's cookbook series, "Les Grands Chefs"; among other great cooks to be recognized are Escoffier, Bocuse and Lenôtre. Three cookbooks that Faye wrote in Hebrew were published in Israel where she is also the monthly culinary columnist of the country's foremost women's magazine.

Faye works with her husband and close associate, Yakir, amid the cookbook-lined walls of their Santa Monica, California, residence. Whenever they do manage to break away from the stove and word processor, they relax by trying out new restaurants in the Los Angeles area or, if time permits, Europe and the Orient! Traveling and food are their twin passions and the delicious results of both are presented here for your enjoyment in this fabulous collection of pasta recipes.

Other Books by Faye Levy:
Faye Levy's Chocolate Sensations
Fresh from France: Vegetable Creations
Classic Cooking Techniques
La Cuisine du Poisson (in French, with Fernand Chambrette)
French Cooking Without Meat (in Hebrew)
French Desserts (in Hebrew)
French Cakes, Pastries and Cookies (in Hebrew)
The La Varenne Tour Book

INTRODUCTION

There is an explosion of creativity among pasta producers. We see more colors of pasta than anyone even dreamed of several years ago—purple pasta, black pasta, even confetti pasta, to name a few. There are many new flavored pastas—Cajun, garlic, lemon, smoked salmon, carrot-thyme, and tomato-basil-red pepper, for example. More pasta shapes, such as wheels, butterflies and even little radiators, are available than before. A variety of fresh stuffed pastas—tortellini, tortelloni, ravioli and agnolotti—with numerous fillings can now be found easily at the market.

A mere glance at restaurant menus, take-out displays, covers of the cooking magazines and cooking-school brochures will tell that pasta has become one of America's favorite foods. All over the country cooks are striving to present exciting, original pasta dishes.

There are good reasons for this popularity. Pasta possesses the qualities that make it the perfect modern food. It cooks very quickly. It is economical. And it is being recommended as a

Linguine with Shrimp Scampi & Broccoli, page 78

staple more and more by nutritionists as Americans move from a high-protein to a higher-carbohydrate diet. Most important, pasta is delicious with every other ingredient, from carrots to caviar.

Perhaps the most versatile of all foods, pasta is wonderful with seafood, meats and vegetables. It can be seasoned with an endless variety of flavorings, from French and Italian cheeses to nuts to fresh herbs and even to unusual spice mixtures like those of India and the American Southwest. Rich sauces are fabulous with pasta, but pasta dishes can be low in calories as well.

Pasta has been my favorite food for as long as I can remember. When I was growing up in Washington, D.C., whenever my mother asked what I would like for supper, the answer was macaroni and cheese. As a young adult, I moved to the Middle East and discovered new flavors and a multitude of pasta dishes. For 12 years I lived in countries bordering the Mediterranean and spent most of this time studying the cooking of the region. I also traveled extensively in Italy, France and much of Europe, and whenever I came across an interesting pasta dish on a menu, I ordered it. Later I visited the Orient and was intrigued by the exciting pasta dishes I found because they varied greatly from those I had tasted in Chinese, Thai, Vietnamese and other Oriental restaurants in the West.

Because of my background, I have taken a broad international approach to pasta, rather than sticking only to classic Italian recipes. Of course, fine Italian-style pasta is well represented, but so is pasta from a variety of cuisines, from Eastern European to Oriental, as well as creative American and exquisite contemporary French pasta dishes.

When I returned to the United States and moved to California, I looked for original ideas for my cooking classes. I had just arrived from France where I had noticed a new focus on preparing innovative pasta dishes. I began to teach French pasta classes and my students were most enthusiastic about them. Later these teaching recipes were the basis for an article I wrote for *Gourmet* magazine on French pasta dishes which became the cover story of the magazine. My French favorites are included here.

Recipes in this book range from the fastest and easiest ones in which a flavored oil or butter is added to pasta, to pastas tossed with quick sautés of meats and vegetables, to more elaborate layered pastas with sauces.

I have used as many types of ingredients as possible to give a wide array of flavors. The flavorings in my recipes are primarily fresh, although I have suggested packaged substitutes for ingredients that are not always available or in season or that are somewhat time-consuming to prepare.

Pasta is delicious with a generous amount of oil or butter. Many of us are used to this richness from dining at good restaurants, and of course when we eat out we do not actually see how much fat went into our food. Because we often prefer not to use large amounts of butter and oil at home, I have given a range when possible.

Although I have included instructions for making homemade pasta in many flavors, the focus of this book is on how to *use* pasta, whether homemade or fine-quality purchased, whether fresh or dried, to make delectable, enticing dishes. Many of the recipes give alternatives to the suggested shape, and sometimes flavor, of pasta. Since most people have busy schedules, I have included information on what part of a dish can be prepared ahead and how to reheat it.

Each recipe has its own sauce or topping and so the only sauces that are referred to occasionally are the tomato sauces in the Basics chapter.

HOW TO BUY PASTA

Pasta is a general term for all sorts of noodles, spaghetti and other shapes made from a stiff flour-and-water or flour-and-egg dough. Even though it consists of such basic, simple ingredients, there are differences among brands.

Many people insist that pasta imported from Italy is the best, and it is generally of high quality, but I have found domestic brands that are also delicious, some of which feature creative new types of pasta. Once in a while you might come across pasta that falls apart in the cooking water; if that happens, you know which brand to avoid.

Nearly all Western-style dried pasta, whether made in Italy or America, uses durum, or hard-wheat, semolina—it gives the pasta a good flavor and texture and a light-golden color. Most dried pasta, except for egg noodles, used to be made of semolina and water but now there is also egg spaghetti, egg linguine and other pasta shapes of semolina and egg dough.

In America even much of the fresh pasta is made of semolina, although in Italy it is usually made of flour. Fresh pasta used to be shaped mainly as fettuccine or noodles, but now spaghetti, linguine and angel-hair and even some of the more complex shapes like spirals and wheels are available fresh.

Oriental pastas make use of wheat flour and other types of flour rather than semolina and the resulting pasta is quite different. See Exotic Pasta, page 144.

Generally, cooks allow about 2 ounces dried pasta as a side dish, 2 to 3 ounces as a first course and about 4 ounces as a main course, with slightly larger amounts of fresh pasta. But this depends entirely on what other ingredients are combined with the pasta and on the rest of the menu.

GLOSSARY OF COMMON PASTA SHAPES

A wide variety of pasta shapes is available, although the selection differs from one market to another. If you can't find a pasta shape specified in a recipe, use this glossary to choose another one of a similar type. Not all manufacturers use the same name for the same shape of pasta, and sizes often vary as well, but usually you can see the pasta in its package to determine what it is. More and more shapes are being made both dried and fresh, and in an increasing variety of flavors.

SPAGHETTIS OR STRING SHAPES

capelli d'angelo or capellini: angel-hair pasta, the thinnest spaghetti

fedelini: very thin spaghetti, similar to vermicelli or can be slightly thinner

fideos: thin Spanish pasta, resembles vermicelli but is coiled

spaghetti: long, thin cylindrical pasta

spaghettini: thin spaghetti

vermicelli: very thin spaghetti, slightly thinner than spaghettini

FLAT AND RIBBON SHAPES

These are generally referred to as "noodles" and are often made with a pasta dough that contains egg.

fettucce: wide noodles, about ½ inch wide

fettuccelle: narrow fettuccine

fettuccine: thin noodles, ⅛ to ¼ inch wide; sold both as straight rods and loosely coiled.

lasagne: long, broad noodles, 2 to 3 inches wide

linguine: very narrow, flat, straight pasta or "flat spaghetti," ⅛ inch wide or less

mafalda, mafalde, mezza lasagne or lasagnette: wide, ripple-edged noodles

noodles: vary greatly in width, from under 1/16 to over 1 inch wide. Fettuccine are the equivalent of medium noodles. Noodles also come as extra-fine, fine and wide but how these categories are used depends on the manufacturer.

pappardelle: wide noodles, often cut with a fluted pastry wheel to give them a crinkled edge

tagliatelle: medium-wide noodles; sometimes used interchangeably with fettuccine, sometimes wider

tagliolini or tagliarini: very fine, thin noodles

TUBULAR OR HOLLOW SHAPES

Although we often think of "macaroni" as elbow-shaped, the word is used to refer to a whole family of hollow pasta of varying sizes and thicknesses. Many are labeled "rigati," ribbed or grooved.

bucatini: long, straight macaroni or hollow spaghetti

cannaroni: wide tubes; also called *zitoni*

cavatappi: spiral macaroni

ditali: small, short macaroni or "thimbles"

ditalini: smaller ditali

elbow macaroni: comes in several sizes, small for pasta and soup, medium for casseroles

maccheroni: Italian spelling for macaroni

penne: diagonal- or slant-cut or quill-shaped macaroni, also called *mostaccioli;* these are medium pasta tubes, about 2 inches long

perciatelle: similar to bucatini

rigatoni: large, grooved macaroni

tubetti: little tubes

ziti: large, straight or slightly curved tubes; they can be very long, or cut in straight pieces, in which case they are sometimes labeled *ziti tagliati*

1. Cavatelli/gnocchetti, 2. Gnocchi, 3. Fusilli, 4. Gemelli, 5. Orecchiette, 6. Angel hair, 7. Spinach fettuccine, 8. Egg fettuccine, 9. Canneloni, 10. Beet tagliarini, 11. Artichoke tagliarini, 12. Rigatoni, 13. Cavatappi, 14. Rotelle, 15. Ziti, 16. Bow ties, 17. Whole-wheat, spinach and egg lasagne, 18. Bucatini, 19. Marfalda, 20. Pappardelle, 21. Tomato-basil linguine, 22. Spinach linguine

FANCY SHAPES

cavatelli: small, narrow, ripple-edged shells

conchiglie: seashells; sometimes called *maruzze.* Shells are also available in jumbo size for stuffing. Shells can be grooved or plain.

conchigliette: tiny shells

farfalle: bow ties or butterflies

farfalline: small butterflies

fusilli: corkscrews or spiral-shaped pasta

gemelli: "twins"; pasta twists that look like 2 pieces of spaghetti twisted together.

gnocchi: shells, similar to cavatelli

orecchiette: "little ears"; resemble hats or discs

orzo: rice-shaped pasta; sometimes called "barley" pasta

radiatore: little radiators

riso: rice-shaped pasta, like orzo

rotelle: wheel-shaped pasta, or corkscrews or spirals

rotini: spirals

ruote: wheels

semi de melone: pasta shaped like melon seeds

tripolini: small, rounded bow ties

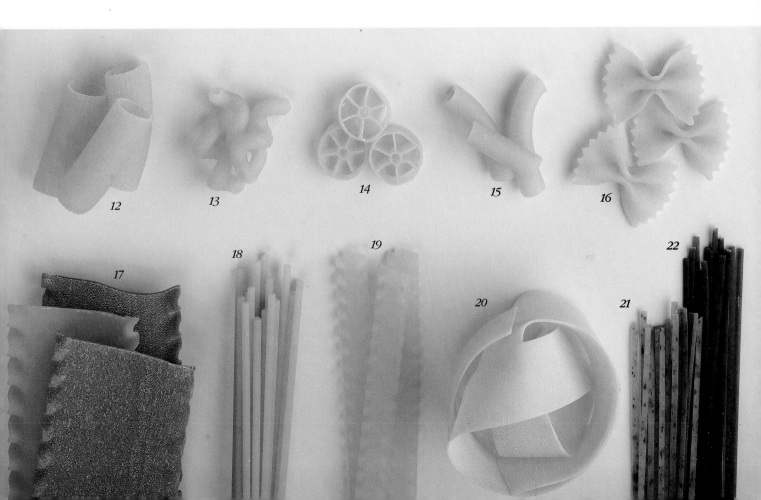

FLAVORED PASTA

Cooks and manufacturers have come up with numerous new pasta flavors and colors in recent years. From black pasta made with squid ink or olives to seaweed pasta to jalapeño pasta, there is no end in sight. In both fresh and dried forms, flavored pastas are much more popular in America than anywhere else and are available in specialty shops and increasingly in supermarkets.

Of course, not all flavored pasta is new—green pasta made with spinach or other leafy greens is traditional and tomato pasta has been around for a long time too.

I have included recipes that use flavored pastas and instructions for making them at home. You will no doubt discover other new flavors at the market. All can be tossed simply with olive oil or butter so the taste of the pasta comes through, or with a light tomato sauce. Try substituting flavored pasta for plain pasta in your favorite recipes—you will have new presentations with no extra work. (See also the Guide to Using Flavored Pastas, page 183.)

Do not expect the flavors in these pastas to be strong, however. Vegetables are generally added only for color. Certain herbs add some taste but it is mainly spices that give flavor to pasta. For this reason some companies are producing combination-flavor pastas, often using a vegetable for color and herbs or spices for taste. The result has been such pastas as carrot-ginger, tomato-basil-garlic and spinach-nutmeg.

SAUCES

Pasta loves sauces. It is equally at home with classic brown sauces, rich cream sauces, fragrant tomato sauces, and modern French butter sauces, as well as with pestos, dressings and seasoned butters. A wide range of flavorings complement pasta sauces, from delicate herbs such as dill to spicy curries to Chinese-style combinations of soy sauce and sesame oil. Sautéed or toasted nuts of all types are especially good with pasta because their crunchiness and rich taste provide a marvelous contrast of texture. Diced vegetables provide moistness, lightness and color. With pasta providing the background, the number of creations is limited only by the cook's imagination.

Sauces should be very well seasoned for matching with pasta. They may appear too spicy or sharp when tasted on their own, but taste just right when mixed with the pasta. For example, the sauce for Quick & Zesty Macaroni with Garlic, Olives & Capers, page 43, seems quite strong flavored when tasted alone, but is delicious with the pasta.

On the other hand, a sauce may taste perfect on its own but, after being mixed with pasta, will seem bland. This is why it is essential to taste again after tossing the pasta with the sauce. Freshly ground black or white pepper added at the last minute or at the table gives the pasta a pleasant zip.

Pasta should be tossed with just enough sauce to coat and moisten it—there should not be a puddle of sauce at the bottom of the bowl or platter. Whenever possible, it is best to serve a little of the sauce on the side, especially with strong-flavored sauces.

In some dishes pasta is tossed with butter or olive oil before a sauce is added, even if the sauce already contains some butter or oil. The reason is that unheated butter or fine olive oil gives the best, most natural taste for enriching the pasta.

Tossing the pasta with the sauce is usually the best procedure, not only because the pasta is flavored more evenly but also because the sauce prevents the strands from sticking together. Some thick sauces, especially very chunky ones, are better spooned over each portion of pasta on the plate.

Many pasta shapes are interchangeable. If you don't happen to have the pasta specified in a recipe, you can usually substitute another. The most important rule is that relatively thick pastas such as lasagne, mafalda, rigatoni, large macaroni and rather large pasta shells are better for baked dishes and with robust sauces. Delicate, thin pasta, especially fresh pasta, is better with lighter, more subtle sauces. Pastas of unusual shapes are best with light sauces so that their shapes are apparent. Spaghetti, vermicelli and linguine are good with almost any type of sauce.

SERVING PASTA

Americans love pasta so much that we use it throughout the meal. Besides serving it as a first course according to the Italian custom, we make it into main courses, salads and sometimes even desserts.

Cooked pasta can be tossed with the sauce either in a heated bowl or in the pan of sauce or the pasta cooking pot, if it does not have a colander insert. It is best to use a large fork for tossing pasta with sauce and other ingredients to avoid crushing the pasta and sticking the pieces together.

Hot pasta should be served in heated shallow bowls or on heated plates because it cools rapidly. When serving pasta, it is good to have a peppermill on the table with black, white or mixed peppercorns. Freshly grated cheese is also a popular accompaniment for most pastas. Although unconventional, hot-tasting or spicy sauces are also good with many pastas. When serving dishes containing soy sauce, provide a small bottle of soy sauce on the table as well.

QUICK PASTA IDEAS

Part of the reason for pasta's popularity is that it makes possible a delicious meal very quickly, without the need for special ingredients or equipment.

While the pasta cooks, the seasoning ingredients can be combined in a bowl—olive oil or soft butter, diced tomatoes, feta cheese or other flavorful foods like tuna or smoked fish and fresh or dried herbs, for example. Diced cooked vegetables, meats or seafood can also be added. Once the pasta is cooked, it is drained, added to the bowl and tossed. This is the key to preparing a delightful, natural pasta dish in 10 minutes or less. To save time, choose pastas that cook fastest, such as thin noodles or fresh pastas.

Many ingredients that are either salty or powerful in flavor are perfect for pasta—anchovies, prosciutto, Parmesan, Roquefort and other sharp cheeses are a few examples. Some of these store well and can be kept on hand for making pasta dishes at the last minute.

Here are a few suggestions:

olive oil	nuts
sesame oil	dried herbs and spices
Chinese chili oil or other flavored oils such as garlic oil or herb oil	dried mushrooms
	frozen vegetables
butter	onions
oil-packed sun-dried tomatoes	garlic
black olives	lemons
tuna in olive oil	canned tomatoes
roasted peppers in jars	tomato sauce
capers	

PASTA SALADS

Although there are a few cold pasta dishes in Italy, pasta salads are rarely seen in Europe. They are primarily an American development. Sadly, for many years the choice was restricted to mainly macaroni salad with pickles, pimentos and a slightly sweet, slightly vinegary mayonnaise. No wonder some people claimed they didn't like pasta salad!

Now an impressive variety of imaginative, colorful, lively salads made with fresh vegetables, fresh herbs and light dressings, have led to the great popularity of pasta salads. Food writers often discuss whether they are "in" or "out" during a particular year, but, judging from gourmet take-out windows and restaurant menus, there is no question they are constantly in demand. Perhaps their biggest advantage is that most of them are so easy to prepare at home.

For salads the pasta is tossed with fish, meat, vegetables or some combination of these. Depending on the ingredients added and the amounts you serve, most of them are suitable as either first courses or main courses. Simple pasta salads with vegetables, such as Napoli

Salmon & Black-Pasta Salad with Caviar, page 27

17

Vermicelli Salad, also make refreshing side dishes, especially in summer.

There is no need to use fresh pasta for most salads because after sitting and absorbing the dressing, the delicate texture of fresh pasta is not apparent. In fact, dried pasta is still available in a greater variety of interesting shapes and is perfect for salads because the shapes show well.

Dressings for pasta salads can be light, in which case they are generally variations of vinaigrette, as in Shrimp & Spinach-Fettuccine Salad with Tarragon and in Crab & Linguine Salad with Sesame Dressing. Because pasta is delicate in flavor, a vinaigrette made with a little less vinegar than the classic three parts oil to one part vinegar is usually preferable. Richer dressings are made from mayonnaise, cream or both. Many pasta salads, such as Tortellini Salad with Roasted Peppers, Parmesan & Fresh Basil, do not need a true "dressing," but just enough fine olive oil to moisten the ingredients.

Pasta salads are often thought of as cold pasta dishes, but they actually taste best when served cool or at room temperature rather than cold. Salads made ahead should be removed from the refrigerator 30 minutes to an hour before serving. This is especially important for those with creamy dressings, such as Pasta & Tuna Salad with Avocado Aioli, which otherwise would become too thick.

Most pasta salads are served informally in a bowl. In fine restaurants, salads are often arranged, and the pasta alone is first tossed with dressing. The advantage of doing this is that each ingredient keeps its color. For some elegant salads, such as Lobster & Angel-Hair Pasta Salad with Fines Herbes, it is good to set aside some of each colorful ingredient and place them on top of each portion when serving.

For this light, elegant spring-time salad, I like to cut the asparagus on the diagonal to match the shape of the mostaccioli or penne, which are smooth or grooved, quill-shaped macaroni.

Asparagus, Chicken & Pasta Salad with Hazelnuts

1 quart chicken stock or broth
Pinch of salt, if desired
1¾ pounds chicken thighs or drumsticks
2 tablespoons white-wine vinegar
Salt and freshly ground pepper to taste
3 tablespoons vegetable oil
3 tablespoons hazelnut oil

8 ounces mostaccioli or penne (about 2¾ cups)
1¼ pounds asparagus, peeled, about 1½ inches of bases trimmed
2 tablespoons chopped fresh parsley leaves
1 hard-cooked egg, chopped
⅓ cup toasted hazelnuts, chopped (see page 174)

Bring stock to a boil in a medium saucepan. Add chicken, cover and poach over low heat about 20 minutes or until tender. Remove chicken; broth can be reused for soup or stock. Cool chicken; discard skin. Remove meat from bones. Cut in thin strips, about 1½ inches long. In a large bowl, whisk vinegar with salt and pepper. Whisk in oils. Add chicken.

Bring a large pot of water to a boil; add salt, then pasta. Cook uncovered over high heat, stirring occasionally, about 9 minutes or until tender but firm to the bite. Drain, rinse with cold water and drain well.

If asparagus is wide, halve lengthwise. Cut diagonally in 1½-inch lengths. Add asparagus to a medium saucepan of enough boiling salted water to cover generously. Cook uncovered over high heat about 2 minutes or until crisp-tender.

Rinse with cold water; drain. Reserve 12 asparagus tips for garnish. Add pasta, parsley and asparagus to chicken mixture; toss well. Taste and adjust seasoning. Add hard-cooked egg and toss lightly. (Salad can be kept, covered, up to 1 day in refrigerator. Bring to room temperature before serving.)

To serve, spoon salad onto plates and garnish with asparagus tips. Sprinkle about 1 tablespoon chopped toasted hazelnuts on each serving.
Makes 4 to 6 main-course servings.

Mediterranean Chicken Pasta Salad

Lemon-Oregano Dressing, see below
1 pound boneless chicken breast, with skin on, patted dry
2 teaspoons olive oil
½ teaspoon dried leaf oregano, crumbled
Salt and freshly ground pepper to taste
8 ounces medium pasta shells (about 3 cups)

1 (6-oz.) jar or 1 cup drained marinated artichokes, quartered
½ cup Niçoise or other black olives, halved, pitted
¼ cup chopped Italian parsley leaves or regular parsley
1 large or 2 small ripe tomatoes, diced (about 8 oz.)

Marinated artichokes, black olives and other favorite Mediterranean ingredients combine here with chunks of grilled chicken. Medium pasta shells are ideal because they suit the shapes and sizes of the other ingredients. Tomato pasta shells or spirals also give a pretty result. Instead of grilling chicken breasts, you can use 2 cups diced roast chicken or turkey. Marinated mushrooms can be substituted for the artichokes.

Prepare Lemon-Oregano Dressing; set aside. Preheat broiler or grill with rack about 4 inches from heat source; or heat stove-top ridged grill over medium-high heat. Rub chicken with 2 teaspoons olive oil on meat side and sprinkle with oregano, salt and pepper. Set chicken breast on broiler rack or grill with skin side down. Broil or grill about 4 minutes per side, pressing occasionally on thickest part of chicken with a spatula, or until meat in thickest part is no longer pink when cut. Cool to room temperature and discard any juices that escape. Discard skin. Cut meat in about ¾-inch cubes.

Add chicken to dressing; taste and adjust seasoning. Marinate in dressing, stirring occasionally, about 1 hour at room temperature.

Bring a large pot of water to a boil; add salt, then pasta. Cook uncovered over high heat, stirring occasionally, 5 to 8 minutes or until tender but firm to the bite. Drain, rinse with cold water and drain well. Add to bowl of chicken. Add artichokes, olives, parsley and tomatoes to salad; toss gently. Taste and adjust seasoning. (Salad can be kept, covered, up to 1 day in refrigerator.)
Makes 4 main-course servings.

Lemon-Oregano Dressing

3 tablespoons strained fresh lemon juice
Red (cayenne) pepper to taste
1 teaspoon dried leaf oregano, crumbled

Salt and freshly ground pepper to taste
½ cup extra-virgin olive oil
¼ cup minced red onion

In a large bowl, whisk lemon juice with red pepper, oregano, salt and pepper. Whisk in olive oil. Stir in onion.

"Pistou," the southern French cousin of pesto, is made of olive oil, garlic and basil but does not usually include pine nuts or cheese like the most common Italian version. The pistou is the basis for a pale-green, easy-to-make, creamy dressing.

Turkey Salad with Pistou Dressing in Jumbo Shells

2 turkey drumsticks (about 2½ lbs. total)
1 large onion, sliced
2 large garlic cloves, peeled
1 teaspoon dried leaf thyme, crumbled
1 teaspoon dried leaf basil, crumbled
Salt and freshly ground pepper to taste
2 bay leaves
½ cup dry white wine
6 cups water
Pistou Dressing, opposite
2 hard-cooked eggs, chopped
32 to 35 jumbo pasta shells, each 2 to 2¼ inches long (8 oz., about 5¼ cups)
Romaine lettuce leaves
5 or 8 cherry tomatoes

Put turkey in a large casserole in which it can fit snugly. Add onion, garlic, thyme, basil, salt, pepper, bay leaves, wine and 6 cups water or enough to nearly cover; bring to a boil. Cover and simmer over low heat, turning turkey pieces over from time to time, about 1½ hours or until very tender when pierced in thickest part with a knife. Uncover and cool in cooking liquid about 30 minutes.

Remove turkey from liquid and let stand until cool enough to handle. (Turkey liquid can be used as chicken stock or soup.) Remove skin with the aid of a paring knife. Remove meat from bones; discard any cartilage and fat. Cut meat in small dice, slightly under ½ inch. Transfer to a large bowl.

Prepare Pistou Dressing. Combine turkey with hard-cooked eggs and 1¼ cups dressing. Toss until well blended. Taste and adjust seasoning; season mixture well.

Bring a large pot of water to a boil; add salt, then pasta. Cook uncovered over high heat, stirring occasionally, about 11 minutes or until tender but firm to the bite. To check, remove 1 shell, cut a small piece from an end and taste; it should be tender and only slightly firm. Drain, rinse with cold water and drain well. Drain each shell individually so water does not remain inside. Set on a plate in 1 layer. (Some of shells may tear but there are a few extra.)

Holding each shell open, put about 1½ tablespoons filling inside each, filling shells so turkey mixture shows slightly. (Filled shells can be kept, covered, up to 1 day in refrigerator. Bring to room temperature before serving.)

To serve, arrange lettuce leaves on each plate. Allow 3 shells per first-course serving or 5 shells as a main course. Arrange shells, filling side up, on lettuce, pointing to center of plate. Add a cherry tomato in center. Serve remaining dressing separately.

Makes 5 main-course or 8 first-course servings.

Turkey Salad with Pistou Dressing in Jumbo Shells

Holding a shell open, put about 1¹/₂ tablespoons filling inside, filling shell so turkey mixture shows slightly.

Pistou Dressing

4 medium garlic cloves, peeled
3 cups lightly packed fresh basil leaves (about 2 large bunches of 1¹/₂ oz. each), rinsed, thoroughly dried
1 cup olive oil

2 large eggs, room temperature
4 teaspoons strained fresh lemon juice
Salt and freshly ground pepper to taste
1 cup vegetable oil

With the blade of a food processor turning, drop garlic cloves, 1 at a time, through feed tube and process until finely chopped. Add basil and ¹/₄ cup olive oil. Process by on/off turns until basil is coarsely chopped, scraping down often. Transfer to a medium bowl; mixture will not be smooth.

In food processor, combine eggs, 2 teaspoons lemon juice, 2 tablespoons olive oil and a little salt and pepper. Process until thoroughly blended; scrape bottom and sides of processor container several times. With blade turning, gradually pour in ¹/₄ cup olive oil drop by drop. Scrape down sides of processor. Remaining olive oil and vegetable oil can be poured in a little faster, in a fine stream. Add about ¹/₂ of basil mixture and process until blended. Add remaining basil mixture and process. Add remaining 2 teaspoons lemon juice and process until blended. Taste and adjust seasoning. Transfer to a large bowl. (Dressing can be made 2 days ahead and kept, covered, in refrigerator; garlic flavor will intensify.)

Inspired by "salade Paris-ienne," a potato and beef salad made to use leftover pot au feu or poached beef, this salad combines beef with pasta spirals. Since most of us don't usually have poached beef around the house, a quick, and in many people's opinion, tastier, substitute is roast beef from your favorite deli.

Parisian Pasta Salad

Mustard-Caper Vinaigrette, see below
1 pound pasta spirals or spaghetti twists (gemelli)
8 ounces very thin slices roast beef, cut in 3" x ½" strips
8 ounces green beans, ends removed, cut diagonally in 2-inch pieces

½ cup watercress leaves
3 hard-cooked eggs
2 ripe medium tomatoes, quartered, if desired
Watercress sprigs, if desired

Prepare Mustard-Caper Vinaigrette; set aside. Bring a large pot of water to a boil; add salt, then pasta. Cook uncovered over high heat, stirring occasionally, about 8 minutes or until tender but firm to the bite. Drain, rinse with cold water and drain well. Transfer to a large bowl. Add vinaigrette and toss. Add beef and toss. Cover and refrigerate 1 hour or up to 1 day.

Add green beans to a large saucepan of enough boiling salted water to cover generously. Cook uncovered over high heat about 5 minutes or until crisp-tender. Drain, rinse with cold water and drain well.

Add green beans and watercress to salad; toss. Chop 1 egg and add to salad; toss. Taste and adjust seasoning. Quarter remaining 2 eggs. Garnish salad with quartered eggs, tomatoes and watercress sprigs, if desired.
Makes 4 to 6 main-course servings.

Mustard-Caper Vinaigrette

4 teaspoons Dijon mustard
3 tablespoons white-wine vinegar
Salt and freshly ground pepper to taste
½ cup plus 1 tablespoon vegetable oil

3 tablespoons minced green onions
3 tablespoons minced fresh parsley leaves
2 tablespoons finely chopped rinsed drained capers
1 garlic clove, minced

Whisk mustard in a small bowl with vinegar, salt and pepper. Whisk in oil. Stir in green onions, parsley, capers and garlic. Taste and adjust seasoning.

In this new variation on the classic theme of duck with orange sauce, the duck is tossed with orange pasta, citrus dressing and a few orange segments.

Roast-Duck Salad with Orange Fettuccine

1 (4¹/₂- to 5-lb.) duckling, thawed if frozen, patted dry
Salt and freshly ground pepper to taste
Citrus Dressing, see below
¹/₄ cup finely chopped red onion
12 ounces fresh orange or egg fettuccine, homemade, page 181 (see Note with Orange Pasta), or packaged, or 10 ounces dried

2 tablespoons minced fresh parsley leaves
12 snow peas
1 large orange

Position rack in center of oven and preheat to 450F (230C). Pull out 2 pads of fat from inside duck near tail and remove excess fat from under neck skin. Remove giblets and neck from inside duck and discard or reserve for stock (except for liver, which can be sautéed). Sprinkle duck inside and out with salt and pepper. Prick duck skin all over with a trussing needle or skewer at intervals of about ¹/₂ inch, being sure to thoroughly prick skin of thighs, back and lower part of breast, where fat is thickest; do not pierce meat.

Set a rack in a heavy medium roasting pan and set duck breast side down on rack. Roast 30 minutes. Using a bulb baster or large spoon, remove fat from pan. Set duck on its back and roast 10 minutes. Reduce oven temperature to 400F (205C). Roast duck 30 to 40 minutes or until done to taste. To check, use trussing needle, skewer or carving fork to prick thigh meat in plumpest part: if juices that escape are still red, duck is not done; if they are slightly pink, duck is rare; if they are clear, duck is well done. Remove duck from pan.

Prepare Citrus Dressing. Discard duck skin. Remove meat from bones and cut in strips, about 2" x ¹/₂" x ¹/₄". Add duck and onion to dressing; let stand while finishing salad.

Bring a large pot of water to a boil; add salt, then pasta. Cook uncovered over high heat, separating strands occasionally with a fork, 30 seconds to 2 minutes for fresh pasta or 2 to 5 minutes for dried, or until tender but firm to the bite. Drain, rinse with cold water and drain well. Transfer to bowl of duck mixture and toss. Add parsley and toss. (Salad can be kept, covered, up to 1 day in refrigerator.)

Pull off stem end of each snow pea, removing strings. Add to a medium saucepan of enough boiling salted water to cover generously. Cook uncovered over high heat 30 seconds. Drain, rinse with cold water and drain thoroughly.

Just before serving, use a serrated knife to cut skin and pith from orange. Separate sections by cutting on each side of membrane between them, inward to center; see photos page 173. Fold back membrane and cut to remove segment. Continue until all segments have been removed; discard membranes. Cut orange segments in three. Add to salad; toss. Taste and adjust seasoning.

To serve, spoon salad onto each of 4 plates. Set snow peas together on edge of plate, fanning out from salad and pointing outward.
Makes 4 servings as a light main course.

Citrus Dressing

¹/₄ cup strained fresh lemon juice
¹/₄ cup strained fresh orange juice
Salt and freshly ground pepper to taste

³/₄ cup vegetable oil
1 teaspoon finely grated orange zest (if using plain pasta)

In a large bowl, whisk lemon juice, orange juice, salt and pepper. Whisk in oil. Add grated orange zest if using plain pasta. Taste and adjust seasoning.

Macaroni Salad with Blue-Cheese Dressing & Smoked Turkey

This updated version of the traditional American favorite makes use of a smooth blue-cheese dressing that is lighter than the usual mayonnaise, and combines the macaroni with smoked turkey and fresh colorful vegetables. Smoked turkey breast or chicken breast give a much more flavorful result than chopped pressed turkey.

Blue-Cheese Dressing, see below
8 ounces elbow macaroni (about 2 cups)
1 tablespoon vegetable oil
1 medium carrot, cut in 2" x ⅛" x ⅛" strips
1 small zucchini, cut in 2" x ¼" x ⅛" strips
1 cup cooked fresh or frozen peas

5 ounces sliced smoked turkey or chicken breast, cut in 2" x ¼" strips
3 tablespoons chopped green onions
¼ cup chopped fresh parsley leaves
Romaine lettuce leaves
3 tablespoons coarsely chopped toasted walnuts

Prepare Blue-Cheese Dressing; set aside. Bring a large pot of water to a boil; add salt, then pasta. Cook uncovered over high heat, stirring occasionally, about 6 minutes or until tender but firm to the bite. Drain, rinse with cold water and drain well. Transfer to a large bowl. Add 1 tablespoon oil and toss to combine.

Add carrot pieces to a medium saucepan of enough boiling salted water to cover generously. Cook uncovered over high heat 2 minutes or until nearly tender. Add zucchini and cook 1 minute or until both vegetables are crisp-tender; do not overcook. Drain, rinse with cold water and drain well. Transfer to bowl of pasta.

Add peas, turkey or chicken, green onions and 3 tablespoons parsley to pasta; toss gently. (Salad can be kept, covered, up to 1 day in refrigerator; refrigerate dressing separately. Bring to room temperature before serving.)

Set aside ¼ cup Blue-Cheese Dressing. Add remaining dressing to pasta salad and toss gently to combine. Taste and adjust seasoning. To serve, arrange a bed of Romaine lettuce leaves on each of 6 plates and mound salad in the center. Spoon 1 tablespoon reserved dressing on each serving. Sprinkle a little parsley on dressing and sprinkle toasted walnuts around it.
Makes 6 first-course servings.

Blue-Cheese Dressing

2 teaspoons white- or red-wine vinegar
3 tablespoons vegetable oil
¼ cup whipping cream
⅓ cup sour cream

⅓ cup crumbled or mashed blue cheese
Salt, if desired, and freshly ground pepper to taste

Combine vinegar and oil in a medium bowl. Whisk briefly. Gradually whisk in whipping cream. Continue whisking until dressing is well blended. Gradually whisk in sour cream. Whisk in blue cheese; small pieces will remain. Taste; add salt, if desired, and pepper.

You can use heavy cream instead of whipping cream but do not substitute half and half or milk.

COOKING TIP

Crab & Linguine Salad with Sesame Dressing

Sesame Dressing, see below
8 ounces fresh crabmeat
2 tablespoons sesame seeds
8 ounces dried linguine
3 tablespoons minced fresh parsley leaves
3 tablespoons chopped green onions

2 tablespoons chopped cilantro (fresh coriander) leaves, if desired
½ teaspoon Oriental chili oil or Tabasco sauce or to taste

Prepare Sesame Dressing. Pick through crabmeat and discard any pieces of shell or cartilage. Reserve a few large pieces of crabmeat for garnish. Add 1 tablespoon dressing to remaining crabmeat and let stand about 15 minutes.

Toast sesame seeds in a dry small heavy skillet over medium-low heat, stirring until golden brown, about 4 minutes; transfer to a small bowl.

Bring a large pot of water to a boil; add salt, then pasta. Cook uncovered over high heat, separating strands occasionally with a fork, about 8 minutes or until tender but firm to the bite. Drain, rinse with cold water and drain well.

Transfer linguine to a large bowl. Add remaining dressing, parsley, green onions and cilantro if desired; toss. Add crab mixture and toss. Taste and adjust seasoning, adding more chili oil or Tabasco and salt if needed. (Salad can be kept, covered, up to 8 hours in refrigerator. Bring to room temperature before serving.) Just before serving, add sesame seeds and toss. Garnish with reserved pieces of crabmeat.

Makes 2 or 3 main-course or 4 or 5 first-course servings.

Sesame Dressing

¼ cup vegetable oil
2 tablespoons Oriental sesame oil
2 tablespoons rice vinegar

½ teaspoon Oriental chili oil or Tabasco sauce
Salt to taste

Combine vegetable oil, sesame oil, vinegar, ½ teaspoon chili oil or Tabasco sauce and salt in a small bowl. Whisk until blended.

COOKING TIP

If a vinaigrette-dressed salad is made 1 day ahead, some of the dressing will be absorbed by the salad. To freshen and moisten the salad, add 1 to 2 tablespoons oil and 1 to 2 teaspoons lemon juice or vinegar before serving.

Salmon & Black-Pasta Salad with Caviar

½ cup dry white wine
3 cups water
¼ teaspoon salt
Pinch of pepper
1 thyme sprig or ¼ teaspoon dried leaf, crumbled
1 bay leaf
1¼ pounds salmon steaks, about 1 inch thick
Vinaigrette, see below
9 to 10 ounces fresh black pasta, homemade, page 181, or packaged, or 8 ounces dried

2 tablespoons olive oil
Salt and pepper to taste
2 tablespoons snipped fresh chives
½ to ¾ cup sour cream
4 teaspoons black or golden caviar
Whole chives, if desired
More caviar, if desired (for serving)

It's hard to believe that such an exquisite entree could be so easy to make—it is simply black pasta tossed with pink poached salmon and a basic vinaigrette dressing, topped with sour cream and a spoonful of caviar. Black pasta made with squid ink is available in both dry and fresh form and you can even make it yourself, or you can substitute spinach, smoked-salmon or beet pasta.

◆ *Photo on page 16.*

Combine wine, water, salt, pepper, thyme and bay leaf in a medium sauté pan or deep medium skillet. Bring to a simmer. Add salmon. Cover and cook over low heat about 9 minutes; to check if salmon is cooked, insert a skewer into it and touch skewer to underside of your wrist—it should feel hot. Remove salmon with a slotted spoon and let cool.

Prepare Vinaigrette; set aside. Bring a large pot of water to a boil; add salt, then pasta. Cook uncovered over high heat, separating strands occasionally with a fork, 30 seconds to 2 minutes for fresh or 2 to 5 minutes for dried or until tender but firm to the bite. Drain well. Transfer to a large bowl and toss with olive oil. Spread out on a baking sheet and refrigerate, tossing every few minutes, about 30 minutes or until cool.

Meanwhile, remove skin and any bones from salmon. Pull meat into bite-size chunks. Put salmon in a bowl, pour vinaigrette over it and toss. Taste and adjust seasoning.

When pasta is cool, season with salt and pepper. Add salmon-vinaigrette mixture and chives; toss gently. (Salad can be kept, covered, up to 1 day in refrigerator. Bring to room temperature before serving.)

To serve, divide pasta salad among 3 or 4 plates. Top each portion with a dollop of sour cream, then with a teaspoon of caviar. Garnish with whole chives, if desired. Serve more caviar separately, if desired.
Makes 3 to 4 main-course servings.

Vinaigrette

4 teaspoons sherry vinegar or white-wine vinegar

Salt and pepper to taste
¼ cup vegetable oil

In a small bowl, whisk vinegar with salt and pepper until blended. Whisk in vegetable oil. Taste and adjust seasoning.

Pasta & Tuna Salad with Avocado Aioli

Aioli is a garlic sauce of mayonnaise consistency popular in Provence in southern France. I developed this new version using avocado which makes the sauce exceptionally creamy, colors it a cool green hue and turns tuna and pasta into a festive appetizer.

Avocado Aioli, see below
¼ cup slivered almonds
8 ounces medium pasta shells (about 3 cups)
1 tablespoon vegetable oil
1 (6½-oz.) can oil-packed tuna, preferably in olive oil
3 tablespoons minced fresh parsley leaves
½ cup finely diced celery
⅓ cup diced oil-packed sun-dried tomatoes, if desired
1 small avocado
About 16 leaves tender lettuce, such as red-leaf or butter lettuce

Prepare Avocado Aioli; set aside. Preheat oven to 350F (175C). Toast almonds on a small baking sheet in oven until light brown, about 4 minutes. Transfer to a plate and cool.

Bring a large pot of water to a boil; add salt, then pasta. Cook uncovered over high heat, stirring occasionally, 5 to 8 minutes or until tender but firm to the bite. Drain, rinse with cold water and drain well. Transfer to a large bowl. Add oil and toss to combine.

Drain and flake tuna. Add to pasta and toss. Add 1 cup Avocado Aioli. Add parsley, celery and sun-dried tomatoes if desired, to salad; toss. (Salad and remaining Avocado Aioli can be kept in covered containers up to 4 hours in refrigerator. Bring to room temperature before serving.)

A short time before serving, halve small avocado and remove pit. Use a small melon-ball cutter to shape avocado flesh in balls. Make a bed of lettuce on each of 4 plates. Spoon salad onto lettuce. Scatter balls of avocado on salad and sprinkle top with toasted almonds. Serve remaining sauce separately.
Makes 4 servings as a first course or light main course.

Avocado Aioli

3 large garlic cloves, peeled
1 ripe medium avocado (8 oz.), preferably Haas, room temperature
1 large egg yolk, room temperature
1 to 2 tablespoons strained fresh lemon juice
Salt and freshly ground pepper to taste
½ cup vegetable oil
¼ cup olive oil, room temperature
Red (cayenne) pepper to taste

Cut off brown end of garlic and any brown spots. Halve garlic cloves lengthwise and remove any green sprouts from center. Halve avocado, remove pit and scoop out flesh.

With the blade of a food processor turning, drop garlic cloves, 1 at a time, through feed tube and process until finely chopped. Add egg yolk, avocado flesh, 1 tablespoon lemon juice and a pinch of salt and pepper. Process until thoroughly blended; scrape bottom and sides of processor container several times. With blade turning, gradually pour in ¼ cup vegetable oil drop by drop. Scrape down sides of processor. Remaining vegetable oil and olive oil can be poured in a little faster, in a fine stream. Taste; if desired add up to 1 tablespoon lemon juice, 1 teaspoon at a time, processing after each addition. Add red pepper. Taste and adjust seasoning. Transfer to a medium bowl.

Note: If making Avocado Aioli in a blender, first mince garlic with a knife.

Lobster & Angel-Hair Pasta Salad with Fines Herbes

Creamy Herb Vinaigrette, see
  below
¾ cup dry white wine
¾ cup water
2 tarragon stems (without leaves)
1 bay leaf
1 thyme sprig or ¼ teaspoon
  dried leaf
Salt and freshly ground pepper to
  taste

8 ounces sole fillets
1 cooked lobster (1½ to 1¾ lbs.)
  or 1 cooked lobster tail (12 oz.
  to 1 lb.)
4 ounces haricots verts (very thin
  French green beans) or regular
  green beans
8 ounces angel-hair pasta or
  capellini
2 ripe plum tomatoes, diced

Prepare this sumptuous pasta salad for special occasions. The creamy vinaigrette is richer and more satisfying than plain vinaigrette, but is much lighter than mayonnaise and shows the colors of the ingredients well. I learned to make this dressing when I trained at a small restaurant in Paris. I have adapted it here for the food processor and added the classic "fines herbes," a fresh herb mixture of chives, tarragon and chervil or parsley.

Prepare Creamy Herb Vinaigrette; set aside. Combine wine, water, tarragon stems, bay leaf, thyme and a pinch of salt and pepper in a medium saucepan. Bring to a boil. Cover and simmer 5 minutes. Fold sole fillets in half. Add to simmering liquid. Cover and cook over low heat 3 minutes, or until a skewer inserted into thickest part comes out hot; to check, touch skewer to underside of your wrist. Transfer sole to a plate with a slotted spatula. Cool fish. Discard liquid that escapes onto plate. Cut sole in about ¾-inch dice.

Remove lobster meat from shell. Cut tail meat in attractive crosswise slices, if possible, about ¼ inch thick or less. If using a whole lobster, dice remaining meat. Set aside ½ of lobster pieces for garnish.

Remove ends from green beans and break beans in half. Add green beans to a medium saucepan of enough boiling salted water to cover generously. Cook uncovered over high heat until crisp-tender, about 2 minutes for French green beans or about 4 minutes for regular beans. Drain, rinse with cold water until cool and drain well.

Bring a large pot of water to a boil; add salt, then pasta. Cook uncovered over high heat, separating strands occasionally with a fork, about 4 minutes or until tender but firm to the bite. Drain, rinse with cold water and drain well.

Using 2 forks, toss pasta thoroughly with vinaigrette. Add tomatoes and green beans; toss gently. Taste and adjust seasoning. Add sole and remaining lobster pieces; toss gently. Garnish with reserved lobster. (Salad can be kept, covered, up to 8 hours in refrigerator. Bring to room temperature before serving.) When serving salad, put some vegetables and seafood on top of each portion of pasta. Makes 4 servings as a light main course.

Creamy Herb Vinaigrette

1 large egg yolk
1 teaspoon Dijon mustard
1 medium shallot
Salt and freshly ground pepper to
  taste
3 tablespoons herb vinegar or
  tarragon vinegar
5 tablespoons olive oil
5 tablespoons vegetable oil

1 tablespoon snipped fresh
  chives
1 tablespoon chopped fresh
  tarragon leaves, stems reserved
1 tablespoon chopped fresh
  chervil leaves, if desired
1 tablespoon chopped fresh
  parsley leaves

Combine egg yolk, mustard, shallot, salt, pepper and vinegar in a food processor. Process until shallot is minced and ingredients are blended. With the blade turning, gradually pour in olive oil and vegetable oil; scrape down sides of processor occasionally. Transfer vinaigrette to a medium bowl. Stir in herbs. Taste and adjust seasoning.

Shrimp & Spinach-Fettuccine Salad with Tarragon

Tarragon Vinaigrette, see below
**8 ounces medium shrimp,
  unshelled**
**2 yellow zucchini or crookneck
  squash, cut in 2¹/₂" x ¹/₂" x ¹/₄"
  strips**
**1 medium carrot, cut in strips
  about same size as squash**

**8 ounces good-quality spinach
  fettuccine or noodles,
  preferably fresh, homemade,
  page 180, or packaged**
**2 tablespoons chopped fresh
  tarragon leaves**

Prepare Tarragon Vinaigrette; set aside. Cook shrimp in a medium saucepan of boiling salted water over medium heat about 1¹/₂ minutes or until they turn pink. Rinse with cold water, drain and peel. Add shrimp to vinaigrette and let stand while finishing salad.

Add squash to a medium saucepan of enough boiling salted water to cover generously. Cook uncovered over high heat about 1 minute or until crisp-tender. Drain, rinse with cold water and drain well. Cook carrot strips in a medium saucepan of boiling salted water about 2 minutes or until crisp-tender. Drain well.

Bring a large pot of water to a boil; add salt, then pasta. Cook uncovered over high heat, separating strands occasionally with a fork, 30 seconds to 2 minutes for fresh or 2 to 5 minutes for dried or until tender but firm to the bite. Drain, rinse with cold water and drain well. Transfer to a large bowl. Add shrimp-vinaigrette mixture and toss. Add tarragon, squash and carrot; toss again. Taste and adjust seasoning. (Salad can be kept, covered, up to 8 hours in refrigerator. Bring to room temperature before serving.)
Makes 4 first-course or 2 main-course servings.

Tarragon Vinaigrette

2 tablespoons tarragon vinegar
2 teaspoons Dijon mustard
**Salt and freshly ground pepper to
  taste**

¹/₄ cup vegetable oil
3 tablespoons olive oil
**1 tablespoon chopped fresh
  tarragon leaves**

In a medium bowl, whisk vinegar with mustard, salt and pepper until blended. Whisk in vegetable oil and olive oil. Stir in tarragon. Taste and adjust seasoning.

Clockwise from top right: Smoked Haddock & Pasta Salad with Chive-Caper Vinaigrette, page 32; Tortellini Salad with Roasted Peppers, Parmesan & Fresh Basil, page 36; Shrimp & Spinach-Fettuccine Salad with Tarragon.

Arrange this salad on individual plates or serve it in a glass bowl to show its pretty shapes and colors—the bright-orange smoked fish, the black olives, the bright-red tomatoes, the pale-green avocado and the light-yellow pasta bow ties.

◆ *Photo on page 31.*

Smoked Haddock & Pasta Salad with Chive-Caper Vinaigrette

12 ounces smoked haddock (sometimes called finnan haddie), smoked cod, scrod, whitefish or halibut
About 3 cups milk, if using finnan haddie
8 ounces pasta bow ties or wheels (about 4 cups)
1 small green bell pepper, seeds and ribs discarded, diced

2 large ripe tomatoes, diced
1 cup (about 3½ oz.) pitted medium-size black olives, halved
Chive-Caper Vinaigrette, see below
1 ripe avocado, if desired

Remove any skin and bones from fish. If using finnan haddie, but not other types of smoked fish, put fish in a saucepan and add enough milk to cover. Bring just to a simmer. Poach uncovered over low heat, turning once, 7 minutes. Remove finnan haddie with a slotted spoon and let cool.

Bring a large pot of water to a boil; add salt, then pasta. Cook uncovered over high heat, stirring occasionally, 6 to 8 minutes or until tender but firm to the bite. Drain, rinse with cold water and drain well.

Put diced pepper in a medium saucepan of boiling water to cover and boil 1 minute. Rinse under cold running water and drain well.

Dice or flake fish, discarding any remaining skin and bones. Place fish in a serving bowl. Add pasta, green pepper, tomatoes and olives.

Prepare Chive-Caper Vinaigrette; add to salad and mix gently. (Salad can be kept, covered, up to 1 day in refrigerator. Bring to room temperature before serving.)

A short time before serving, peel and dice avocado, if using. Add to salad and toss. Taste and adjust seasoning. Serve salad at room temperature or cool but not chilled.

Makes 6 first-course servings.

Chive-Caper Vinaigrette

2 tablespoons plus 2 teaspoons white-wine vinegar or herb vinegar
Salt and freshly ground pepper to taste

½ cup extra-virgin olive oil
2 tablespoons rinsed drained capers
2 tablespoons snipped fresh chives

In a medium bowl, whisk vinegar with salt and pepper. Whisk in oil. Stir in capers and chives.

COOKING TIP   Hot pasta dishes flavored with vegetables, herbs and oil, but not with butter or melted cheese, can be easily made into salads by being served cold or at room temperature.

Napoli Vermicelli Salad

8 ounces small ripe plum
   tomatoes
4 to 5 tablespoons virgin or
   extra-virgin olive oil
1 small garlic clove, minced
1 tablespoon chopped fresh basil
   leaves

Salt and freshly ground pepper to
   taste
¼ teaspoon dried leaf oregano,
   crumbled
8 ounces vermicelli
Basil sprigs for garnish

Cut tomatoes in half lengthwise, squeeze well and remove seeds. Cut each piece in half again lengthwise. Put in a large bowl. Add 4 tablespoons oil, garlic, chopped basil, salt, pepper and oregano. Let stand 1 or 2 hours at room temperature.

Bring a large pot of water to a boil; add salt, then pasta. Cook uncovered over high heat, separating strands occasionally with a fork, 6 to 7 minutes or until tender but firm to the bite. Drain well. Add to tomato mixture and mix well. Taste and adjust seasoning; add more olive oil if desired. Garnish with basil sprigs. Serve warm or at room temperature.
Makes 4 first-course servings.

When I visited Naples, I was fascinated by the lively markets and impressed by the importance of the region's beautiful tomatoes to its tasty food. This simple dish from the Naples area with its easy dressing of marinated tomatoes is one of the few pasta salads made in Italy. Perfect for summer, it makes use of ripe tomatoes and fresh basil at their peak. It can be served at room temperature as a salad or hot as a colorful first course.

Spinach-Tortelloni Salad with Walnut-Oil Dressing

Walnut-Oil Dressing, see below
8 or 9 ounces or 1 (9-oz.)
   package cheese- or meat-filled
   spinach tortelloni, fresh or
   frozen
1 small cauliflower (1 to 1¼ lbs.)
¼ cup minced fresh parsley
   leaves

1 cup red cherry tomatoes,
   halved
1 cup yellow or additional 1 cup
   red cherry tomatoes, halved
2 to 3 tablespoons chopped
   walnuts, if desired

Prepare Walnut-Oil Dressing; set aside. Bring a large pot of water to a boil; add salt, then pasta. Cook uncovered over medium-high heat, stirring occasionally, about 7 minutes or until tender. Drain, rinse gently with cold water and drain well. Transfer to a large bowl. Add dressing and toss to combine.

Divide cauliflower into small flowerets, about size of tortelloni. Add cauliflower to a large saucepan of enough boiling salted water to cover generously. Cook uncovered over high heat about 5 minutes or until crisp-tender. Drain, rinse with cold water and drain well.

Add cauliflower, parsley and tomatoes to bowl of tortelloni; toss gently. Taste and adjust seasoning. (Salad can be kept, covered, up to 1 day in refrigerator. Bring to room temperature before serving.) Taste; if you would like a stronger walnut flavor, sprinkle chopped walnuts over each serving.
Makes 2 or 3 main-course or 5 or 6 first-course servings.

For this colorful salad, meat- or cheese-filled spinach tortelloni are tossed with small crisp-tender cauliflowerets, red and yellow cherry tomatoes and a vinaigrette dressing made with walnut oil. Because walnut oil varies in strength, you can add chopped walnuts to the finished salad if you prefer a more intense taste.

Walnut-Oil Dressing

1 tablespoon white-wine vinegar
Salt and freshly ground pepper to
   taste

⅓ cup walnut oil

Whisk vinegar with a pinch of salt and pepper in a small bowl. Whisk in walnut oil. Taste and adjust seasoning.

Ziti with Zucchini & Cilantro

This simple aromatic pasta with lightly sautéed zucchini and Jack cheese is good as a cold side dish with chicken or lamb chops, or as one of several salads on a buffet. If you prefer a sharp cheese, substitute pecorino-romano.

12 ounces zucchini
12 ounces crookneck squash or yellow zucchini
3 ripe plum tomatoes
⅓ cup virgin or extra-virgin olive oil
2 large garlic cloves, minced
1 or 2 medium jalapeño peppers, seeds and ribs discarded, minced

Salt and freshly ground pepper to taste
1 pound ziti or other tubular pasta such as mostaccioli
¼ cup chopped cilantro (fresh coriander) leaves
2 cups shredded Monterey Jack cheese (about 8 oz.) or ½ cup grated pecorino-romano cheese (about 1½ oz.)

Cut zucchini and yellow squash in sticks, about 2" x ¼" x ¼". Cut tomatoes in eighths, then in thin strips.

Heat oil in a large skillet over medium heat. Add garlic, jalapeño pepper, both types of squash, salt and pepper. Cook, stirring, about 2 minutes or until zucchini are just tender. Add tomato strips and toss a few seconds over heat. Transfer mixture to a serving bowl.

If ziti are long, break each in 3 pieces. Bring a large pot of water to a boil; add salt, then pasta. Cook uncovered over high heat, stirring occasionally, about 9 minutes or until tender but firm to the bite. Drain well.

Add pasta to bowl of zucchini mixture and toss. Add cilantro. Cool to room temperature. Add cheese; toss well. Taste, adjust seasoning and serve.
Makes 6 side-dish servings.

Triple-Tomato Pasta Salad

A celebration of summer, this three-tone tomato salad combines fresh tomatoes, tomato pasta and sun-dried tomatoes with avocado cubes to give a pleasing color and texture. Small dice of fontina or mozzarella cheese can also be added. The sun-dried tomatoes are packed in a flavored oil of which 1 or 2 tablespoons can be used for part of the dressing, as long as enough oil is left in the jar to cover the remaining tomatoes so they will keep.

Herb Vinaigrette, see below
8 ounces dried tomato spirals or fusilli (about 3½ cups), tomato noodles or tri-colored noodles

12 ounces ripe tomatoes, diced
⅓ cup chopped oil-packed sun-dried tomatoes
1 large ripe avocado

Prepare Herb Vinaigrette; set aside. Bring a large pot of water to a boil; add salt, then pasta. Cook uncovered over high heat, stirring occasionally, about 7 minutes or until tender but firm to the bite. Drain, rinse with cold water and drain well. Add to vinaigrette and toss. Add fresh and dried tomatoes. (Salad can be kept, covered, up to 1 day in refrigerator.)

A short time before serving, halve avocado and remove pit. Cut avocado flesh in small dice. Add to salad. Taste and adjust seasoning.
Makes 4 first-course servings.

Herb Vinaigrette

1 tablespoon strained fresh lemon juice or herb vinegar
Salt and freshly ground pepper to taste
6 tablespoons olive oil, preferably virgin or extra-virgin

3 tablespoons chopped green onions
2 tablespoons chopped fresh parsley leaves
1 tablespoon chopped fresh basil leaves or 1 teaspoon dried leaf, crumbled

Combine lemon juice or vinegar with salt and pepper in a large bowl. Whisk in oil. Stir in green onions, parsley and basil.

Goat-Cheese, Spinach & Whole-Wheat Pasta Salad

½ cup pecans or ⅓ cup pine nuts
4 ounces spinach, stems removed, leaves rinsed well, patted dry (about 5 cups leaves)
4 ripe plum tomatoes, diced
2 teaspoons chopped fresh thyme leaves or ¾ teaspoon dried leaf, crumbled
6 to 8 tablespoons olive oil, preferably extra-virgin
Freshly ground pepper to taste

12 ounces whole-wheat or regular macaroni tubes, straight (cannaroni) or diagonal-cut (penne) (about 6 cups)
2 medium zucchini, (about 8 oz. total), cut in about 2" x ¼" x ¼" strips
8 ounces French-style goat cheese, diced or crumbled (about 1½ cups)
Salt, if desired

Preheat oven to 350F (175C). Toast nuts in oven, about 3 minutes for pine nuts and about 5 minutes for pecans. Break pecans in pieces.

Cut spinach leaves in thin strips, about 3" x ½". Combine tomatoes, spinach, thyme and 6 tablespoons olive oil in a large bowl. Season with freshly ground pepper.

Bring a large pot of water to a boil; add salt, then pasta. Cook uncovered over high heat, stirring occasionally, about 8 minutes or until tender but firm to the bite. Before draining, add zucchini and cook another 2 or 3 seconds. Drain together, rinse with cold water and drain well. Add to bowl of spinach mixture and toss. Taste and add remaining 2 tablespoons olive oil if desired. Add goat cheese and toasted nuts; toss lightly. Adjust seasoning; salt may not be needed if cheese is salty. Serve warm or at room temperature. (Salad can be kept, covered, up to 8 hours in refrigerator.)
Makes 4 main-course servings.

VARIATION
Feta Cheese, Spinach & Whole-Wheat Pasta Salad: Substitute 8 ounces crumbled feta cheese (2 cups) for goat cheese.

Flavorful whole-wheat pasta is now available in many shapes—in addition to noodles and spaghetti, there are corkscrews, shells, quills and straight and curved macaroni. Its nutritional value is often emphasized but it also tastes great, especially when matched with toasted nuts, cheeses and vegetables. Here it is used in a quick, easy salad with plenty of green vegetables and a simple seasoning of thyme and olive oil. For a colorful alternative, substitute Beet Fettuccine, page 181, for the whole-wheat pasta and add 1 or 2 peeled sliced baked beets at the last minute.

"Pure" olive oil is the most common type of olive oil and is generally used for cooking. The finer "virgin" olive oil, and the finest "extra virgin" taste best when used raw or warmed only briefly. Most cooks find it practical to keep on hand a bottle of pure oil and use it for cooking, and a bottle of the more expensive "extra virgin" for last minute flavoring. I have not usually specified two types of olive oil in a single recipe, but if you do have both types, this is the way to use them to best advantage.

COOKING TIP

No cooking at all is required for this refreshing salad of couscous with tomatoes, celery, mint and toasted pine nuts; boiling water is poured over the couscous, which then needs only a few minutes to soften. The salad is even better when dressed with an extra-virgin olive oil.

Couscous Salad with Tomatoes, Pine Nuts & Mint

2 tablespoons strained fresh lemon juice
Salt and freshly ground pepper to taste
6 tablespoons olive oil
1 cup couscous
2/3 cup boiling water
2 tablespoons pine nuts
2 ripe medium tomatoes, diced (about 12 oz. total)

2 small celery stalks, peeled, diced finely
3 tablespoons chopped fresh mint leaves
10 leaves of leaf lettuce or butter lettuce
8 cherry tomatoes
Mint sprig for garnish

Whisk lemon juice with a pinch of salt and pepper in a medium bowl. Whisk in oil.

Combine couscous with salt to taste in a medium saucepan. Shake saucepan to spread couscous in an even layer. Pour boiling water evenly over couscous and immediately cover saucepan tightly. Shake to distribute water evenly; let stand 5 minutes. Whisk dressing again and drizzle 2 tablespoons dressing over couscous. Cover and let stand 2 minutes. Transfer couscous to a ceramic or glass bowl. Break up any lumps and fluff with a fork. Let cool completely.

Toast pine nuts in a dry small heavy skillet over medium heat, shaking skillet often, until lightly browned, about 3 minutes. Transfer to a bowl and let cool.

Whisk remaining dressing. Drizzle over couscous and toss gently with a fork. Add diced tomatoes, celery and chopped mint; toss salad gently. Cover and refrigerate 1 hour. (Salad can be kept, covered, up to 1 day in refrigerator.)

Add pine nuts and toss salad. Taste and adjust seasoning. To serve, make a bed of lettuce on a platter. Spoon couscous mixture in a mound in center. Arrange cherry tomatoes on lettuce around couscous; set a mint sprig on top. Makes 4 side-dish servings.

This is a favorite at gourmet take-outs. It is very easy to prepare—the pasta is simply tossed with the flavorings and no separate dressing is needed. What makes it special is fine-quality ingredients— fresh pasta, extra-virgin olive oil, basil leaves, roasted peppers and imported Parmesan cheese. Cheese- or meat-filled tortellini or the larger tortelloni are excellent here because the filling adds taste and texture to the salad but it can also be made with rotelle or other pasta shapes.

◆ Photo on page 31.

Tortellini Salad with Roasted Peppers, Parmesan & Fresh Basil

1 pound or 2 (9-oz.) packages cheese-filled tortellini or tortelloni, fresh or frozen
2/3 cup extra-virgin olive oil
1 red bell pepper
1 green bell pepper

6 tablespoons freshly grated Parmesan cheese, preferably imported
1/2 cup chopped fresh basil leaves
Salt, if desired, and freshly ground pepper to taste

Bring a large pot of water to a boil; add salt, then pasta. Cook uncovered over medium-high heat, stirring occasionally, about 8 minutes or according to package directions or until tender. Drain, rinse gently with cold water and drain well. Transfer to a large bowl. Add olive oil and toss to combine. (It might appear that there is too much oil but it will be absorbed by remaining ingredients.)

Preheat broiler. Broil bell peppers about 2 inches from heat source, turning about every 5 minutes with tongs, until pepper skin is blistered and charred, 15 to 25 minutes. Transfer to a plastic bag and close bag. Let stand 10 minutes. Peel using a paring knife, see photo page 95. Halve peppers lengthwise and discard seeds and ribs. Drain well and pat dry. Halve pepper pieces crosswise; cut each half in thin lengthwise strips about ¼ inch wide.

Add Parmesan cheese to salad and toss. Add pepper strips and basil; toss until combined. Season to taste with salt, if desired, and freshly ground pepper. (Salad can be kept, covered, up to 1 day in refrigerator. Bring to room temperature before serving.)

Makes 4 main-course or 8 first-course servings.

Corn, Bean & Pasta Salad with Extra-Virgin Olive Oil & Tomatoes

This colorful Mediterranean-flavored salad makes a delightful vegetarian main course or accompaniment for grilled chicken or steak. Because it keeps well, it is ideal for taking on picnics.

¹/₂ cup dried garbanzo beans (also called chick peas) or 1 (15-oz.) can garbanzo beans
1 green bell pepper, if desired
1¹/₂ to 1³/₄ pounds fresh lima beans, shelled, or 1¹/₂ cups (about 8 oz.) frozen
1¹/₄ cups fresh or frozen corn kernels
8 ounces medium pasta shells (about 3 cups)
¹/₄ cup minced green onions
8 ounces ripe tomatoes, cut in ¹/₂-inch dice
2 tablespoons chopped fresh parsley leaves

2 tablespoons chopped fresh basil leaves or 2 teaspoons dried leaf, crumbled, or 1 tablespoon chopped fresh marjoram leaves or 1 teaspoon dried leaf, crumbled
3 tablespoons strained fresh lemon juice
7 tablespoons extra-virgin olive oil
Salt and freshly ground pepper to taste
1 cup pitted black olives, halved

Sort dried garbanzo beans. Soak in a bowl of 1¹/₂ cups cold water in a cool place 8 hours or overnight. Drain and rinse. Put beans in a medium saucepan and add 2 cups water. Bring to a boil. Reduce heat to low, cover and simmer 45 minutes. Add a pinch of salt and simmer about 30 minutes or until tender. Drain thoroughly. If using canned garbanzo beans, rinse and drain.

If using bell pepper, preheat broiler. Broil pepper about 2 inches from heat source, turning about every 5 minutes with tongs, until pepper skin is blistered and charred, 15 to 25 minutes. If you prefer, roast pepper directly on burner and turn often with tongs until skin blackens. Transfer to a plastic bag and close bag. Let stand 10 minutes. Peel using a paring knife, see photo page 95. Halve pepper lengthwise and discard seeds and ribs. Drain well and pat dry. Cut in ¹/₂-inch dice.

Add lima beans to a medium saucepan of enough boiling salted water to cover generously. Cook uncovered over medium-high heat until just tender, 15 to 20 minutes for fresh beans or about 10 minutes for frozen. Drain thoroughly. Cook corn uncovered in a medium saucepan of boiling water to cover generously over high heat about 1 minute or until just tender. Drain thoroughly.

Bring a large pot of water to a boil; add salt, then pasta. Cook uncovered over high heat, stirring occasionally, 5 to 8 minutes or until tender but firm to the bite. Drain, rinse with cold water and drain well.

Combine garbanzo beans, lima beans, corn, pasta, green onions, tomatoes, parsley and basil or marjoram in a large bowl; toss lightly.

In a small bowl, whisk lemon juice with olive oil, salt and pepper. Add to salad and toss until ingredients are coated. Add olives and green pepper. Taste and adjust seasoning. Serve warm or at room temperature. (Salad can be kept, covered, up to 1 day in refrigerator; if it appears dry, add 1 or 2 tablespoons olive oil and 1 or 2 teaspoons lemon juice before serving.)

Makes 6 to 8 side-dish servings.

PASTA WITH VEGETABLES & CHEESE

Over the years, cooks have developed an enormous variety of pasta dishes featuring cheeses and vegetables. And no wonder—these are often the quickest pasta recipes. The pasta is simply tossed with oil or butter and a flavorful cheese, or with a single or several sautéed vegetables, and it's ready! Many of these creations can play several roles in the menu—as first courses, side dishes or vegetarian main courses.

It might be surprising that such simple dishes can be so delicious. Yet to make a good dish, there is no need to have a long list of ingredients but rather to use ingredients of good quality. Sauces, especially tomato sauces or creamy sauces, can be included but often are not needed.

Many of the classic Italian pasta dishes follow this pattern. *Pasta a l'aglio e olio,* page 185, in which pasta is simply tossed with garlic-scented oil, and *spaghetti al cacio e pepe,* with grated cheese and black pepper, are outstanding examples. Even for the famous *fettuccine Alfredo* the pasta is tossed only with softened butter and cheese, not an elaborate sauce. A

Spaghettini with Japanese Eggplant & Sweet Peppers,
page 48

39

delightful, simple dish I tasted in the lovely town of Spoleto in central Italy was of thin noodles tossed only with a little butter, diced tomato, parsley and the area's specialty, aromatic black truffles.

PASTA WITH VEGETABLES

All vegetables are good with pasta. They can be cooked in a variety of ways: simmered in cream, as in Angel-Hair Pasta with Creamy Mushroom Sauce & Fresh Herbs; sautéed in olive oil, as in Spaghettini with Japanese Eggplant & Sweet Peppers; heated in sauce, as in Vermicelli with Indian Vegetable Sauce; or lightly cooked in boiling salted water, like the asparagus in Lemon Fettuccine with Asparagus, Smoked Salmon & Herb Butter.

The vegetable most commonly paired with pasta is the tomato, which is often cooked into sauce, page 186, but can also be lightly sautéed or just diced and added raw, as in Spinach Pasta with Goat Cheese, Tomatoes & Thyme.

In addition to fresh vegetables, it is practical to keep other forms of vegetables on hand for making quick pasta dishes. Sun-dried tomatoes in both their loose, dried form and packed in olive oil, make wonderful additions to pasta, as do dried mushrooms. Jars of roasted peppers and canned, whole plum tomatoes are also time-saving and valuable ingredients for numerous recipes, and so are frozen vegetables, especially peas, artichoke hearts and spinach.

Although all pasta shapes can be paired with vegetables, you might want to consider the shapes of the ingredients you are using and how they will look together. For example, if all the vegetables will be cut in strips, it is good to pair them with long thin pastas like linguine or fettuccine. On the other hand, if the vegetables will not have much shape once cooked, choose an interesting form of pasta, as in Pasta Spirals with Butter-Cooked Onions.

For a few dishes vermicelli and very thin types of pasta like fideos are cooked by a special technique: the pasta is sautéed and cooked gently in just the amount of broth it will absorb, rather like risotto or rice pilaf. Examples of these types are Sautéed Pasta with Skillet-Toasted Almonds & Raisins and Mexican Sautéed Noodles with Tomatoes & Mild Chiles.

PASTA WITH CHEESE

Cheese, of course, is the most popular flavoring for pasta—its saltiness and richness are just what a bowl of plain pasta needs. The cheese can be blended into a creamy sauce, as in Spaghetti with Spicy Gorgonzola Sauce, grated and tossed with the pasta, as in Linguine with Broccoli, Sun-Dried Tomatoes & Pecorino Cheese, or sprinkled on top, as in Penne with Peas & Parmesan.

In addition to Parmesan and romano, other grating cheeses like Gruyère, kashkaval and asiago are flavorful additions. For best results, buy the finest quality imported cheeses and grate them just before use. Softer cheeses like creamy goat cheese, feta cheese and Roquefort are also good partners for pasta. Many stuffed and baked pastas are generously flavored with cheeses, including creamy cheeses like ricotta. (See Stuffed & Baked Pasta, page 118.)

Linguine with Mushrooms, Pesto & Plum Tomatoes

Pesto, see below
3 tablespoons pine nuts
8 ounces small ripe plum
  tomatoes
3 tablespoons olive oil
4 ounces mushrooms, halved,
  sliced thin

½ teaspoon dried leaf basil,
  crumbled
Salt and freshly ground pepper to
  taste
8 ounces dried linguine
Bowl of freshly grated Parmesan
  cheese (for serving)

It is hard to think of a better match for pasta than homemade pesto redolent of fresh basil. Here the traditional pair is embellished by mushrooms and tomatoes and garnished with toasted pine nuts which highlight the flavor of the pesto.

Prepare Pesto; set aside. Preheat oven to 350F (175C). Toast pine nuts on a small baking sheet in oven until lightly browned, about 3 minutes. If you prefer, toast pine nuts in a dry small heavy skillet over medium heat, shaking skillet often, until lightly browned, about 3 minutes. Transfer pine nuts to a plate and let cool.

Cut tomatoes in half lengthwise, squeeze well and remove seeds. Cut each piece in four lengthwise; set aside.

Heat 2 tablespoons oil in a medium skillet over medium heat. Add mushrooms, dried basil, salt and pepper. Sauté, stirring, about 3 minutes or until lightly browned. Remove mushrooms to a plate. Add 1 tablespoon oil to skillet and heat over medium-high heat. Add tomato pieces and sauté about 30 seconds or until just heated through. Transfer to a plate.

Bring a large pot of water to a boil; add salt, then pasta. Cook uncovered over high heat, separating strands occasionally with a fork, about 8 minutes or until tender but firm to the bite. Drain well. Transfer to a heated serving bowl.

Add ½ cup Pesto to pasta and toss. Add mushrooms and tomatoes; toss again. Taste and adjust seasoning. Sprinkle with toasted pine nuts and garnish with basil sprig. Serve immediately with more Parmesan cheese and remaining Pesto separately.

Makes 4 to 6 first-course or 2 or 3 main-course servings.

Pesto

1 cup basil leaves (1½-oz. bunch)
3 medium garlic cloves, peeled
2 tablespoons pine nuts
½ cup freshly grated Parmesan
  cheese (about 1½ oz.)

⅓ cup fine-quality olive oil,
  preferably extra virgin

Reserve 1 basil sprig for garnish. With the blade of a food processor turning, drop garlic cloves, 1 at a time, through feed tube and process until finely chopped. Add pine nuts, remaining basil and Parmesan cheese; process until basil is chopped. With blade turning, gradually add olive oil. Scrape down sides and process until mixture is well blended. Transfer to a small bowl. (Pesto can be kept, covered, 2 days in refrigerator. Bring to room temperature before using.)

A toaster oven is useful for toasting small amounts of nuts.

COOKING TIP

Whole-Wheat Spaghetti with Ginger-Scented Vegetables

8 ounces whole-wheat spaghetti
1 tablespoon sesame seeds
2 tablespoons soy sauce
2 tablespoons mirin (syrupy rice wine)
1 tablespoon Oriental sesame oil
Omelet Strips, see below
4 tablespoons vegetable oil
1 large carrot, peeled, cut in 2-inch julienne strips
3 large green onions, sliced thin

2 tablespoons minced peeled gingerroot
2 small zucchini, cut in 2-inch julienne strips
4 ounces snow peas, ends removed, cut diagonally in thin strips about ¼ inch wide
Oriental chili oil or Tabasco sauce to taste, if desired
Cilantro (fresh coriander) or parsley sprigs

Bring a large pot of water to a boil; add salt, then pasta. Cook uncovered over high heat, separating strands occasionally with a fork, 8 to 9 minutes or until tender but firm to the bite. Drain, rinse with cold water and drain well.

Toast sesame seeds in a dry small heavy skillet over medium-low heat, stirring, until light brown, 2 to 3 minutes; transfer to a small bowl.

Combine soy sauce, mirin and sesame oil in a small bowl; blend well. Set aside. Prepare Omelet Strips; set aside. (Recipe can be prepared to this point up to 2 hours ahead and kept at room temperature.)

Heat 3 tablespoons vegetable oil in a large skillet over medium-high heat. Add carrot, green onions and gingerroot. Sauté, stirring, 2 minutes. Add zucchini and snow peas. Sauté 1 minute. Transfer vegetables to a bowl.

Add remaining 1 tablespoon oil to skillet and heat over medium heat. Add spaghetti and sauté, tossing lightly with a slotted spatula, until hot. Remove from heat. Gently stir in soy-sauce mixture and transfer to a heated dish. Add vegetables and ⅔ of Omelet Strips to spaghetti; toss. Taste and adjust seasoning, adding chili oil or Tabasco if desired. Transfer mixture to a platter and sprinkle with sesame seeds. Garnish with remaining Omelet Strips and with cilantro or parsley sprigs. Serve hot.

Makes 6 first-course or side-dish or 3 main-course servings.

Omelet Strips

2 teaspoons vegetable oil
2 large eggs

Salt and freshly ground pepper to taste

Heat oil in a 10-inch skillet, preferably nonstick, over medium heat. Tilt skillet to coat with oil. Beat eggs with salt and pepper to taste. Add egg mixture to hot oil and cook, loosening sides often with a pancake turner to allow uncooked egg mixture to flow to edge of skillet, 2 minutes or until set. Slide pancake turner carefully underneath to release omelet. Cut omelet in half with pancake turner. Turn each half omelet over and cook it 30 seconds longer. Transfer omelet halves carefully to a plate and let cool to room temperature. Cut each omelet half in half lengthwise, then in crosswise strips about ¼ inch wide.

Quick & Zesty Macaroni with Garlic, Olives & Capers

5 to 6 tablespoons extra-virgin olive oil

4 large garlic cloves, minced

8 ounces ripe plum tomatoes, peeled, seeded, chopped

3 anchovy fillets, chopped

1/4 teaspoon hot red-pepper flakes, if desired

8 ounces long macaroni, bucatini or perciatelli

1/2 cup pitted oil-cured black olives, or 1 (3¼-oz.) can pitted olives in brine, drained

Freshly ground black pepper to taste

2 tablespoons chopped fresh parsley leaves, if desired

1 tablespoon drained capers, rinsed

6 tablespoons thin strips fresh basil leaves or 3 tablespoons chopped cilantro (fresh coriander) leaves, if desired

Heat 2 tablespoons oil in a medium skillet over medium heat. Add garlic and sauté 30 seconds. Add tomatoes, anchovies and red-pepper flakes, if desired. Sauté over medium-high heat about 3 minutes or until tomatoes soften.

Bring a large pot of water to a boil; add salt, then pasta. Cook uncovered over high heat, stirring occasionally, about 8 minutes or until tender but firm to the bite. Meanwhile, reheat tomato mixture if necessary. Add olives and heat a few seconds. Drain pasta well. Transfer to a heated bowl.

Toss pasta with 3 tablespoons olive oil, tomato mixture, freshly ground pepper and parsley. Taste and adjust seasoning; add another 1 tablespoon olive oil if desired. Spoon into serving dish. Top with capers. If desired, sprinkle with basil strips or chopped cilantro. Serve hot or at room temperature.

Makes 4 first-course servings.

Pasta Puttanesca, or "prostitute's pasta," is the Italian name of this dish, though nobody knows exactly why! In the classic version, the pasta is tossed with lightly sautéed tomatoes as well as garlic, anchovies, olives and capers. Although the sauce is quite pungent on its own, it is perfect when mixed with the pasta. I sometimes like to add basil or, for a total break with tradition, cilantro.

Pasta with Avocado Pesto

2 medium garlic cloves, halved

1 cup fresh basil leaves

1/4 cup packed Italian parsley leaves or small sprigs regular parsley

2 tablespoons pine nuts

2 tablespoons freshly grated Parmesan cheese

1 ripe medium avocado, preferably Haas (8 oz.)

6 tablespoons pure olive oil or avocado oil

Salt and freshly ground pepper to taste

8 ounces pasta wheels, shells or other small round pasta shapes (about 3½ cups)

1/4 cup toasted pine nuts, page 36

2 medium tomatoes, diced

With the blade of a food processor turning, drop garlic cloves, 1 at a time, through feed tube and process until finely chopped. Add basil, parsley, pine nuts and Parmesan cheese; process until basil and parsley are chopped. Peel and pit avocado; cut flesh in a few chunks. Add to mixture in processor and puree. With blade turning, gradually add oil. Scrape down sides and process until mixture is well blended. Season with salt and freshly ground pepper. Transfer to a bowl.

Bring a large pot of water to a boil; add salt, then pasta. Cook uncovered over high heat, stirring occasionally, about 7 minutes or until tender but firm to the bite. Drain well. Transfer to a heated serving dish. Add pesto and fold in with a rubber spatula. If mixture is too thick to blend easily, add 1 tablespoon hot water and toss until blended. Taste and adjust seasoning. Add 2 tablespoons toasted pine nuts and about ½ of diced tomato; toss again. Sprinkle with remaining diced tomato and remaining pine nuts and serve.

Makes 4 first-course servings.

Cooks are now developing variations on the popular pesto sauce of basil, garlic and olive oil—you can find cilantro pesto, mint pesto and chili pesto, all made by blending an herb or spice with oil and usually garlic. Here I have added avocado to the traditional basil to make a rich creamy sauce for the pasta wheels. Avocado pesto is lighter in color and creamier than classic pesto. Use mild or "pure" olive oil rather than virgin or extra virgin for a more delicate taste that does not overpower the avocado. I would not purchase a bottle of avocado oil just for this recipe, but if you already have it, use it.

Angel-Hair Pasta with Creamy Mushroom Sauce & Fresh Herbs

1 tablespoon butter
2 medium shallots, minced
1¾ to 2 cups whipping cream
8 ounces mushrooms, halved, sliced
Salt and freshly ground pepper to taste
8 ounces dried angel-hair pasta or capellini

2 or 3 tablespoons minced fresh tarragon leaves, to taste
3 tablespoons snipped fresh chives
3 tablespoons minced fresh parsley leaves

Melt butter in a heavy medium saucepan over low heat. Add shallots and cook 1 minute. Add 1¾ cups cream and bring to a simmer, stirring. Add mushrooms, salt and pepper. Cook uncovered over low heat, stirring often, about 30 minutes or until mushrooms are very tender and cream is well flavored. (Sauce can be kept, covered, up to 1 day in refrigerator.)

Bring a large pot of water to a boil; add salt, then pasta. Cook uncovered over high heat, separating strands occasionally with a fork, about 4 minutes or until tender but firm to the bite. Meanwhile, reheat sauce to a simmer over medium heat, stirring. Drain pasta well. Transfer to a large serving bowl.

Add tarragon, chives and 2 tablespoons parsley to sauce. Taste and adjust seasoning. Add sauce to pasta and toss until thoroughly coated. Taste again for seasoning. For creamier pasta, heat remaining ¼ cup cream in a very small saucepan over medium heat until simmering. Pour hot cream over pasta and toss well. Sprinkle with remaining parsley and serve immediately.
Makes 6 first-course or side-dish servings.

Pasta Spirals with Butter-Cooked Onions

1 tablespoon vegetable oil
4 tablespoons butter
2 large onions (1 lb. total), halved, sliced thin
Salt and freshly ground pepper to taste
2 teaspoons fresh thyme leaves or ¾ teaspoon dried leaf, crumbled

1 bay leaf
8 ounces fusilli, rotini or other spiral-shaped pasta (about 3½ cups)
2 tablespoons grated Parmesan cheese, if desired
Bowl of freshly grated Parmesan cheese (for serving), if desired

Heat oil and 3 tablespoons butter in a large skillet over medium-low heat. Add onions, salt, pepper, thyme and bay leaf. Sauté, stirring often, about 25 minutes or until soft. Increase heat to medium-high and sauté, stirring, until onions are light brown, about 5 minutes. Discard bay leaf. (Onions can be kept, covered, up to 2 days in refrigerator; reheat in large skillet over low heat before continuing.)

Bring a large pot of water to a boil; add salt, then pasta. Cook uncovered over high heat, stirring occasionally, about 7 minutes or until tender but firm to the bite. Drain well.

Add pasta to skillet of onions. Add remaining 1 tablespoon butter and toss gently over low heat until well combined and butter melts. Transfer to a heated serving dish and add 2 tablespoons Parmesan cheese if desired. Taste and adjust seasoning. Serve with more Parmesan cheese, if desired.
Makes 4 side-dish servings.

Herb Fettuccine with Wild Mushrooms

6 ounces fresh shiitake mushrooms, chanterelles, oyster mushrooms, cèpes, or porcini mushrooms
2 tablespoons vegetable oil
7 tablespoons butter
Salt and freshly ground pepper to taste
2 tablespoons minced shallots
1¹/₂ teaspoons chopped fresh thyme leaves or ¹/₂ teaspoon dried leaf, crumbled

9 to 10 ounces fresh herb-flavored or egg fettuccine, homemade, page 182, or packaged, or 8 ounces dried
2 tablespoons chopped fresh parsley leaves
Bowl of freshly grated Parmesan cheese (for serving)

This is a simple recipe for using fresh "wild" mushrooms inspired by a lovely dish of rigatoni with fresh porcini mushrooms that I enjoyed in Florence. For those like me who prefer to look for wild mushrooms at the market rather than in the forest, it is fortunate that exotic mushrooms can now be found in fine supermarkets and produce shops. Although often referred to as "wild," quite a few types are now cultivated. Very little else is added to this pasta dish so the mushrooms stand out.

Gently rinse mushrooms and dry on paper towels. If using shiitake mushrooms, remove stems. Cut large mushrooms lengthwise in pieces about ¹/₂ inch wide.

In a large skillet, heat oil and 4 tablespoons butter over medium heat. Add mushrooms, salt and pepper. Sauté about 3 minutes. Add shallots and thyme. Sauté over medium-high heat, tossing often, about 3 minutes longer or until mushrooms are browned and tender and any liquid that may have escaped from them has evaporated. (Sautéed mushrooms can be kept, covered, 1 to 2 hours at room temperature.)

Bring a large pot of water to a boil; add salt, then pasta. Cook uncovered over high heat, separating strands occasionally with a fork, 30 seconds to 2 minutes for fresh or 2 to 5 minutes for dried or until tender but firm to the bite. Meanwhile, reheat mushrooms, uncovered. Taste and adjust seasoning.

Drain pasta well. Transfer to a heated serving dish. Add remaining 3 tablespoons butter, parsley, salt and pepper; toss until coated. Spoon mushroom mixture on top and serve with Parmesan cheese.
Makes 4 first-course servings.

For a quick dish using dried pasta, you can add quick-cooking cut vegetables to the pot of cooking pasta at the appropriate point according to their cooking times.

COOKING TIP

Vermicelli with Indian Vegetable Sauce

Indian Tomato Sauce, see below
1 thin carrot, cut in diagonal
   slices about ½ inch thick
12 ounces fresh peas, shelled, or
   ¾ cup frozen

1½ cups small cauliflowerets
¼ cup whipping cream, if desired
5 tablespoons chopped cilantro
   (fresh coriander) leaves
12 ounces vermicelli

Prepare Indian Tomato Sauce; set aside. Put carrot slices in a medium sauce-pan and cover generously with water. Bring to a boil and cook 3 minutes or until softened slightly but not quite tender. Transfer to a medium bowl with a slotted spoon. Add peas to carrot cooking liquid and cook 30 seconds. Transfer to bowl with slotted spoon. Add cauliflower to cooking liquid and cook about 3 minutes; it should still be crisp as it will continue to cook in sauce. Drain thoroughly.

Add vegetables to Indian Tomato Sauce. Cover and cook over low heat about 5 minutes or until just tender. Add cream, if desired, and simmer uncovered 2 minutes. Stir in 4 tablespoons cilantro. Taste and adjust seasoning.

Bring a large pot of water to a boil; add salt, then pasta. Cook uncovered over high heat, separating strands occasionally with a fork, 6 to 7 minutes or until tender but firm to the bite. Meanwhile, reheat sauce over low heat.

Drain pasta well. Transfer to a heated serving bowl. Toss with 2½ cups vegetable sauce. Sprinkle with remaining 1 tablespoon cilantro. Serve remaining sauce separately.

Makes 6 to 8 first-course or side-dish servings.

Indian Tomato Sauce

2 tablespoons vegetable oil
2 tablespoons butter
1 medium onion, chopped
4 teaspoons minced peeled
   gingerroot
4 teaspoons minced garlic
1 to 3 fresh jalapeño peppers,
   seeds and ribs discarded,
   minced (see Note below)

1 tablespoon ground cumin
½ teaspoon ground turmeric
1 teaspoon ground coriander
2 pounds ripe tomatoes, peeled,
   seeded, chopped, or 2 (28-oz.)
   cans whole plum tomatoes,
   drained
Salt and freshly ground pepper to
   taste

Heat oil and butter in a heavy medium saucepan over low heat. Add onion and cook, stirring, about 7 minutes or until soft but not browned. Add gingerroot, garlic and jalapeño peppers. Cook 1 minute. Add cumin, turmeric and coriander. Cook, stirring, 30 seconds. Add tomatoes, salt and pepper. Stir well to combine with spice mixture. Bring to a boil. Cover and cook over low heat, stirring occasionally (and crushing canned tomatoes if using), about 30 minutes or until tomatoes are very soft. (Sauce can be kept, covered, up to 2 days in refrigerator or can be frozen; reheat in medium saucepan before continuing.)

Note: Wear gloves when handling jalapeño peppers. After cutting, wash your hands, cutting board and any utensils that came in contact with jalapeño pepper, with soap and hot water.

Lemon Fettuccine with Asparagus, Smoked Salmon & Herb Butter

For this festive first course, choose homemade or fine-quality packaged pasta. The abundance of herbs gives this elegant dish a fresh character. Smoked salmon and lemon pasta are a natural pair but you can substitute herb pasta, plain egg fettuccine or even smoked-salmon pasta.

✦ *Photo on cover.*

Herb Butter, see below
1 pound thin asparagus
9 to 10 ounces fresh lemon or egg fettuccine or tagliarini, homemade, page 181, or packaged, or 8 ounces dried
3 ounces sliced smoked salmon or lox, cut in about 2" x ¼" strips
1 teaspoon chopped fresh tarragon leaves
½ teaspoon snipped fresh chives
1 teaspoon chopped fresh parsley leaves
Tarragon sprigs, parsley sprigs and whole chives, if desired
Lemon slices, if desired

Prepare Herb Butter; set aside at room temperature. Peel asparagus if over ¼ inch thick and trim about 1½ inches off ends. Set aside a few spears for garnish. Cut remaining asparagus in 2-inch lengths; reserve tips separately. Add stems and whole spears to a medium saucepan of enough boiling salted water to cover generously. Cook uncovered over high heat about 2 minutes; add tips and cook 2 minutes or until crisp-tender. Drain, rinse with cold water and drain well. Return to saucepan and add 1 tablespoon Herb Butter.

Bring a large pot of water to a boil; add salt, then pasta. Cook uncovered over high heat, separating strands occasionally with a fork, 30 seconds to 2 minutes for fresh pasta or 2 to 5 minutes for dried or until tender but firm to the bite. Drain well.

Return pasta to pot or to a medium saucepan. Add remaining Herb Butter in pieces and toss over low heat until pasta is coated with butter. Meanwhile, reheat asparagus in its butter. Transfer pasta to a large heated serving platter. Add asparagus pieces and smoked salmon; toss gently. Taste and adjust seasoning. Sprinkle with tarragon, chives and parsley. Garnish with asparagus spears. If desired, garnish with herb sprigs and lemon slices before serving.
Makes 4 or 5 first-course servings.

Herb Butter

6 or 7 tablespoons unsalted butter, softened
2 tablespoons chopped fresh tarragon leaves
2 tablespoons snipped fresh chives
1 tablespoon chopped fresh parsley leaves
2 teaspoons chopped fresh thyme leaves or ¾ teaspoon dried leaf, crumbled
2 teaspoons tarragon vinegar or herb vinegar, if desired
Salt and freshly ground pepper to taste

Combine butter, tarragon, chives, parsley and thyme in a medium bowl. Beat with a wooden spoon until blended. Add vinegar if desired. Season with salt and pepper. (Flavored butter can be kept, covered, up to 1 day in refrigerator. Bring to room temperature before using.)

Spaghettini with Japanese Eggplant & Sweet Peppers

8 ounces Japanese eggplants
2 green or red bell peppers, or 1 green and 1 red, seeds and ribs discarded
7 tablespoons olive oil, preferably virgin or extra virgin
Salt and freshly ground pepper to taste
2 large garlic cloves, minced
12 ounces ripe plum tomatoes, peeled, seeded, chopped, or 1¼ cups chopped drained canned plum tomatoes

8 ounces spaghettini
¼ cup thin strips fresh basil leaves
¼ cup freshly grated Parmesan cheese
Bowl of freshly grated Parmesan cheese (for serving)

Cut eggplants in crosswise slices about ¼ inch thick. Cut bell peppers in about 2" x ¼" strips. Heat 2 tablespoons oil in a large skillet over medium-high heat. Add eggplant and quickly sprinkle with salt and pepper. Sauté about 2 minutes per side or until tender when pierced with a fork. Transfer to an ovenproof platter. Add 2 tablespoons oil to skillet and heat over medium heat. Add peppers and sauté about 10 minutes or until tender. Transfer to platter. Cover eggplant and peppers; keep warm in a 350F (175C) oven.

Add 1 tablespoon oil to skillet and heat over medium-low heat. Add garlic and sauté 30 seconds. Add tomatoes, salt and pepper. Cook over high heat, stirring often (and crushing canned tomatoes, if using), about 10 minutes or until soft and thick. Taste and adjust seasoning. Keep warm over low heat.

Bring a large pot of water to a boil; add salt, then pasta. Cook uncovered over high heat, separating strands occasionally with a fork, about 7 minutes or until tender but firm to the bite. Drain well. Transfer to a heated serving platter or bowl.

Add remaining 2 tablespoons olive oil to pasta and toss. Add tomato sauce and toss. Reserve a few eggplant slices, pepper strips and basil strips for garnish. Add remaining eggplant and peppers to pasta; toss. Add ¼ cup Parmesan cheese and basil; toss again. Taste and adjust seasoning. Arrange reserved pepper strips over top. Garnish with reserved eggplant slices. Sprinkle basil strips in center. Serve with more Parmesan cheese.
Makes 4 first-course servings.

Note: A small regular eggplant can be substituted for the Japanese type but the slices should be cut in half after they are sautéed.

COOKING TIP

To keep a bowl warm for serving pasta, an old Italian trick is to keep it full of very hot water and to pour out the water just before adding the pasta.

Vermicelli-Vegetable Medley with Sautéed Pecans

2 teaspoons vegetable oil
½ cup pecan halves
Salt to taste
1 large red bell pepper, seeds and ribs discarded
1 small zucchini
1 small yellow zucchini or crookneck squash
1 small eggplant (about 12 oz.)
7 tablespoons olive oil
2 tablespoons butter or 2 additional tablespoons olive oil
1 medium onion, halved, sliced thin
Freshly ground pepper to taste
8 ounces vermicelli
4 large garlic cloves, minced
5 tablespoons minced fresh oregano leaves or 1 tablespoon plus 2 teaspoons dried leaf, crumbled
2 tablespoons minced fresh parsley leaves

You can treat this colorful dish as a basic recipe and vary the herbs and vegetables according to their seasons, and choose different nuts according to your fancy. It is also great with whole-wheat spaghetti.

Heat vegetable oil in a small heavy skillet over medium-low heat. Add pecans and a pinch of salt. Sauté, tossing often with a slotted spoon, until lightly browned, about 3 minutes. Transfer to a plate and set aside.

Halve bell pepper crosswise and cut in ¼-inch-wide strips. Cut zucchini in 3 pieces crosswise, then in lengthwise strips about ¼ inch wide and ¼ inch thick. Cut squash like zucchini. Cut peel from eggplant, discard ends and cut eggplant in 2" x ½" x ¼" strips.

Heat 2 tablespoons olive oil in a large skillet over medium heat. Add eggplant and sprinkle with salt. Sauté, tossing constantly, about 7 minutes or until just tender. Transfer to a bowl.

Add 2 tablespoons olive oil and 2 tablespoons butter or additional oil to skillet. Heat over medium-low heat. Add onion and cook, stirring often, about 7 minutes or until softened but not brown. Add pepper strips, salt and pepper. Cook, tossing often, about 5 minutes or until onions and peppers are nearly tender. Add zucchini, yellow squash and eggplant. Cook, tossing often, until zucchini is crisp-tender, about 3 minutes. Transfer vegetables to a large bowl and keep warm. Wipe skillet clean and set aside.

Bring a large pot of water to a boil; add salt, then pasta. Cook uncovered over high heat, separating strands occasionally with a fork, 6 to 7 minutes or until tender but firm to the bite. Drain well. Add to bowl of vegetables and toss.

Add remaining 3 tablespoons olive oil to skillet from cooking vegetables and heat over low heat. Add garlic and cook about 30 seconds. Add oregano and heat 2 or 3 seconds. Pour mixture over vegetables and pasta. Add parsley and toss well. Taste and adjust seasoning. Garnish with some of sautéed pecans and serve remaining pecans separately.

Makes 4 first-course or side-dish servings.

Creamy Fettuccine with Porcini, Prosciutto & Peas

1 pound ripe tomatoes, peeled, seeded, chopped, or 1 (28-oz.) can whole plum tomatoes, drained, chopped
$2/3$ to 1 ounce dried porcini mushrooms
6 tablespoons butter, cut in pieces, room temperature
Salt and freshly ground pepper to taste
$1/2$ cup cooked fresh or thawed frozen peas
1 ounce prosciutto, cut in thin strips

1 small crookneck squash or yellow zucchini, halved, cut crosswise in $1/4$-inch slices
9 to 10 ounces fresh fettuccine, homemade, page 178, or packaged, or 8 ounces dried
$1/3$ cup sour cream, room temperature
5 tablespoons freshly grated Parmesan cheese
Bowl of freshly grated Parmesan cheese (for serving)

Put chopped tomatoes in a strainer to drain while preparing remaining ingredients. Soak porcini in enough hot water to cover about 30 minutes or until tender; drain well. Remove porcini and rinse. Discard any hard parts. Chop porcini.

Melt 1 tablespoon butter in a medium skillet over medium heat. Add chopped porcini and stir. Add tomatoes, salt and pepper. Cook, stirring often, 10 to 12 minutes or until mixture is thick. Stir in peas and prosciutto. Heat 1 to 2 minutes. Taste and adjust seasoning. Keep warm over low heat.

Meanwhile, melt 2 tablespoons butter in a medium skillet over medium heat. Add squash and sauté about 2 minutes or until just tender. Remove squash with its cooking butter to a bowl. Cover and keep warm.

Bring a large pot of water to a boil; add salt, then pasta. Cook uncovered over high heat, separating strands occasionally with a fork, 30 seconds to 2 minutes for fresh or 2 to 5 minutes for dried or until tender but firm to the bite. Drain well and transfer to a large heated serving bowl.

Add remaining 3 tablespoons butter to pasta and toss. Add sour cream and squash; toss. Sprinkle with $1/4$ cup Parmesan cheese and spoon tomato mixture on top. Sprinkle with remaining 1 tablespoon cheese. Toss at the table. Serve on hot plates with Parmesan cheese.
Makes 5 or 6 first-course servings.

VARIATION
Add $1/3$ cup strips of roasted peeled green bell pepper, page 95, or strips of roasted red peppers from a jar, at same time as peas.

Artichoke Spaghetti with Artichokes

5 or 6 medium artichokes or 1
  (9-oz.) package frozen
  artichoke quarters (19 or 20
  pieces)
1 lemon (if using fresh
  artichokes) or 1 teaspoon
  strained fresh lemon juice (if
  using frozen)
4 to 5 tablespoons olive oil,
  preferably extra virgin
4 ounces mushrooms, halved,
  sliced
Salt and freshly ground pepper to
  taste

3 large garlic cloves, minced
1 medium shallot, minced
8 ounces artichoke spaghetti or
  artichoke-heart tagliarini,
  fresh or dried
⅓ cup freshly grated Parmesan
  cheese
¼ cup minced fresh parsley
  leaves
Bowl of freshly grated Parmesan
  or pecorino-romano cheese
  (for serving)

Artichoke spaghetti is sometimes made with sunchokes (Jerusalem artichokes), but finer versions are made with artichoke hearts. You can also find whole-wheat artichoke pasta. Use any type or substitute whole-wheat or regular spaghetti for this dish with its simple topping of garlic-scented sautéed artichokes, mushrooms and Parmesan cheese.

If using fresh artichokes, squeeze juice of ½ lemon into a medium bowl of cold water. Break off stem of 1 artichoke and largest leaves at bottom. Put artichoke on its side on a board. Holding a very sharp knife or small serrated knife against side of artichoke (parallel to leaves), cut lower circle of leaves off, up to edge of artichoke heart; turn artichoke slightly after each cut. Rub cut edges of artichoke heart with cut lemon. Cut off leaves under base. Trim base, removing all dark-green areas. Rub again with lemon. Cut off central cone of leaves just above artichoke heart. Put artichoke in bowl of lemon water. Repeat with remaining artichokes.

Prepare a medium saucepan of boiling salted water and squeeze in any juice remaining in lemon (if using fresh artichokes) or add 1 teaspoon lemon juice (if using frozen). Add fresh or frozen artichoke hearts to saucepan. Cover and simmer over low heat until just tender when pierced with knife, 15 to 20 minutes for fresh ones and about 7 minutes for frozen ones. Remove, reserving liquid, and cool. Using a teaspoon, scoop out hairlike "choke" from center of each fresh artichoke heart. Return artichokes to liquid until ready to use. (They can be kept 1 or 2 hours at room temperature.) Drain and cut each fresh artichoke into 8 pieces. If frozen artichoke pieces are large, cut in half after draining.

Heat 1 tablespoon oil in a medium skillet over medium-high heat. Add mushrooms, salt and pepper. Sauté about 5 minutes or until tender and lightly browned. Transfer to a medium bowl.

Add 3 tablespoons oil to skillet and heat over medium heat. Add artichokes, salt and pepper. Sauté 2 minutes. Add garlic and shallot. Sauté 30 seconds. Transfer mixture to bowl of mushrooms; reserve skillet.

Bring a large pot of water to a boil; add salt, then pasta. Cook uncovered over high heat, separating strands occasionally with a fork, 2 to 4 minutes for fresh or 5 to 7 minutes for dried or until tender but firm to the bite. Drain well. Transfer to a heated serving bowl. Add remaining 1 or 2 tablespoons oil and toss. Sprinkle with ⅓ cup Parmesan cheese and freshly ground pepper.

Return artichoke and mushroom mixture to skillet; reheat over low heat. Add 2 tablespoons parsley and spoon mixture over pasta; toss. Sprinkle with remaining 2 tablespoons parsley and serve with more cheese.
Makes 3 main-course or 4 or 5 side-dish servings.

Holding knife against side of artichoke (parallel to leaves), cut lower circle of leaves off up to edge of artichoke heart; turn artichoke slightly after each cut. Rub cut edges of artichoke heart with cut lemon.

Cut off leaves under base. Trim base, removing all dark-green areas. Rub again with lemon. Cut off central cone of leaves just above artichoke heart. Put artichoke heart in a bowl of lemon water.

For this Middle Eastern dish, traditionally served with roast leg of lamb, the cooking technique for the pasta is unusual and bears a certain resemblance to the procedure for risotto or rice pilaf—the noodles are sautéed, then simmered slowly in just enough chicken broth to cook them. It works only with very thin noodles and tiny pastas like orzo.

Sautéed Pasta with Skillet-Toasted Almonds & Raisins

¼ cup dark raisins
2 small zucchini
3 tablespoons plus 1 teaspoon butter
½ cup slivered almonds
Salt to taste
1 tablespoon vegetable oil
8 ounces very thin egg noodles for soup (4 cups)

2 cups unsalted chicken stock or broth, homemade, page 187, or packaged
2 tablespoons chopped fresh parsley leaves
Freshly ground pepper to taste

Pour enough boiling water over raisins to cover. Let stand 5 minutes to plump; drain well. Cut zucchini in 3 crosswise; cut each chunk in lengthwise strips ¼ inch wide and ¼ inch thick. Set aside.

Melt 1 teaspoon butter in a small heavy skillet over medium heat. Add almonds and a pinch of salt. Sauté, stirring, until light golden, about 3 minutes. Transfer to a plate. Wipe skillet clean if butter turned brown. Add oil to skillet and heat over medium heat. Add zucchini and sauté about 2 minutes or until barely tender. Transfer to a plate.

Melt remaining 3 tablespoons butter in a large heavy deep skillet or sauté pan over medium heat. Add pasta and sauté, stirring constantly, until golden, about 7 minutes. Add ½ cup stock and a pinch of salt. Cook over medium heat, uncovered, stirring often and turning pasta over with tongs. Add more stock in ½-cup portions as it is absorbed and cook about 7 minutes or until pasta is tender.

Stir in zucchini, parsley and pepper. Taste and adjust seasoning. Serve pasta on a heated platter or heated plates and top with almonds and raisins.
Makes 4 to 6 side-dish servings.

These noodles are a good accompaniment for chicken or meat. The dish is even more fun to present with a variety of toppings, such as avocado, sour cream and cilantro, as suggested below, to mix and match as a first course. The thin Spanish noodles called fideos are available in many supermarkets but regular vermicelli makes a fine substitute.

Mexican Sautéed Noodles with Tomatoes & Mild Chiles

1 fresh mild green chile (also called California or Anaheim chile) or ⅓ cup chopped canned green chile
8 ounces fideos (coiled thin noodles) or vermicelli
4 or 5 tablespoons vegetable oil
⅓ cup minced onion
2 medium garlic cloves, minced
1 pound ripe tomatoes, peeled, seeded, chopped, or 1 (28-oz.) can whole plum tomatoes, drained, chopped

1 teaspoon dried leaf oregano, crumbled
About 1½ cups unsalted chicken stock or broth, homemade, page 187, or packaged
Salt and freshly ground pepper to taste
Toppings, opposite
4 tablespoons chopped cilantro (fresh coriander) leaves or fresh parsley leaves

If using a fresh chile, discard seeds and ribs. Chop finely and set aside. Break noodles in 2- or 3-inch pieces. Heat 4 tablespoons oil in a large skillet over medium heat. Add noodles and sauté, stirring constantly and turning over from time to time, until golden, about 7 minutes. Transfer to a bowl with tongs or a slotted spoon. (A few noodles may remain in skillet.)

Mexican Sautéed Noodles with Tomatoes & Mild Chiles

Add noodles to hot oil in a large skillet. Sauté until golden, stirring constantly and turning from time to time, about 7 minutes.

Add 1 tablespoon oil if skillet is dry and heat over low heat. Add onion and chile. Cook, stirring often, about 5 minutes or until onion softens. Add garlic, tomatoes and oregano; stir well and bring to a boil. Add 1½ cups broth and a pinch of salt; bring to a boil. Add pasta and stir. Reduce heat to low, cover and simmer, stirring occasionally, about 12 minutes or until liquid is absorbed and pasta is tender. If skillet becomes dry before pasta is tender, add a few table-spoons stock or water. Meanwhile, prepare Toppings, if desired. Add 3 table-spoons cilantro or parsley to pasta. Taste and adjust seasoning. Sprinkle with remaining 1 tablespoon cilantro or parsley and serve in a heated bowl with Toppings if desired.
Makes 4 first-course or side-dish servings.

Toppings

1 small avocado, preferably Haas
Sour cream
Chopped green onions

Chopped cilantro leaves
Cherry tomatoes
Shredded Monterey Jack cheese

If using avocado, peel and slice or dice it just before serving. Serve pasta with bowls of avocado, sour cream, green onion, cilantro, cherry tomatoes and shred-ded Monterey Jack cheese.

Jalapeño peppers cook gently in cream and add zip to the rich Gorgonzola sauce, while a small amount of pureed tomato gives a fresh taste and a pale-pink tint. Try the sauce also on tomato noodles or whole-wheat spaghetti.

Spaghetti with Spicy Gorgonzola Sauce

2 fresh jalapeño peppers
1 ripe plum tomato, peeled, seeded or 1 canned plum tomato
1 cup whipping cream
2 medium garlic cloves, coarsely chopped
4 ounces Gorgonzola cheese, rind removed, cut in a few pieces

Salt to taste, if desired
Red (cayenne) pepper to taste, if desired
8 ounces spaghetti
2 tablespoons unsalted butter, room temperature
1 tablespoon minced fresh parsley leaves

Wearing gloves, halve jalapeño peppers and discard seeds and ribs; coarsely chop. Wash hands, cutting board and any utensils that came in contact with jalapeño peppers, with soap and hot water.

Puree tomato in a food processor and set aside; there is no need to clean food processor as it will be used in next step.

Bring cream to a boil in a small saucepan. Add jalapeño peppers and garlic. Reduce heat to low and simmer, uncovered, stirring occasionally, 10 minutes. Put Gorgonzola cheese in food processor. Add ½ cup hot cream mixture and process until blended. Gradually add remaining cream and process mixture until smooth. Return to saucepan. Taste and add salt and red pepper, if desired.

Bring a large pot of water to a boil; add salt, then pasta. Cook uncovered over high heat, separating strands occasionally with a fork, 8 to 9 minutes or until tender but firm to the bite. Drain well. Transfer to a heated serving bowl.

Meanwhile, reheat sauce to a simmer. Remove from heat; stir in butter and pureed tomato. Add to pasta and toss. Taste and adjust seasoning. Sprinkle with parsley and serve.

Makes 4 first-course servings.

Here the penne, or diagonal-cut macaroni, and peas are not served in a bowl but are spooned onto a platter, sprinkled with a generous amount of cheese and doused with hot butter which melts the cheese. The simple flavoring of good cheese, butter and a colorful vegetable is great with pasta. I like to serve this dish as a lunch or supper main course, accompanied by a tomato salad.

Penne with Peas & Parmesan

2 pounds fresh peas, shelled, or 2 cups frozen
8 ounces penne or mostaccioli (diagonal-cut macaroni) (about 2¾ cups)
6 tablespoons butter
2 medium shallots, minced

1½ teaspoons chopped fresh marjoram or thyme leaves or ½ teaspoon dried leaf, crumbled
Salt and freshly ground pepper to taste
¾ cup freshly grated Parmesan cheese (about 2¼ oz.)

Add peas to a large saucepan of enough boiling salted water to cover generously. Cook uncovered over high heat about 5 minutes for fresh peas or 2 minutes for frozen, or until just tender but still bright green. Drain, rinse with cold water and drain well.

Bring a large pot of water to a boil; add salt, then pasta. Cook uncovered over high heat, stirring occasionally, about 9 minutes or until tender but firm to the bite. Drain well.

Meanwhile, melt 2 tablespoons butter over low heat in saucepan used to cook peas. Add shallots and cook 2 minutes, stirring, until softened but not brown. Add peas, marjoram or thyme, salt and pepper; heat gently 1 minute. Melt remaining 4 tablespoons butter in a small saucepan.

Transfer pasta to saucepan of peas and toss well. Transfer to a large heated platter. Sprinkle with Parmesan cheese. Heat melted butter over medium heat until sizzling and pour evenly over top. Serve immediately.

Makes 4 to 6 first-course or 3 main-course servings.

Bow Ties with Spinach Sauce & Gruyère Cheese

The creamy spinach sauce, made by simmering lightly cooked spinach in cream and seasoning it with its best partners—nutmeg and cheese—is a bright-green complement to the butterfly-shaped pasta.

1 pound spinach, stems removed, leaves rinsed well
3 tablespoons butter
2 medium shallots, minced
1 cup whipping cream
Freshly grated nutmeg to taste
Salt and freshly ground pepper to taste

8 ounces pasta bow ties or farfalle (about 4 cups), or spirals
1 cup finely grated Gruyère cheese, preferably imported (about 3 oz.)
Bowl of finely grated Gruyère cheese (for serving)

Add spinach to a large saucepan of enough boiling salted water to cover generously. Cook uncovered over high heat about 2 minutes or until wilted. Drain, rinse with cold water and drain well. Squeeze out as much liquid as possible. Chop spinach.

Melt 1 tablespoon butter in a medium saucepan over low heat. Add shallots and cook, stirring often, until soft but not brown. Add spinach and cook 1 minute. Stir in ¾ cup cream, nutmeg, salt and pepper; heat over low heat until just heated through. Taste and adjust amounts of salt, pepper and nutmeg. (Sauce can be kept, covered, up to 1 day in refrigerator.)

Bring a large pot of water to a boil; add salt, then pasta. Cook uncovered over high heat, stirring occasionally, 6 to 8 minutes or until tender but firm to the bite. Meanwhile, heat sauce to a simmer over low heat. Add remaining ¼ cup cream and bring to a simmer. Add remaining 2 tablespoons butter and heat until blended.

Drain pasta well. Transfer to a heated serving dish. Add sauce and toss to blend. Add 1 cup Gruyère cheese and toss again. Taste and adjust seasoning. Serve immediately with more Gruyère cheese.

Makes 4 first-course servings.

Leftover pasta can be reheated in a heavy skillet with a little oil or butter over very low heat, tossing often with a fork. The pasta will no longer be al dente, and if it has a creamy sauce, it will turn to butter, but the pasta will taste good anyway!

COOKING TIP

Salsa means sauce, but is often used in California to mean a spicy uncooked sauce of chopped vegetables, especially tomatoes, and happens to be marvelous with pasta. Here it is combined with feta cheese to create a quick dish bursting with flavor. Whole-wheat pasta is perfect with these zesty ingredients.

Spinach Penne with Feta Cheese, Tomato Salsa & Green Beans

Tomato-Garlic Salsa, see below
4 ounces green beans, trimmed, broken in 2 or 3 pieces
4 ounces wax beans or additional green beans, trimmed, broken in 2 or 3 pieces
8 ounces spinach penne or whole-wheat noodles

2 to 4 tablespoons olive oil, preferably extra virgin or virgin
1 cup crumbled feta cheese (4 oz.)
Oregano sprigs, if desired

Prepare Tomato-Garlic Salsa; set aside. Add green beans and wax beans to a large saucepan of enough boiling salted water to cover generously. Cook uncovered over high heat about 4 minutes or until crisp-tender. Drain thoroughly.

Bring a large pot of water to a boil; add salt, then pasta. Cook uncovered over high heat, stirring occasionally, about 6 minutes or until tender but firm to the bite. Meanwhile, heat 2 tablespoons oil in a skillet. Add beans and keep warm over very low heat.

Drain pasta well. Transfer to a large heated serving bowl. Toss with 2 tablespoons oil, if desired, then with salsa. Reserve 2 to 3 tablespoons feta cheese for garnish. Add bean mixture and remaining cheese to pasta; toss. Taste and adjust seasoning. Top with reserved feta and oregano sprigs if desired. Serve hot or at room temperature.

Makes 3 or 4 servings as a light main course.

Tomato-Garlic Salsa

1 pound ripe tomatoes, peeled, seeded, diced
2 large garlic cloves, minced
1 jalapeño pepper, fresh or canned, seeded, ribs removed, minced
Salt to taste
3 tablespoons minced green onions

3 tablespoons minced fresh oregano leaves or 1 tablespoon dried leaf, crumbled
2 tablespoons olive oil, preferably extra virgin or virgin

Combine ingredients in a small bowl and stir. Let stand about 30 minutes at room temperature or up to 4 hours in refrigerator. Bring to room temperature before using.

Spinach Penne with Feta Cheese, Tomato Salsa & Green Beans

The linguine is flecked with bits of bright-green broccoli and vivid-red sun-dried tomatoes. Pecorino-romano cheese, made from sheep's milk, has a distinctive taste but you can also use the milder and more widely available American-made romano, which is made from cow's milk.

Linguine with Broccoli, Sun-Dried Tomatoes & Pecorino Cheese

1½ to 1¾ pounds broccoli, divided in medium flowerets, stems discarded
8 ounces dried linguine
5 tablespoons olive oil
2 large garlic cloves, minced
Salt and freshly ground pepper to taste

¼ cup coarsely chopped or diced oil-packed sun-dried tomatoes
½ cup grated pecorino-romano cheese (about 1½ oz.)
¼ cup chopped fresh basil leaves, if desired
Bowl of grated pecorino-romano cheese (for serving), if desired

Add broccoli flowerets to a large saucepan of enough boiling salted water to cover generously. Cook uncovered over high heat about 2 minutes or until crisp-tender. Drain, rinse with cold water and drain well. Chop coarsely so some of flowerets break up.

Bring a large pot of water to a boil; add salt, then pasta. Cook uncovered over high heat, separating strands occasionally with a fork, about 8 minutes or until tender but firm to the bite. Drain well. Transfer to a large heated serving bowl. Toss with 1 tablespoon olive oil.

Heat remaining 4 tablespoons olive oil in a large heavy skillet over medium heat. Add garlic and sauté a few seconds. Add broccoli, salt and pepper. Sauté about 2 minutes or until heated through.

Add broccoli mixture to pasta bowl and toss. Add sun-dried tomatoes, ½ cup pecorino-romano cheese and basil, if desired; toss again. Taste and adjust seasoning. Serve hot or at room temperature with more cheese, if desired.
Makes 4 servings as a first course or light main course.

When I tasted the famous fettuccine dish at Alfredo's restaurant in Rome, where it originated, I expected it to be made with cream the way I've often had it in Italian restaurants in America. But to my surprise it was made only with butter and cheese. The pasta arrived on a platter, topped with a generous amount of butter pieces and then covered with cheese, and was tossed at the table. What was remarkable was the thinness of the fresh noodles and the richness of the dish, known as fettuccine al triplo burro, or with triple the amount of butter you would usually add to fettuccine. Here I have added vegetables to give color and texture.

Fettuccine Alfredo with Vegetable Julienne

1 medium leek, split lengthwise, rinsed well
1 celery stalk, peeled, cut in 2" x ⅛" x ⅛" strips
4 large mushrooms
½ cup plus 2 tablespoons (5 oz.) unsalted butter
1 large carrot, peeled, cut in 2" x ⅛" x ⅛" strips
Salt and freshly ground pepper to taste

1 pound thin asparagus, tips only (about 2-inch tips)
9 to 10 ounces thin fresh fettuccine, homemade, page 178, or packaged
1¼ cups freshly grated Parmesan cheese, preferably imported (about 4 oz.)
Bowl of freshly grated Parmesan cheese (for serving)

Discard dark-green part of leek. Cut white and light-green part in strips about same size as celery strips. Cut mushrooms in thin slices, then in strips about ¼ inch thick; some will break up but they won't be noticeable.

Put 7 tablespoons butter in a large serving bowl and set aside in a warm place. Melt remaining 3 tablespoons butter in a large skillet over low heat. Stir in leek, carrot and celery; sprinkle with salt and pepper. Cover and cook, stirring often, about 9 minutes or until just tender. Add mushrooms and cook uncovered, stirring often, about 3 minutes or until just tender. Taste and adjust seasoning.

Cook asparagus tips in a medium saucepan of boiling salted water uncovered about 2 minutes or until crisp-tender. Drain well. Add to vegetable mixture.

Bring a large pot of water to a boil; add salt, then pasta. Cook uncovered over high heat, separating strands occasionally with a fork, 30 seconds to 2 minutes or until tender but firm to the bite. Drain well. Transfer to serving bowl containing butter. Add vegetable mixture and toss. Add 1¼ cups Parmesan cheese and toss again. Serve immediately with freshly ground pepper and more Parmesan cheese.

Makes 4 first-course servings.

Spinach Pasta with Goat Cheese, Tomatoes & Thyme

4 ounces creamy goat cheese
   (chèvre), such as Montrachet
   (about ¾ cup)
1 tablespoon butter
1 large shallot, minced
1 cup whipping cream
1 tablespoon minced fresh thyme
   leaves or 1 teaspoon dried leaf,
   crumbled
8 ounces spinach pasta shapes,
   such as penne, fusilli or
   medium shells (3 to 3½ cups)

Red (cayenne) pepper to taste
Salt to taste
2 tablespoons minced green
   onions
8 ounces ripe tomatoes, peeled,
   seeded, diced
3 tablespoons minced fresh
   parsley leaves

Pasta with goat cheese make a popular pair in modern cuisine on both sides of the Atlantic. Goat cheese flavors this dish in two ways: in a creamy, easy-to-prepare sauce that is tossed with the pasta tubes and, for an additional accent, in small chunks scattered over the top. French-style goat cheese is now made in America and is becoming increasingly available in supermarkets.

If goat cheese has a dark rind, cut it off. Crumble or dice enough cheese to obtain ¼ cup and set aside for garnish. Crumble or dice remaining cheese.

Melt butter in a small saucepan over low heat. Add shallot and cook, stirring often, about 3 minutes or until soft. Add cream and bring to a boil. Reduce heat to low. Stir larger amount goat cheese into cream. Add thyme. Heat over medium heat, stirring, until smooth.

Bring a large pot of water to a boil; add salt, then pasta. Cook uncovered over high heat, stirring occasionally, about 9 minutes for penne or 5 to 8 minutes for other shapes, or until tender but firm to the bite. While pasta is cooking, reheat sauce over medium heat to a simmer, stirring. Season to taste with red pepper and salt, if desired. Remove from heat and stir in green onions.

Drain pasta well. Transfer to a heated serving dish and toss with sauce. Add ¾ of tomatoes, 2 tablespoons parsley and salt and red pepper to taste; toss. Sprinkle with parsley, then with remaining tomatoes, last with reserved crumbled or diced cheese. Serve immediately.

Makes 4 to 6 first-course or 3 main-course servings.

VARIATION
Spinach Pasta with Goat Cheese & Red Pepper: Omit tomatoes. Add 1 roasted peeled red bell pepper, page 95, cut in thin strips.

Pasta with Chard & Cheese

1 bunch Swiss chard (about 10 oz.)
5 tablespoons olive oil
Salt and freshly ground pepper to taste
2 medium garlic cloves, minced
8 ounces orecchiette (about 3 cups), medium shells or other pasta shapes

½ cup grated provolone cheese, preferably imported (about 1½ oz.)
Bowl of grated provolone cheese (for serving)

Remove chard leaves and discard stalks or reserve for other uses. Rinse leaves thoroughly. Stack chard leaves. Cut in four lengthwise and cut crosswise in ½-inch-wide pieces; you will have squares.

Heat 2 tablespoons oil in a large skillet over low heat. Add about ½ of chard and a pinch of salt and pepper. Cook, stirring often, about 6 minutes or until tender. Transfer to a plate with a slotted spoon. Add 1 tablespoon oil to skillet and heat over low heat. Cook remaining chard in same way and remove. Add 1 tablespoon oil to skillet and heat over low heat. Add garlic and sauté about 1 minute. Return chard to skillet.

Bring a large pot of water to a boil; add salt, then pasta. Cook uncovered over high heat, stirring occasionally, about 10 minutes for orecchiette or 5 to 8 minutes for shells or until tender but firm to the bite. Drain well. Transfer to a heated serving bowl. Toss with remaining 1 tablespoon oil.

Meanwhile, reheat chard, stirring. Add to pasta and toss. Add ½ cup provolone cheese and toss. Taste and adjust seasoning. Serve immediately with more provolone cheese.

Makes 4 first-course or side-dish servings.

Bucatini with Two Cheeses, Tomatoes & Basil

⅓ cup olive oil
1 small onion, minced (about ⅔ cup)
2 pounds ripe tomatoes, peeled, seeded, coarsely chopped, or 2 (28-oz.) cans whole plum tomatoes, drained, coarsely chopped
Salt and freshly ground pepper to taste

3 tablespoons chopped fresh basil leaves
1 pound bucatini, perciatelli, long macaroni or ziti
1¼ cups finely grated kashkaval or Parmesan cheese (about 4 oz.)
3 ounces mozzarella cheese, cut in ¼-inch cubes (¾ cup cubes)

Heat ¼ cup oil in a large skillet over medium heat. Add onion and sauté about 5 minutes or until just beginning to brown. Add tomatoes and salt. Cook over medium-high heat about 10 minutes or until tender and thick. Stir in 2 tablespoons basil. Taste and adjust seasoning.

Bring a large pot of water to a boil; add salt, then pasta. Cook uncovered over high heat, stirring occasionally, about 8 or 9 minutes or until tender but firm to the bite. Drain well.

Transfer pasta to a heated serving bowl. Add remaining oil and tomato sauce; toss. Sprinkle with grated kashkaval or Parmesan cheese and freshly ground pepper; toss again. Add mozzarella cubes and continue tossing until they just start to melt. Sprinkle with remaining 1 tablespoon basil and serve.

Makes 4 main-course servings.

Classic Spaghetti Carbonara

4 ounces pancetta, cut in ¼-inch
  slices
1 garlic clove, peeled
3 tablespoons unsalted butter
4 large egg yolks, room
  temperature
¼ cup whipping cream, room
  temperature

½ cup grated Parmesan cheese
  (about 1½ oz.)
Freshly ground pepper to taste
1 tablespoon olive oil
12 ounces spaghetti
Bowl of freshly grated Parmesan
  or pecorino-romano cheese
  (for serving)

Cut pancetta in ½-inch squares. Lightly crush garlic so it remains in 1 piece. Cut 2 tablespoons butter in 2 pieces and set aside at room temperature. Combine egg yolks, cream, ½ cup cheese and pepper in a medium bowl; whisk until blended. Heat oil and remaining 1 tablespoon butter with garlic in a medium skillet over medium-low heat. Add pancetta and cook, stirring occasionally, about 5 minutes or until it just begins to brown; discard garlic. Reserve pancetta in skillet; cover to keep warm.

Bring a large pot of water to a boil; add salt, then pasta. Cook uncovered over high heat, separating strands occasionally with a fork, 8 to 9 minutes or until tender but firm to the bite. Drain well. Transfer to a heated serving bowl. Add reserved butter and toss quickly.

Reheat pancetta in its fat over medium heat just until hot. Add cheese mixture to pasta and toss vigorously and thoroughly so mixture becomes saucelike but eggs don't scramble. Add pancetta mixture and toss. Serve immediately.
Makes 4 first-course servings.

VARIATION
Substitute 6 ounces thick-sliced bacon for pancetta. Cut bacon in ½-inch squares. Omit oil and 1 tablespoon butter. Sauté bacon in dry skillet over medium heat 5 minutes; add garlic and sauté 5 minutes. Pour into a strainer set over a bowl. Discard garlic. Return bacon to skillet with 2 tablespoons of its fat.

This is one of my favorite pasta dishes—it is quick, easy and rich. Although it originated in Lazio, the region that includes Rome, it always reminds me of Paris where I first tasted it and where I enjoyed it on numerous occasions in casual Italian restaurants. Like other time-honored dishes, it has many versions. It is sometimes prepared with bucatini or long macaroni instead of spaghetti. Some cooks use pancetta, the unsmoked salt-cured Italian bacon, but regular bacon also gives a delicious result. Pancetta is available in Italian foods shops and specialty stores.

Spaetzle with Nutmeg & Butter

1½ cups all-purpose flour
½ teaspoon salt
Pinch of freshly grated nutmeg
2 large eggs
¼ cup milk

¼ cup water
4 to 6 tablespoons melted butter
Freshly ground pepper to taste
Grated Swiss or Parmesan cheese,
  if desired

Mix flour, salt and nutmeg in a large bowl; make a well in center. Add eggs, milk and water to well; whisk to combine. Draw in flour with a wooden spoon and beat just until smooth; batter will be quite thick. Let rest 15 minutes.

Put melted butter in a medium baking dish or ovenproof serving dish.

Bring a medium saucepan of salted water to a simmer. Use a colander or flat grater to make spaetzle; if using grater, set it on pan so it is easier to handle. Using a rubber spatula, push 2 to 3 tablespoons batter through holes of colander or large holes of grater so that batter falls in small pieces into simmering water; move spatula back and forth to push batter through holes. Move colander or grater so all of batter does not fall in same place. Continue to make spaetzle until about ¼ of batter is used.

After spaetzle float to top of pan, cook over medium heat about 2 minutes or until no longer doughy; taste to check. Remove with a slotted spoon and drain well. Transfer to dish of melted butter. Keep warm in a 200F (95C) oven while cooking remaining spaetzle in batches. Season spaetzle with salt, if desired, pepper and nutmeg. Serve with cheese if desired.
Makes 4 side-dish servings.

A specialty of Germany, Austria and the Alsace region of France, spaetzle are fresh pasta prepared without the aid of a pasta machine. They are made from a thick batter rather than a dough. It is pushed through the holes of a slotted spoon or colander or a special spaetzle machine into boiling water and cooks into little curls which are halfway between noodles and dumplings. Unlike most pastas, spaetzle can be kept warm or reheated without loosing their texture. Serve them as a side dish with meat or chicken.

PASTA WITH SEAFOOD

The most festive of pasta dishes are those made with seafood. One of the best I ever tasted was a tender sole fillet set on a bed of fresh noodles and moistened with a superb French butter sauce. This is the model for Sole with Spinach Pasta & White-Wine Butter Sauce. Recently at a seafood restaurant in Rome I enjoyed a delicate pasta dish with a light vegetable sauce and little flakes of fresh fish, which inspired Linguine with Leek & Salmon Sauce.

Many seafood-and-pasta dishes are easy to prepare because seafood cooks quickly. Some types, especially fresh lobster and crabmeat, can be purchased cooked and still be of good quality. Try, for example, Capellini with Crab, Tomatoes & Basil Butter for a lovely colorful dish that is ready in minutes.

For special occasions, seafood-pasta dishes with complex flavors and lavish sauces are a real treat. The sauces can be based on cream, as in Spiral Pasta with Creamy Curried Lobster; tomatoes, as in Marinated Monkfish with Rigatoni & Tomatoes; or butter, as in Scallops with Saffron Butter Sauce on a Bed of Pasta.

Clockwise from the top: Capellini with Crab, Tomatoes & Basil Butter, page 72; Scallops with Saffron Butter Sauce on a Bed of Pasta, page 74; Cajun-Spiced Shrimp with Rotelle, page 73

As with all seafood recipes, the key to delicious seafood-and-pasta dishes is good-quality fish and shellfish. Shopping at the best fish markets is most important. Seafood can be fresh or frozen, but should be moist and not smell strong.

Smoked fish and shellfish add an intriguing flavor to pasta and can be the basis for some very quick and easy dishes, such as Noodles with Smoked Salmon & Dill Sauce, and Smoked Oysters with Tomato Noodles & Fresh Herbs. Even canned tuna can become glamorous when combined with a good sauce and pasta, as in Roman Spaghetti with Tuna, Tomatoes & Mushrooms.

PASTA WITH FISH

Fish, like meat, can be paired with pasta in a variety of ways. It can be served on a bed of seasoned pasta as in Tomato Fettuccine with Sole Fillets & Lemon Butter, or can be flaked into the sauce and tossed with the pasta, as in Vermicelli with Mediterranean Sea-Bass Sauce. If the pasta has a special shape, it can also be served on the side, as in Salmon & Bow Ties with Cumin-Garlic Butter.

PASTA WITH SHELLFISH

Shrimp is a great favorite with pasta. I prefer to buy shrimp uncooked, because it is easy to prepare, cooks quickly and tastes so much better when freshly cooked. Raw shrimp also has the advantage of being able to absorb the flavors of a marinade, as in Cajun-Spiced Shrimp with Rotelle, or Linguine with Shrimp Scampi & Broccoli. The marinade can then be used to flavor the pasta.

Clams and mussels should also be purchased in the shell for maximum freshness. When they are cooked, their cooking liquid is the basis for lovely sauces for the pasta. One of the best southern Italian pasta dishes, *spaghetti alle vongole,* is composed simply of pasta tossed with tender tiny clams cooked only briefly then combined with a little olive oil, garlic, pepper and parsley.

Serve this delicate dish, flecked with pink salmon, green leeks and parsley, as a first course. No cheese is necessary; good Italian and French cooks rarely serve cheese with a pasta featuring a subtle fish sauce.

Linguine with Leek & Salmon Sauce

1 pound salmon fillet
4 medium leeks, split, rinsed thoroughly (1¾ to 2 lbs. total)
6 tablespoons butter
Salt and freshly ground pepper to taste
⅓ cup dry white wine
6 to 8 tablespoons whipping cream
½ cup bottled clam juice
1 tablespoon chopped fresh thyme leaves or 1 teaspoon dried leaf, crumbled
8 ounces dried linguine
3 tablespoons chopped fresh parsley leaves

Remove skin from salmon fillet and pull out any bones. Cut salmon in about ½-inch cubes.

Discard dark-green part of leeks. Cut white and light-green parts in thin slices. Melt 3 tablespoons butter in a large skillet. Add leeks and a pinch of salt and pepper. Cover and cook over low heat, stirring occasionally, 7 minutes or until tender but not brown.

Add wine, 6 tablespoons cream and clam juice to leeks; bring to a boil. Reduce heat to low. Add salmon and sprinkle lightly with salt, pepper and thyme. Cook uncovered, stirring often, just until color of fish becomes lighter, about 3 minutes. Remove from heat.

Cut remaining 3 tablespoons butter in pieces and put in a large heated bowl. Bring a large pot of water to a boil; add salt, then pasta. Cook uncovered over high heat, separating strands occasionally with a fork, about 8 minutes or until tender but firm to the bite. Drain well. Transfer to bowl and toss with butter.

Reheat sauce if necessary. Add 2 tablespoons cream if desired. Pour over pasta and toss. Taste and adjust seasoning. Sprinkle with parsley and serve. Makes 4 to 6 first-course servings.

Tomato Fettuccine with Sole Fillets & Lemon Butter

Lemon Butter, see below
1¼ pounds sole fillets
Salt and freshly ground pepper to taste
¼ cup all-purpose flour
2 to 3 tablespoons vegetable oil

1 to 1½ tablespoons butter
9 to 10 ounces fresh tomato fettuccine or tri-color noodles, homemade, page 181, or packaged, or 8 ounces dried
Lemon wedges (for serving)

One of the best and easiest ways to flavor pasta is with a seasoned butter. Here the lemon and parsley butter enhances both the pasta and the sautéed sole. The dish is also pretty with tomato fusilli.

Prepare Lemon Butter; set aside about half for serving with fish. Run your finger over sole fillets to check for bones; remove any bones carefully with tweezers, a pastry crimper or paring knife. Sprinkle fillets with salt and pepper. Dredge in flour, tapping to remove excess. Set on a plate in 1 layer. Heat 2 tablespoons oil and 1 tablespoon butter in a large heavy skillet over medium heat. Add ½ of sole and sauté until light golden, about 1 minute per side. Transfer to a platter in 1 layer. Cover and keep warm in a 200F (95C) oven. Add more oil and butter if skillet becomes dry. Repeat with remaining sole.

Bring a large pot of water to a boil; add salt, then pasta. Cook uncovered over high heat, separating strands occasionally with a fork, 30 seconds to 2 minutes for fresh pasta or 2 to 5 minutes for dried or until tender but firm to the bite. Drain well. Transfer to a large heated platter and toss with remaining ½ of Lemon Butter.

To serve, arrange sole on top of pasta or alongside. Spoon reserved Lemon Butter on top of each sole fillet by teaspoonfuls. Serve immediately; flavored butter melts quickly from contact with hot fish. Serve with lemon wedges. Makes 4 main-course servings.

Lemon Butter

½ cup (4 oz.) butter, softened
1½ teaspoons strained fresh lemon juice
1½ teaspoons finely grated lemon zest

1 tablespoon minced fresh parsley leaves
Salt and freshly ground pepper to taste

Beat butter in a medium bowl until smooth. Gradually stir in lemon juice, then lemon zest and parsley. Season with salt and pepper. (Flavored butter can be prepared 1 day ahead and refrigerated. Bring to room temperature before using.)

Some excellent recipes are created because of the need to use leftovers. At La Varenne, the Parisian cooking school where I studied, we learned so much on Friday, "refrigerator cleaning day," from watching the chef make new dishes from the bits and pieces he found in the kitchen. This is a colorful and easy recipe I developed this way. Besides barbecued cod, which is available in packages and which turns the sauce bright orange, it is good with lox, smoked fish and smoked poultry.

Herb Noodles with Smoked Cod & Roasted Pepper

1 green bell pepper
6 ounces smoked or barbecued cod, bones and skin removed
2 tablespoons butter
½ cup whipping cream
8 ounces dried herb-flavored or egg noodles or fettuccine

2 tablespoons chopped green onions
4 teaspoons chopped fresh tarragon leaves or ¼ cup thin strips of fresh basil leaves
Salt and freshly ground pepper to taste

Broil pepper about 2 inches from heat source, turning about every 5 minutes with tongs, until pepper skin is blistered and charred, 15 to 25 minutes. If you prefer, roast pepper directly on burner and turn often with tongs, until skin blackens. Transfer to a plastic bag and close bag. Let stand 10 minutes. Peel using a paring knife, see photo page 95. Halve pepper and discard seeds and ribs. Drain well and pat dry. Cut in ¼-inch strips.

Cut cod in about ½" x ½" x ¼" dice; set aside. Bring butter and cream to a bare simmer in a small saucepan. Add cod and heat through over low heat.

Bring a large pot of water to a boil; add salt, then pasta. Cook uncovered over high heat, separating strands occasionally with a fork, about 5 minutes or until tender but firm to the bite. Drain well. Transfer to a heated bowl.

Add cod mixture and toss. Reserve a few pepper strips. Add green onions, remaining pepper strips and tarragon or basil to pasta. Taste and adjust seasoning. Top with reserved pepper strips and serve.
Makes 4 first-course servings.

The zesty Moroccan marinade, flavored with cilantro, cumin and garlic, seasons both the fish and the robust tomato sauce for the pasta.

Marinated Monkfish with Rigatoni & Tomatoes

Cilantro-Garlic Marinade, opposite
4 pieces monkfish fillet or 4 steaks of halibut or other firm lean fish, cut about 1 inch thick (about 1½ lbs.)
2 tablespoons olive oil
2 garlic cloves, chopped
1½ pounds tomatoes, peeled, seeded, chopped, or 1 (28-oz.) can and 1 (14-oz.) can whole plum tomatoes, drained

Salt to taste
¼ teaspoon hot red-pepper flakes or pinch of red (cayenne) pepper
8 ounces rigatoni (about 3½ cups)
1 teaspoon strained fresh lemon juice
1 tablespoon chopped cilantro leaves

Prepare Cilantro-Garlic Marinade. If using monkfish, trim any grayish skin with a sharp thin-bladed flexible knife, so fillet is white. Put fish pieces in a tray in 1 layer. Rub marinade over both sides of fish pieces. Cover and marinate in refrigerator about 2 hours, turning pieces occasionally. (Fish can be marinated up to 8 hours.)

In a sauté pan large enough to hold fish in 1 layer, heat 1 tablespoon oil over low heat. Add garlic and cook, stirring, 30 seconds. Add tomatoes, salt and red-pepper flakes or red pepper; bring to a boil. Cook over medium heat, stirring often (and crushing canned tomatoes, if using), about 12 minutes or until soft and thickened. (Sauce can be kept, covered, 2 days in refrigerator; reheat before continuing.)

Add fish with its marinade to sauce. Cover and cook over very low heat about 4 minutes per side or until fish is just tender. A thin skewer inserted into center of fish should be hot when touched to underside of your wrist. Transfer fish to a platter, using a slotted spoon. Cover and keep warm.

Bring a large pot of water to a boil; add salt, then pasta. Cook uncovered over high heat, stirring occasionally, about 10 minutes or until tender but firm to the bite. Drain well. Transfer to a large heated bowl and toss with remaining 1 tablespoon olive oil.

Add lemon juice and cilantro to sauce. Taste and adjust seasoning. Add to pasta and toss. Arrange on a heated platter or plates and set fish next to pasta. Serve hot.

Makes 4 main-course servings.

Cilantro-Garlic Marinade

4 medium garlic cloves, peeled
1/3 cup packed cilantro (fresh coriander) sprigs
1 tablespoon ground cumin

1 tablespoon paprika
1/4 cup olive oil
Salt and freshly ground pepper to taste

With the blade of a food processor turning, drop garlic cloves, 1 at a time, through feed tube and process until chopped. Add cilantro, cumin, paprika, olive oil, salt and pepper; process until cilantro is chopped and mixture is blended. Or, chop garlic and cilantro by hand and transfer to a small bowl. Add remaining ingredients and stir until blended.

Roman Spaghetti with Tuna, Tomatoes & Mushrooms

2 teaspoons anchovy paste
1/4 cup butter, softened
1 (6½-oz.) can oil-packed tuna, preferably in olive oil
5 tablespoons olive oil
6 ounces mushrooms, halved, sliced thin
Salt and freshly ground pepper to taste

4 large garlic cloves, minced
1 pound ripe tomatoes, peeled, seeded, coarsely chopped, or 1 (28-oz.) can whole plum tomatoes, drained, chopped
12 ounces spaghetti
3 tablespoons minced fresh parsley leaves

Considering the simple ingredients it uses, this quick entree is amazingly delicious. Anchovy-flavored butter is the "secret" element that gives a subtle accent to this dish and makes it memorable.

Beat anchovy paste with butter in a small bowl until blended; set aside at room temperature. Drain and flake tuna; set aside.

Heat 3 tablespoons oil in a large skillet over medium heat. Add mushrooms and a pinch of salt. Sauté about 5 minutes or until tender. Add about 1/3 of garlic and sauté 30 seconds. Transfer to a plate.

Add remaining 2 tablespoons oil to skillet and heat over medium heat. Stir in remaining garlic, then tomatoes, salt and pepper. Cook 12 to 15 minutes or until mixture is thick.

Bring a large pot of water to a boil; add salt, then pasta. Cook uncovered over high heat, separating strands occasionally with a fork, 8 to 9 minutes or until tender but firm to the bite. Drain well, reserving a little pasta water. Transfer pasta to a large heated bowl. Add anchovy butter and toss.

Reheat tomato sauce, if necessary, over low heat. Stir in tuna and mushrooms. Season with freshly ground pepper. If mixture is dry, add 1 to 3 tablespoons pasta water, 1 tablespoon at a time. Spoon over spaghetti. Sprinkle with parsley and bring to the table. Toss and serve immediately.

Makes 4 or 5 main-course servings.

Vermicelli with Mediterranean Sea-Bass Sauce

4 tablespoons olive oil
1 small onion, finely chopped
1 small carrot, finely diced
1 medium celery stalk, diced
4 medium garlic cloves, coarsely chopped
4 ripe medium tomatoes (about 1½ lbs. total), or 1 (28-oz.) can and 1 (14-oz.) can whole plum tomatoes, drained
Salt and freshly ground pepper to taste
¼ teaspoon hot red-pepper flakes or red (cayenne) pepper to taste
1 teaspoon chopped fresh thyme leaves or ¼ teaspoon dried leaf, crumbled

1 bay leaf
1¼ pounds sea-bass fillet
1 tablespoon tomato paste
1 tablespoon chopped fresh basil leaves or 1 teaspoon dried leaf, crumbled
¼ cup chopped fresh oregano leaves or 1 tablespoon dried leaf, crumbled
1 yellow or green bell pepper, seeds and ribs discarded, cut in ½-inch squares
8 ounces vermicelli or fedelini

Heat 2 tablespoons olive oil in large deep skillet over medium-low heat. Stir in onion, carrot, celery and garlic. Cook until vegetables soften, about 7 minutes; do not let brown. Cut tomatoes in chunks and add to skillet. Add salt, pepper, red-pepper flakes or red pepper and thyme. Add bay leaf and push into liquid. Bring to a boil. Add sea bass and sprinkle with salt and pepper. Cover and cook over low heat 4 minutes per side, or until a skewer inserted into center of fish is hot when touched to underside of your wrist. Transfer fish to a platter. Cover and keep warm.

Simmer sauce uncovered over medium heat, stirring often, about 10 minutes or until tomatoes are very soft. Add liquid that escapes from fish. Strain sauce, pressing firmly on vegetables in strainer to extract as much juice as possible, until mixture in strainer remains dry.

Return sauce to cleaned skillet used to cook fish. Bring to a boil. Stir tomato paste into sauce until well blended. Remove from heat and stir in basil and oregano.

Heat 1 tablespoon olive oil in a medium skillet over medium-low heat. Add bell pepper and sauté about 7 minutes or until just tender. Add to sauce. Cut fish in bite-size chunks; set aside.

Bring a large pot of water to a boil; add salt, then pasta. Cook uncovered over high heat, separating strands occasionally with a fork, 6 to 7 minutes or until tender but firm to the bite. Meanwhile, reheat sauce and add fish. Taste and adjust seasoning.

Drain pasta well. Transfer to a large heated bowl. Add remaining 1 tablespoon olive oil and toss. Reserve about ½ cup sauce. Add remaining sauce to pasta and toss. Taste and adjust seasoning. Spoon reserved sauce on top and serve.
Makes 4 main-course servings.

Sole with Spinach Pasta & White-Wine Butter Sauce

This French pasta dish is the creation of my favorite teacher, Chef Fernand Chambrette, with whom I studied in Paris for five years. The sole fillets and the buttery sauce flavored with reduced fish stock are a lovely complement for the pasta. This recipe deserves to be prepared with fresh spinach fettuccine.

WHITE-WINE BUTTER SAUCE

3 cups fish stock, homemade, page 188, or packaged
2 large shallots, minced
½ cup dry white wine
3 tablespoons whipping cream
Salt and white pepper to taste
1 cup (8 oz.) cold unsalted butter, cut in 16 pieces
½ to 1 teaspoon strained fresh lemon juice, or to taste

1¼ pounds sole fillets
½ small carrot, cut in julienne strips
1 small celery stalk, peeled, cut in julienne strips
9 to 12 ounces fresh spinach fettuccine, homemade, page 180, or packaged
3 tablespoons butter, room temperature
Salt and freshly ground pepper to taste
¼ cup all-purpose flour
2 tablespoons vegetable oil

White-Wine Butter Sauce: Boil fish stock in a large skillet over medium-high heat until reduced to about ³/₄ cup. Combine reduced fish stock, shallots and wine in a small heavy saucepan. Simmer over medium heat until reduced to about ½ cup. Continue simmering over low heat until liquid is reduced to about 3 tablespoons. Stir in cream and a pinch of salt and white pepper. Simmer, whisking occasionally, until mixture is reduced to about 3 tablespoons. Keep butter pieces in refrigerator until ready to use. (Sauce can be prepared to this point up to 4 hours ahead and kept, covered, at room temperature.)

Run your finger over sole fillets to check for bones; remove any bones carefully with tweezers, a pastry crimper or a paring knife. Set aside in refrigerator.

Cook carrot and celery uncovered in a medium saucepan of boiling salted water over high heat about 2 minutes or until just tender. Drain well. Cover and keep warm.

Bring a large pot of water to a boil; add salt, then pasta. Cook uncovered over high heat, separating strands occasionally with a fork, 30 seconds to 2 minutes or until tender but firm to the bite. Rinse with cold water and drain well. Transfer to a large skillet. Add 2 tablespoons room-temperature butter.

Sprinkle sole fillets with salt and pepper. Dredge in flour, tapping to remove excess. Set on a plate in 1 layer. Heat oil and remaining 1 tablespoon butter in a large heavy skillet over medium heat. Add ½ of sole and sauté until browned, about 1 minute per side. Transfer to a platter in 1 layer. Cover and keep warm in a 200F (95C) oven. Repeat with remaining sole.

To finish butter sauce: Set pan of shallot mixture over low heat and bring to a simmer, whisking. Add 2 pieces chilled butter and whisk quickly until just blended in. Whisk in remaining butter 1 piece at a time, lifting pan from heat occasionally to cool mixture and adding each new piece of butter before previous one is completely blended in. Butter should soften as it is added but sauce should not get hot enough to liquefy. Remove from heat as soon as last butter piece is incorporated. Add lemon juice; taste and adjust seasoning. Keep sauce warm if necessary in an uncovered bowl set on a rack above hot but not simmering water over low heat, or in a thermos; try to serve as soon as possible.

Reheat pasta gently in skillet. Remove from heat. Add ¼ cup sauce and toss. Taste and adjust seasoning.

Transfer pasta to a serving platter or divide among plates. Top with sole fillets. Coat each fillet with sauce and sprinkle a few vegetable pieces over center. Pour remaining sauce into a sauceboat and serve immediately.
Makes 4 main-course servings.

In this flavorful and easy main course, the spiced butter seasons both the farfalle or bow ties and the salmon steaks. Serve with brilliant-green sugar snap peas for a beautiful presentation.

Salmon & Bow Ties with Cumin-Garlic Butter

Cumin-Garlic Butter, see below
4 salmon steaks, 1 inch thick (about 2½ lbs. total)
2 teaspoons ground cumin
1 teaspoon minced garlic
2 tablespoons strained fresh lemon juice
2 tablespoons vegetable oil

Salt and freshly ground pepper to taste
8 ounces pasta bow ties, butterflies or farfalle (about 4 cups)
Italian parsley leaves, if desired
Lemon slices

Prepare Cumin-Garlic Butter; set aside. Remove any scales from salmon steaks. Rinse and pat dry. Put steaks in a shallow oval baking dish. Mix cumin, garlic, lemon juice, oil, and a pinch of salt and pepper thoroughly in a small bowl. Pour over salmon and rub on both sides. Let stand 1 hour, turning occasionally. (Fish can be kept, covered, up to 8 hours in refrigerator.)

Bring Cumin-Garlic Butter and marinated fish to room temperature if necessary. Spoon about ½ of flavored butter into a pastry bag fitted with a medium star tip. Put remaining flavored butter in a large warm bowl.

Preheat broiler or grill with rack about 4 inches from heat source; or heat stove-top ridged grill over medium-high heat. Lightly oil grill or broiler rack. Set fish on broiler rack or grill. Broil or grill about 4 minutes per side, or until a skewer inserted into thickest part of salmon is hot when touched to underside of your wrist. Transfer to a platter. Cover and keep warm.

Bring a large pot of water to a boil; add salt, then pasta. Cook uncovered over high heat, stirring occasionally, 6 to 8 minutes or until tender but firm to the bite. Drain well. Transfer to bowl and toss with Cumin-Garlic Butter.

Remove salmon skin and center bone. Put salmon on heated plates. Spoon pasta next to it. If desired, lay parsley leaves on salmon. Pipe Cumin-Garlic Butter in a decorative line down center of each salmon steak. Garnish with lemon slices. Serve immediately; flavored butter melts quickly from contact with hot fish.

Makes 4 main-course servings.

Cumin-Garlic Butter

⅔ cup butter, softened
2½ teaspoons ground cumin
1 tablespoon finely minced garlic
1 teaspoon paprika
1 teaspoon strained fresh lemon juice

3 tablespoons minced fresh parsley leaves
Red (cayenne) pepper to taste
Salt and freshly ground pepper to taste

Beat butter in a medium bowl until smooth. Stir in cumin, garlic, paprika, lemon juice, parsley and red pepper. Season to taste with salt and pepper. (Flavored butter can be kept, covered, up to 1 day in refrigerator. Bring to room temperature before using).

Note: If you prefer, instead of piping flavored butter on fish, spoon it on top by small teaspoonfuls.

Noodles with Smoked Salmon & Dill Sauce

4 ounces thinly sliced smoked salmon or mild lox
2 tablespoons plus 2 teaspoons minced shallots
1/2 cup dry white wine
1 cup whipping cream
8 ounces fresh noodles or fettuccine, homemade, page 178, or packaged, or 6 ounces dried medium noodles

2 tablespoons snipped fresh dill
Salt, if desired, and freshly ground pepper to taste
A few small dill sprigs

Cut smoked salmon in lengthwise strips about 2" x 3/8", cutting with grain rather than crosswise so strips hold together better.

Combine shallots and wine in a medium saucepan; bring to a boil. Cook over low heat about 5 minutes or until liquid is reduced to about 2 tablespoons. Stir in cream and bring to a boil. Cook over medium heat about 6 minutes or until sauce is thick enough to lightly coat a spoon.

Bring a large pot of water to a boil; add salt, then pasta. Cook uncovered over high heat, separating strands occasionally with a fork, 30 seconds to 2 minutes for fresh pasta or 2 to 5 minutes for dried or until tender but firm to the bite. Drain well. Transfer to a heated platter.

Bring sauce to a boil. Remove from heat and stir in snipped dill. Pour sauce over noodles and toss. Gently stir in salmon, using a large fork. Add pepper and taste; salt may not be needed. Garnish with dill sprigs and serve.
Makes 4 first-course servings.

Capellini with Crab, Tomatoes & Basil Butter

Basil Butter, opposite
1 tablespoon olive oil or vegetable oil
12 ounces ripe tomatoes, peeled, seeded, diced, or 1 1/4 cups diced drained canned whole plum tomatoes
Salt and freshly ground pepper to taste

1 3/4 cups fresh crabmeat (about 8 oz.)
6 ounces dried capellini or angel-hair pasta
3 tablespoons butter
2 tablespoons coarsely chopped fresh basil leaves, or thin strips basil leaves

Prepare Basil Butter; set aside. Heat oil in a medium skillet over medium heat. Add tomatoes, salt and pepper. Cook, stirring, about 10 minutes or until tomatoes soften and mixture is thick. (Cooked tomatoes can be kept, covered, 1 day in refrigerator.)

Cut Basil Butter in small pieces and put in a large warm bowl. Pick through crabmeat and discard any pieces of shell or cartilage. Reserve a few large pieces of crabmeat for garnish; dice remaining pieces.

Bring a large pot of water to a boil; add salt, then pasta. Cook uncovered over high heat, separating strands occasionally with a fork, about 4 minutes or until tender but firm to the bite. Meanwhile, reheat tomato sauce. Drain pasta well. Transfer to bowl of Basil Butter. Set aside tomato sauce to serve on top of pasta and crabmeat mixture, or add to pasta and toss thoroughly.

Melt 2 tablespoons butter in a medium skillet over low heat. Add diced crabmeat and cook, stirring, until heated through, about 2 minutes. Transfer to bowl of pasta. Add remaining 1 tablespoon butter to skillet and cook large pieces crab meat, stirring about 2 minutes. Add about ½ of cut basil to pasta and toss. Taste and adjust seasoning.

Top pasta with tomato sauce, if desired. Sprinkle with remaining basil. Garnish with large crab pieces and bring to the table. Toss before serving.

Makes 4 first-course or 2 or 3 main-course servings.

Basil Butter

1 cup fresh basil leaves (1½-oz. bunch), rinsed, thoroughly dried
¼ cup parsley sprigs
¼ cup butter, softened
Salt and freshly ground pepper to taste

Coarsely chop basil and parsley in a food processor. Add butter and process until basil is finely chopped and mixture is well blended, scraping down sides occasionally. Transfer to a small bowl. (Flavored butter can be kept, covered, up to 1 day in refrigerator. Bring to room temperature before using.)

Cajun-Spiced Shrimp with Rotelle

2 teaspoons paprika
½ teaspoon red (cayenne) pepper
½ teaspoon salt, or to taste
¼ teaspoon ground black or white pepper
1 teaspoon dried leaf oregano, crumbled
1 teaspoon dried leaf thyme, crumbled
6 to 8 tablespoons butter, room temperature
2 medium garlic cloves, minced
1¼ pounds medium or large shrimp, shelled, deveined if desired, rinsed, patted dry
12 ounces rotelle (pasta wheels) or other medium-size pasta shapes (5⅓ cups)
1 small zucchini, cut in ¼-inch dice
¼ cup minced green onions
2 ripe plum tomatoes, cut in ¼-inch dice
¼ cup chopped fresh parsley leaves
Hot-pepper sauce or additional red (cayenne) pepper to taste

This will be a favorite among lovers of hot dishes—it even looks spicy! The peppery butter with garlic and herbs seasons the shrimp and gives the pasta a beautiful reddish-orange color.

◆ *Photo on page 62.*

In a small bowl, mix paprika, red pepper, salt, black or white pepper, oregano and thyme. Melt 4 tablespoons butter in a large skillet over low heat. Add garlic and spice mixture; stir well. Turn off heat. Add shrimp and stir to coat with spices.

Put 1 to 3 tablespoons butter in a large warm bowl for tossing with pasta. Bring a large pot of water to a boil; add salt, then pasta. Cook uncovered over high heat, stirring occasionally, about 7 minutes or until tender but firm to the bite. Drain well. Transfer to bowl and toss with butter.

Sauté shrimp in its spiced butter over medium heat, tossing often, 2 to 2½ minutes or until pink. Add shrimp mixture to pasta and toss.

Add remaining 1 tablespoon butter to skillet from cooking shrimp and melt over medium heat. Add zucchini and green onions. Sauté about 1 minute or until barely tender. Stir in tomatoes and parsley. Cook a few seconds. Add to pasta and toss until blended. Taste and adjust seasoning, adding more red pepper or hot sauce if desired. Serve immediately.

Makes 4 or 5 main-course servings.

Steamed scallops with a luscious saffron sauce and broccoli flowerets can bring any noodle into the realm of "grande cuisine," as long as you use pasta of the best quality.

◆ *Photo on page 62.*

Scallops with Saffron Butter Sauce on a Bed of Pasta

SAFFRON BUTTER SAUCE

¼ teaspoon crumbled saffron threads
2 tablespoons minced shallots
2 tablespoons white-wine vinegar
3 tablespoons dry white wine
3 tablespoons whipping cream
Salt and freshly ground white pepper to taste
1 cup (8 oz.) cold unsalted butter, cut into 16 pieces

1¼ pounds sea scallops, patted dry
12 ounces broccoli, divided into medium flowerets
1 pound fresh fettuccine, homemade, page 178, or packaged, or 12 ounces dried, or 12 ounces pappardelle or fusilli
¼ cup unsalted butter, cut into pieces, room temperature

Saffron Butter Sauce: Combine saffron, shallots, vinegar and wine in a small heavy saucepan. Simmer over medium heat until liquid is reduced to about 2 tablespoons. Stir in cream and a pinch of salt and white pepper. Simmer, whisking occasionally, until liquid is reduced to about 2 tablespoons. Keep butter pieces in refrigerator until ready to use. (Sauce can be prepared to this point up to 4 hours ahead and kept, covered, at room temperature.)

Remove small white muscle from side of each scallop. Cut any large scallops in 2 slices. Add broccoli to a medium saucepan of enough boiling salted water to cover generously. Cook uncovered over high heat about 4 minutes or until crisp-tender. Drain well.

Bring a large pot of water to a boil; add salt, then pasta. Cook uncovered over high heat, separating strands occasionally with a fork, 30 seconds to 2 minutes for fresh pasta or 2 to 7 minutes for dried or until tender but firm to the bite. Rinse with cold water and drain well. Transfer to a large skillet. Add room-temperature butter, broccoli and salt and pepper to taste.

To finish butter sauce: Set pan of shallot mixture over low heat and bring to a simmer, whisking. Add 2 pieces chilled butter and whisk quickly until just blended in. Whisk in remaining butter 1 piece at a time, lifting pan from heat occasionally to cool mixture and adding each new piece of butter before previous one is completely blended in. Butter should soften as it is added but sauce should not get hot enough to liquefy. Remove from heat as soon as last butter piece is incorporated. Taste and adjust seasoning. Keep sauce warm if necessary in an uncovered bowl set on a rack above hot but not simmering water over low heat, or in a thermos; try to serve as soon as possible.

Toss pasta mixture over low heat just until hot. Season scallops lightly with salt and pepper. Put scallops in a steamer over boiling water. Cover and steam 3 minutes or until just tender; transfer to paper towels.

Divide pasta mixture among 6 plates and set scallops on top. Coat each scallop with sauce. Serve remaining sauce separately.
Makes 6 main-course servings.

Scallops with Saffron Butter Sauce on a Bed of Pasta

Add 2 pieces of chilled butter to reduced shallot mixture over low heat; whisk quickly until just blended in. Whisk in remaining butter 1 piece at a time, lifting pan from heat occasionally to cool mixture and adding each new piece of butter before previous one is completely blended in.

Smoked Oysters with Tomato Noodles & Fresh Herbs

3 tablespoons butter
⅓ cup whipping cream
3 ounces smoked oysters, cut in ½-inch dice
6 ounces dried tomato noodles or fusilli
2 tablespoons snipped fresh chives

2 teaspoons chopped fresh tarragon leaves
1 tablespoon chopped fresh parsley leaves
Freshly ground pepper to taste

One of the easiest and most delicious ways to use a special ingredient that has plenty of flavor, such as smoked shellfish or fish, is to serve it with pasta. All you need to do is to heat it briefly with a little butter, cream and fresh herbs, toss the mixture with pasta—and voilà!

Gently heat butter and cream in a small saucepan over low heat. Stir in diced smoked oysters. Keep warm over very low heat.

Bring a large pot of water to a boil; add salt, then pasta. Cook uncovered over high heat, separating strands occasionally with a fork, about 5 minutes for noodles or about 7 minutes for fusilli or until tender but firm to the bite. Drain well. Transfer to a heated medium bowl.

Stir chives, tarragon and parsley into sauce. Add freshly ground pepper. Add sauce to pasta and toss. Taste and adjust seasoning. Serve immediately.
Makes 2 first-course servings.

The strong-flavored clam
cooking liquid, softened with
cream and herbs, makes an
easy yet fine sauce for pasta.

Fettuccine with Creamy Clam Sauce

1 pound small live clams
¼ cup dry white wine
½ cup whipping cream
1½ teaspoons chopped fresh basil
  leaves or ½ teaspoon dried leaf,
  crumbled

4 ounces dried fettuccine
1 tablespoon chopped fresh
  parsley leaves
Salt and freshly ground pepper to
  taste

Discard any open clams. Put clams in a colander and rinse well several times under cold running water, scrubbing thoroughly with a stiff brush. Put clams in a medium saucepan and add wine. Cover and heat over medium-high heat, shaking pan often, about 5 minutes or until clams open. Discard any that do not open. Remove clams from cooking liquid, but reserve liquid. Leave to cool; shell clams. Cut clams in small pieces.

If cooking liquid is sandy, leave it undisturbed 10 minutes; then carefully pour into another medium saucepan, leaving sand behind. Bring cooking liquid to a boil. Stir in cream. If using dried basil, crumble and add with cream. Simmer over medium heat, stirring often, about 7 minutes or until sauce is thick enough to coat a spoon.

Bring a large pot of water to a boil; add salt, then pasta. Cook uncovered over high heat, separating strands occasionally with a fork, 2 to 5 minutes or until tender but firm to the bite. Drain well. Transfer to a heated medium bowl.

Return clams to sauce and reheat very briefly. Add fresh basil, parsley and a pinch of pepper. Taste and adjust seasoning. Pour over pasta and toss. Serve immediately.

Makes 2 first-course servings.

VARIATION

Pasta with Creamy Mussel Sauce: Substitute 1 pound small mussels for clams. Tap any open mussels gently against sink or other surface and discard any that do not close. Put closed mussels in a colander and rinse well several times under cold running water. Use a sturdy knife to scrape shells clean of foreign particles and to pull out pieces of "beard" that joins mussels together. Cook like clams, above. After cooking, shell mussels and leave whole. Continue as recipe above.

COOKING TIP

Store live mussels and clams in a bowl in the refrigerator, not in a plastic bag, because they need to breathe.

76

Angel-Hair Pasta with Scallops, Asparagus & Cilantro Cream

1¼ pounds sea scallops
1 bunch asparagus (¾ to 1 lb.), peeled, about 1½ inches of bases trimmed
1 tablespoon butter
2 tablespoons minced shallot
½ cup dry white wine
½ cup bottled clam juice or fish stock, page 188

1 cup whipping cream
Salt and freshly ground pepper to taste
6 ounces dried angel-hair pasta or capellini
4 tablespoons coarsely chopped cilantro (fresh coriander) leaves

This is a dish for a special occasion. Cilantro might seem unusual in a wine-and-cream sauce, but it adds an intriguing taste. Because the angel-hair pasta absorbs much of the delicate sauce, it becomes very rich in flavor and provides an exquisite background to show off the scallops and asparagus.

Remove white muscle at side of scallops. Rinse scallops and pat dry. Cut each asparagus spear in 3 crosswise pieces. Keep tips separate from stalks.

Add asparagus stalks to a medium saucepan of enough boiling salted water to cover generously. Cook uncovered over high heat 2 minutes. Add tips and cook 2 minutes or until crisp-tender. Transfer asparagus carefully to a colander and drain.

Melt butter in a large saucepan over low heat. Add shallot and cook about 2 minutes or until softened. Add wine and bring to a boil. Add clam juice or fish stock and bring to a boil. Add ½ cup cream and bring to a simmer. Add scallops, salt and pepper. Bring to a simmer. Cover and poach scallops over low heat about 3 minutes or until opaque. Transfer with a slotted spoon to a plate. Cover and keep warm.

Bring scallop cooking liquid to a boil. Stir in remaining ½ cup cream and bring to a boil. Boil sauce, stirring often, until it is thick enough to lightly coat a spoon and is reduced to about 1⅓ cups.

Bring a large pot of water to a boil; add salt, then pasta. Cook uncovered over high heat, separating strands occasionally with a fork, about 4 minutes or until tender but firm to the bite. Meanwhile, bring sauce to a simmer. Use a slotted spoon to add scallops and asparagus. Heat through over low heat. Remove sauce from heat. Stir in 3 tablespoons cilantro. Taste and adjust seasoning.

Drain pasta well. Transfer to a large heated bowl. Add ½ cup sauce and toss. Taste and adjust seasoning. Pour ⅓ cup sauce into a sauceboat for serving separately. Spoon pasta onto a platter. Spoon scallops and asparagus with remaining sauce over pasta. Garnish pasta with remaining 1 tablespoon cilantro. Serve with sauce in sauceboat.

Makes 4 main-course servings.

Linguine with Shrimp Scampi & Broccoli

1¼ pounds medium or large shrimp, shelled, deveined if desired, rinsed, patted dry
3 large garlic cloves, minced
Salt and freshly ground pepper to taste
6 tablespoons olive oil

4 to 6 tablespoons butter, room temperature
1 bunch broccoli (about 1½ lbs.), cut in medium flowerets
9 to 10 ounces fresh linguine or 8 ounces dried

Combine shrimp, garlic, a pinch of salt and pepper and 4 tablespoons olive oil in a medium bowl. Cover and let marinate in refrigerator 1 hour or up to 4 hours.

Remove shrimp from marinade and reserve marinade. Remove garlic pieces adhering to shrimp with a small rubber spatula and return garlic to marinade. Put 2 to 4 tablespoons butter in a large warm bowl for tossing with pasta.

Add broccoli to a large saucepan of enough boiling salted water to cover generously. Cook uncovered over high heat about 5 minutes or until just tender. Drain broccoli well. Return to saucepan. Cover and keep warm.

Meanwhile, heat remaining 2 tablespoons olive oil and 2 tablespoons butter over medium-high heat in a large heavy skillet. Add shrimp and sauté, tossing often, 1½ to 2 minutes or until pink on outside; large shrimp should be white inside when cut. Reserving fat in skillet, transfer shrimp with a slotted spoon to a bowl. Cut some of larger shrimp into thirds. Cover and keep warm.

Bring a large pot of water to a boil; add salt, then pasta. Cook uncovered over high heat, separating strands occasionally with a fork, about 2 minutes for fresh or about 8 minutes for dried or until tender but firm to the bite. Drain well.

Add linguine to bowl containing butter pieces and toss well. Add about ⅔ of shrimp and about ½ of broccoli flowerets; toss.

Add shrimp marinade to skillet used to cook shrimp. Cook over medium heat, stirring, about 1 minute or until garlic is tender but not brown. Immediately pour mixture over pasta and toss until blended. Taste and adjust seasoning.

Mound pasta mixture on a large heated platter and encircle with remaining shrimp and broccoli flowerets.
Makes 4 main-course servings.

Spiral Pasta with Creamy Curried Lobster

Creamy Curry Sauce, opposite
1 large cooked lobster (about 2 lbs.) or 1 large cooked lobster tail (1 to 1¼ lbs.)
8 ounces fusilli, rotini or other spiral-shaped pasta (about 3½ cups)

¼ cup butter, cut into pieces, room temperature
Freshly ground pepper to taste
4 teaspoons minced fresh parsley leaves

Prepare Creamy Curry Sauce; set aside. Remove meat from lobster. Cut about 16 crosswise slices about ⅜ inch thick. Dice remaining lobster meat.

Bring a large pot of water to a boil; add salt, then pasta. Cook uncovered over high heat, stirring occasionally, about 7 minutes or until tender but firm to the bite. Drain well. Transfer to a large heated serving bowl and toss with butter.

Bring sauce to a simmer over medium-low heat. Stir lobster into sauce and heat gently 1 minute or until heated through. Add pepper. Taste and adjust seasoning. Remove lobster slices to a plate with a slotted spoon.

Add sauce to pasta and toss. Taste and adjust seasoning. Set lobster slices on top. Sprinkle with parsley and serve.

Makes 4 main-course servings.

Creamy Curry Sauce

3 or 4 tablespoons butter	1/2 teaspoon turmeric
2/3 cup minced onion	2 teaspoons ground coriander
6 medium garlic cloves, minced	1 1/2 cups whipping cream
4 teaspoons minced peeled gingerroot	Salt to taste
1 tablespoon ground cumin	1/2 teaspoon hot red-pepper flakes

Melt butter in a medium saucepan over medium-low heat. Add onion and cook about 5 minutes or until soft but not brown. Add garlic and gingerroot; cook 1 minute. Stir in cumin, turmeric and coriander; cook a few seconds. Stir in cream, salt and red-pepper flakes; bring to a boil. Simmer over low heat, stirring, until thick enough to lightly coat a spoon, about 5 minutes. (Sauce can be kept, covered, 1 day in refrigerator.)

Shrimp with Chili Pasta

This easy dish is good with all types of noodles, but chili pasta or curry pasta give it a special zip and a lovely color.

4 tablespoons butter	1/4 cup whipping cream
4 ounces medium shrimp, shelled, deveined if desired, rinsed, patted dry	4 ounces fresh chili fettuccine or curry fettuccine, homemade, page 182, or packaged
Salt and freshly ground pepper to taste	3 tablespoons minced fresh parsley leaves
1 medium shallot, minced	1/4 cup finely diced ripe tomatoes
1/4 cup dry white wine	

Melt 2 tablespoons butter in a medium skillet over medium heat. Add shrimp, salt and pepper. Sauté, stirring, about 1 1/2 minutes or until pink. Remove shrimp with tongs or a slotted spoon to a plate. Add shallot to skillet and stir a few seconds over low heat. Add wine. Bring to a boil and simmer over medium heat 2 minutes. Add cream and bring to a simmer. Cook until sauce thickens enough to lightly coat a spoon.

Bring a large pot of water to a boil; add salt, then pasta. Cook uncovered over high heat, separating strands occasionally with a fork, 30 seconds to 2 minutes or until tender but firm to the bite. Drain well. Transfer to a heated medium serving bowl; toss with 1 tablespoon parsley and remaining 2 tablespoons butter. Season to taste with salt and pepper. Spoon a mound of pasta in center of each of 2 heated plates.

Return sauce to a simmer. Add shrimp and tomatoes; heat a few seconds. Taste and adjust seasoning. Spoon sauce around pasta. Sprinkle with remaining parsley and serve.

Makes 2 servings as a first course or light main course.

Black Pasta with Crab Newburg Sauce

The fresh pink crabmeat in its creamy sauce against the background of midnight-black pasta makes this a truly impressive dish. It is hard to believe it takes so little time to prepare! Black pasta is usually made with squid ink but sometimes black olives are used instead; either type is fine for this dish. If black pasta is not available, spinach pasta can be substituted.

1 pound fresh crabmeat, with a few large pieces if possible
2 large egg yolks
1 cup whipping cream
4 tablespoons butter
1 teaspoon paprika
2 tablespoons dry sherry
Red (cayenne) pepper to taste

Salt and freshly ground pepper to taste
9 to 10 ounces fresh black fettuccine, homemade, page 181, or packaged, or 8 ounces dried
2 teaspoons minced fresh parsley leaves

Pick through crabmeat and discard any pieces of shell or cartilage. Whisk egg yolks with 1/2 cup cream in a medium bowl; set aside.

Melt 2 tablespoons butter in a heavy medium saucepan over medium heat. Add crabmeat and sauté 1 minute. Remove large pieces to a bowl; cover and keep warm. Into saucepan stir paprika, sherry and red pepper. Add remaining 1/2 cup cream and a pinch of salt and pepper; bring to a simmer.

Remove from heat and quickly stir in egg-yolk mixture. Return to low heat and cook, stirring constantly, about 2 minutes or until slightly thickened; do not boil. Remove from heat. Transfer to a bowl. Taste and adjust seasoning. Keep sauce warm by setting bowl above hot water; sauce can be kept warm about 30 minutes.

Bring a large pot of water to a boil; add salt, then pasta. Cook uncovered over high heat, separating strands occasionally with a fork, 30 seconds to 2 minutes for fresh pasta or 2 to 5 minutes for dried or until tender but firm to the bite. Drain well. Transfer to a large heated bowl and toss with remaining 2 tablespoons butter. Add salt and pepper to taste.

Reserve 2 to 4 large crab pieces for garnish. Add any remaining pieces to sauce. Arrange pasta in a ring on each plate. Spoon crab sauce in center. Sprinkle parsley on sauce. Put a large piece of crab on top of each portion.
Makes 2 or 3 main-course or 4 first-course servings.

Spaghetti with Provençal Clam & Mussel Ragout

In this colorful dish, the clams and mussels are served in their shells. Instead of using a mixture of shellfish, either clams or mussels alone can be used.

4 tablespoons olive oil
2 large garlic cloves, chopped
1 1/2 pounds ripe tomatoes, peeled, seeded, chopped or 1 (28-oz.) can and 1 (14-oz.) can whole plum tomatoes, drained, chopped
1/2 cup dry white wine
2 teaspoons fresh thyme leaves or 3/4 teaspoon dried leaf, crumbled
1 bay leaf
1/4 teaspoon fennel seeds

Freshly ground pepper to taste
1 pound small live clams
1 pound small live mussels
1/4 cup water
1 tablespoon Pernod, if desired
1/4 cup chopped fresh basil leaves or 4 teaspoons dried leaf, crumbled
8 ounces spaghetti
2 tablespoons minced fresh parsley leaves
Parsley sprigs

Heat 2 tablespoons olive oil in a large heavy skillet over low heat. Stir in garlic and cook 30 seconds. Add tomatoes and cook 2 minutes over medium-high heat. Add wine, thyme, bay leaf, fennel seeds and pepper. Cook, stirring often, about 15 minutes or until thick. Discard bay leaf. (Sauce can be kept, covered, 2 days in refrigerator.)

Spaghetti with Provençal Clam & Mussel Ragout

Cook mussels in a covered pan over high heat, shaking pan often, until mussels open; they will open after about 5 minutes.

Discard any open clams. Put clams in a colander and rinse well several times under cold running water, scrubbing thoroughly with a stiff brush. Tap any open mussels gently against sink or other surface and discard any that do not close. Put closed mussels in a colander and rinse well several times under cold running water. Use a sturdy knife to scrape shells clean and to pull out pieces of "beard" that joins mussels together.

Put mussels in a medium saucepan. Cover and cook over high heat, shaking pan often, about 5 minutes or until mussels open. Remove mussels with tongs or a slotted spoon; discard any that do not open. Cover mussels to keep warm. Carefully pour mussel liquid into a bowl, without adding any of sand remaining at bottom of saucepan. Discard sandy liquid. If cooking liquid in bowl is still sandy, strain it through a strainer lined with moistened cheesecloth, leaving sandy portion behind.

Put clams in saucepan and add water. Cover and cook over medium-high heat, shaking pan often, about 5 minutes or until clams open. Remove clams with a slotted spoon; discard any that do not open. Reserve cooking liquid and strain if sandy.

Gradually add about 1 tablespoon mussel liquid and 2 tablespoons clam liquid to tomato sauce. Heat sauce again about 3 minutes or until thickened but not dry. Stir in Pernod, if desired, and basil.

Shell all but 4 mussels and 4 clams. If any threadlike "beard" is still stuck to mussels, cut it off.

Bring a large pot of water to a boil; add salt, then pasta. Cook uncovered over high heat, separating strands occasionally with a fork, 8 to 9 minutes or until tender but firm to the bite. Drain well. Transfer to a large bowl and toss with remaining 2 tablespoons olive oil.

Add mussels and clams to sauce and heat briefly. Remove unshelled mussels and clams. Toss sauce and 1 tablespoon parsley with spaghetti. Sprinkle with remaining parsley and arrange shellfish in shells on top. Garnish with parsley sprigs. Serve hot or at room temperature.

Makes 2 main-course or 4 first-course servings.

PASTA WITH POULTRY

I grew up with chicken and noodles. Chicken-alphabet soup, chicken fricassee with noodles, even American-style "chicken chow-mein" with canned crispy noodles, made frequent appearances on our table. The poultry-and-pasta combination has long been a favorite in simple home cooking, yet it can also be appropriate for the most elegant of dinners.

One of the most memorable pasta dishes I ever tasted paired fettuccine with poultry. It was at a wonderful Parisian restaurant called *Au Châteaubriant,* which was considered the best Italian restaurant in France during the years my husband and I lived there. This creative dish was made of fresh white and green noodles with a creamy chicken sauce topped with a little bit of foie gras, a French touch on an Italian masterpiece. The foie gras melted into the sauce before our eyes and the pasta tasted heavenly.

Of course you don't need foie gras to make fabulous chicken-and-pasta dishes. When you cook chicken, the juices gain a wonderful flavor and are a natural partner for pasta, whether the chicken is stewed with tomatoes and saf-

Chicken with Raspberries, Fettuccine & Raspberry Butter Sauce, page 90

83

fron, as in Pasta Paella, is poached in coconut milk, as in Vermicelli with Chicken in Peanut Sauce, or is baked in a covered casserole, as in Butter-Baked Chicken with Pasta & Leeks.

Many dishes of poultry and pasta are delightful for entertaining. Try Chicken with Raspberries, Fettuccine & Raspberry Butter Sauce for an impressive and very elegant main course. On a more casual occasion, such as a Fourth of July lunch, enjoy the zesty ginger-scented Fusilli Spirals with Citrus-Barbecued Chicken. For a tasty meal in minutes, smoked turkey or chicken can be tossed with pasta and a little olive oil or a simple sauce as in Chili Pasta with Smoked Turkey.

Besides being served alongside poultry or mixed with it, pasta can be used inside a chicken. Small pasta shapes, from couscous and orzo to elbow macaroni and medium shells, make a delicious stuffing which gains wonderful richness from the poultry roasting juices and is a welcome change from bread stuffing.

If you have visions of peeling 40 garlic cloves—look again! In this pasta version of a Provençal classic there is no need to peel the garlic before cooking and it pops right out of its skin once cooked. Although there is so much garlic, it is not over-powering—its taste becomes mellowed during the slow cooking and its texture meltingly tender. The garlic flavors the rich chicken juices which become a wonderful sauce for the pasta and chicken. Tomato noodles fit the Provençal theme.

Tomato Noodles with Chicken & 40 Cloves of Garlic

1 (3-lb.) chicken, cut in 8 pieces, or 3 pounds chicken pieces, patted dry
Salt and freshly ground pepper to taste
2 tablespoons pure olive oil
2 celery stalks, cut in thin slices
3/4 teaspoon fresh thyme leaves or 1/4 teaspoon dried leaf, crumbled
2 tablespoons olive oil, preferably extra virgin
3 tablespoons chopped fresh parsley leaves

40 medium garlic cloves, unpeeled (about 3 heads)
3 fresh rosemary sprigs
10 large fresh sage leaves
1 bay leaf
1/4 cup Cognac or brandy
9 to 12 ounces fresh tomato noodles, homemade, page 181, or packaged, or 8 to 10 ounces dried tomato or tri-colored noodles

Preheat oven to 350F (175C). Sprinkle chicken pieces with salt and pepper. Choose a large deep heavy casserole with a tight-fitting lid. Heat 2 tablespoons pure olive oil in casserole over medium-high heat. Add chicken pieces in batches and lightly brown, taking about 5 minutes per batch and removing pieces to a plate with tongs as they brown. Pour off any oil in pan. Let pan cool.

Add celery, thyme, extra-virgin olive oil, 1 tablespoon parsley and a pinch of salt to casserole; stir. Add chicken pieces and stir well to coat with oil mixture.

Separate garlic cloves from heads and remove any loose skin. Add garlic, rosemary, sage, bay leaf and Cognac or brandy to casserole. Cover tightly. Bake chicken about 1 hour or until leg pieces are no longer pink when cut. Remove chicken. Cover and keep warm. If largest garlic clove is not tender enough to crush easily, cover and bake garlic about 10 minutes longer; check again.

Remove garlic cloves with a slotted spoon. Press each clove between your fingers over a small bowl to remove pulp from skin; it pops out easily. Mash garlic with a fork. Discard bay leaf and any large pieces of rosemary from chicken juices but leave sage. In a small saucepan, whisk garlic pulp with chicken juices to make sauce.

Bring a large pot of water to a boil; add salt, then pasta. Cook uncovered over high heat, separating strands occasionally with a fork, 30 seconds to 2 minutes for fresh noodles or 2 to 5 minutes for dried or until tender but firm to the bite. Drain well. Transfer to a large heated bowl. Meanwhile, reheat sauce. Stir in remaining parsley. Taste and adjust seasoning.

To serve, transfer chicken to a platter or plates. Reserve ⅓ cup sauce; pour remaining sauce over pasta and toss. Taste and adjust seasoning. Serve pasta next to chicken. Serve reserved sauce separately for pouring over chicken. Makes 4 main-course servings.

Pasta Paella

⅓ cup chicken stock, homemade, page 187, or packaged
½ teaspoon saffron threads
3 tablespoons olive oil
12 chicken drumsticks
1 medium onion, chopped
1 small red bell pepper, seeds and ribs discarded, cut in lengthwise strips about ¼ inch wide
6 medium garlic cloves, minced
1 pound ripe tomatoes, peeled, seeded, chopped, or 1 (28-oz.) can whole plum tomatoes, drained, chopped

Salt and freshly ground pepper to taste
1½ teaspoons paprika
1 pound fresh peas, shelled, or 1 cup frozen peas
8 ounces (about 2½ cups) small pasta shells (sometimes labeled gnocchi)
8 ounces medium shrimp, shelled, deveined if desired, rinsed, patted dry

This is a new and easier version of the fragrant Spanish specialty, made with pasta instead of rice. The paella is perfect for entertaining—the golden pasta in its saffron-tomato chicken sauce, tossed with the bright-colored shrimp and peas and surrounded by the chicken pieces, makes an impressive, great-tasting dish. The chicken and sauce can be prepared ahead.

Bring stock to a simmer in a small saucepan. Crush saffron threads in a small bowl and pour hot stock over them. Let mixture stand about 20 minutes or while continuing next step.

Heat 2 tablespoons oil in a large deep heavy skillet or sauté pan over medium-high heat. Add chicken pieces in batches and brown, transferring to a plate when browned.

Add remaining 1 tablespoon oil to skillet and heat over low heat. Add onion and bell pepper and cook, stirring often, about 10 minutes or until softened. Stir in garlic, then tomatoes and cook mixture over medium-high heat 5 minutes. Add chicken and any juices that have accumulated on plate. Sprinkle chicken with salt, pepper and paprika. Add saffron-flavored stock and bring to a boil. Cover and simmer 15 minutes. Turn chicken pieces over and simmer about 5 minutes or until no longer pink when cut. (Chicken can be prepared to this point 1 day ahead and kept, covered, in refrigerator. Reheat in a large skillet or sauté pan before continuing.)

Remove chicken pieces to a platter. Cover and keep warm. Add peas to sauce and cook uncovered 3 minutes or until nearly tender.

Bring a large pot of water to a boil; add salt, then pasta. Cook uncovered over high heat, stirring occasionally, 5 to 6 minutes or until tender but firm to the bite. Drain well.

Set chicken pieces at edge of a serving dish and spoon a little sauce from skillet over each piece. Add shrimp to sauce in skillet and cook uncovered over high heat, stirring, 1 to 1½ minutes or until they are pink. Add pasta to shrimp mixture and toss. Taste and adjust seasoning.

Transfer pasta and shrimp mixture to center of serving dish and serve. Makes 6 main-course servings.

Noodles with Mustard-Grilled Chicken & Gruyère Cheese

Mustard Butter, see below
4 tablespoons butter
1 small cabbage head (about 2 lbs.), cored, shredded
1 pound boneless chicken breast halves, skin removed
8 ounces dried wide egg noodles
1 tablespoon Dijon mustard

¼ cup minced green onions
¾ cup shredded Gruyère cheese (about 2½ oz.)
3 tablespoons minced fresh parsley leaves
Bowl of shredded Gruyère cheese (for serving)

Prepare Mustard Butter; set aside. Melt 2 tablespoons butter in a large skillet over medium heat. Add ½ of cabbage and cook, stirring often, about 10 minutes or until tender. Transfer to a bowl. Repeat with remaining 2 tablespoons butter and remaining cabbage. Return all of cabbage to skillet. (Mustard Butter and cabbage can be kept, covered, 1 day in refrigerator. Bring to room temperature before continuing.)

Preheat broiler or grill with rack about 4 inches from heat source. Lightly oil broiler rack. Divide 1 tablespoon Mustard Butter among chicken pieces and spread it on 1 side of each piece. Set chicken on broiler rack or grill with mustard side facing heat source. Broil or grill 3 minutes. Turn chicken over using tongs and quickly spread another 2 teaspoons Mustard Butter on second side, dividing it approximately equally among pieces. Broil about 3 minutes or until meat in thickest part is no longer pink when cut. Transfer to a plate. Cover and keep warm.

Bring a large pot of water to a boil; add salt, then pasta. Cook uncovered over high heat, stirring occasionally, about 5 minutes or until tender but firm to the bite. Meanwhile, cut chicken in ¾-inch cubes. Reheat cabbage in skillet over low heat.

Drain pasta well. Transfer to a large heated bowl. Add mustard and remaining Mustard Butter; toss until pasta is coated. Add cabbage, chicken cubes, green onions, ¾ cup Gruyère cheese and parsley; toss. Taste and adjust seasoning. Transfer to a serving dish and serve with more Gruyère cheese.
Makes 3 or 4 main-course servings.

Mustard Butter

¼ cup butter, softened
2 tablespoons Dijon mustard

Salt and freshly ground pepper to taste

Beat butter until smooth. Add mustard, salt and pepper; beat until well blended. Set aside at room temperature.

Spaghetti with Chicken & Zucchini in Curry Cream

5 tablespoons butter
1 large onion, minced (8 oz.)
3 large garlic cloves, minced
2½ teaspoons curry powder
1 cup unsalted chicken stock, homemade, page 187, or packaged
½ cup whipping cream
Salt and freshly ground pepper to taste

1 pound boneless chicken breast halves, skin removed
2 tablespoons vegetable oil
3 small zucchini, unpeeled, halved crosswise, cut in 2" x ⅛" x ⅛" strips
8 ounces spaghetti
3 tablespoons coarsely chopped cilantro (fresh coriander) leaves, if desired

Lightly sautéed chicken and zucchini strips in a bright-orange garlic-scented curry sauce give this spaghetti a new look and taste. A sprinkling of cilantro adds a fresh touch.

Melt 2 tablespoons butter in a heavy medium saucepan over low heat. Add onion and cook, stirring often, about 10 minutes or until soft but not brown. Add garlic and cook, stirring, 1 minute. Add curry powder and cook, stirring, 1 minute. Stir in stock and bring to a boil, stirring. Boil about 3 minutes or until mixture is reduced to 1⅓ cups. Stir in cream and bring to a boil. Cook sauce over medium-high heat until it is thick enough to lightly coat a spoon, 2 to 3 minutes. Add salt and pepper. (Sauce can be kept, covered, 2 days in refrigerator.)

Lay chicken breasts flat. Cut crosswise on diagonal in about 2½" x ½" strips. In a large heavy skillet, heat oil and 1 tablespoon butter over medium-high heat. Add chicken strips in batches and sauté, tossing often, about 3 minutes or until brown on both sides and just tender, transferring when cooked with a slotted spoon to sauce. Melt 1 tablespoon butter in skillet. Add zucchini strips and sauté over medium heat about 1 minute or until barely tender. Transfer to a plate.

Bring a large pot of water to a boil; add salt, then pasta. Cook uncovered over high heat, separating strands occasionally with a fork, 8 to 9 minutes or until tender but firm to the bite. While pasta is cooking, reheat sauce. Drain pasta well. Transfer to a heated shallow serving bowl. Taste sauce and adjust seasoning.

Toss pasta with remaining 1 tablespoon butter. Set aside ½ cup sauce for serving separately and 1 teaspoon cilantro, if desired, for sprinkling. Add remaining sauce and remaining cilantro to pasta; toss. Add zucchini and toss. Taste and adjust seasoning.

To serve, sprinkle pasta with reserved cilantro. Serve reserved sauce separately.
Makes 3 main-course servings.

Be sure to buy fresh herbs that are still fragrant. When fresh herbs are not available, use approximately ⅓ as much in dried herbs. The leaf form of dried herbs keeps its flavor better than the ground form. Dried herbs and spices do not keep their flavor indefinitely; if their aroma is no longer fresh, they should be replaced.

COOKING TIP

Tri-Colored Pasta-Pepper Medley with Chicken

1 pound boneless chicken thighs, skin removed
1 medium-size red bell pepper
1 medium-size green bell pepper
1 medium-size yellow bell pepper or 1 additional red bell pepper
3 green onions
1 or 2 fresh jalapeño peppers

4 medium garlic cloves, peeled
6 tablespoons olive oil
Salt and freshly ground pepper to taste
8 ounces dried tri-colored noodles
1 tablespoon chopped fresh thyme leaves or 1 teaspoon dried leaf, crumbled

Trim chicken of fat, cartilage and tendons. Cut in about 1½" x ½" x ¼" strips. Halve bell peppers lengthwise and remove seeds and ribs. Cut in ¼-inch-wide strips. Quarter white and light-green parts of green onions lengthwise; cut all parts of onions in 1½-inch lengths.

Wearing gloves, halve jalapeño peppers and remove seeds and ribs. With the blade of a food processor turning, add jalapeño peppers and garlic cloves, 1 at a time, through feed tube; finely chop together. Peppers and garlic can also be chopped with a knife. Wash hands, food processor, cutting board and any utensils that came in contact with jalapeño pepper, with soap and hot water.

Heat 3 tablespoons oil in a large skillet over medium-high heat. Add chicken and sprinkle with salt and pepper. Sauté, stirring and turning often, about 4 minutes or until tender. Transfer to a plate with a slotted spoon. Add 2 tablespoons oil to skillet and heat over low heat. Add jalapeño pepper, garlic, bell peppers and a pinch of salt. Cook, stirring often, about 6 minutes. Add green onions and continue cooking about 4 minutes or until vegetables are tender but not brown. Add chicken and any liquid from plate. Taste and adjust seasoning. (Chicken and peppers can be cooked up to 1 hour ahead and kept at room temperature.)

Bring a large pot of water to a boil; add salt, then pasta. Cook uncovered over high heat, separating strands occasionally with a fork, 30 seconds to 2 minutes for fresh pasta or 2 to 5 minutes for dried or until tender but firm to the bite. Drain well. Transfer to a large heated bowl. Toss with remaining 1 tablespoon olive oil.

Meanwhile, reheat chicken mixture over low heat and add thyme. Add to pasta and toss. Taste, adjust seasoning and serve.
Makes 3 or 4 main-course servings.

Pasta Spirals with Chicken Livers & Onions

6 tablespoons vegetable oil
1 large onion, halved, sliced
1 large red bell pepper, seeds and ribs discarded, cut in about 2" x ½" strips
8 ounces chicken livers, halved, patted dry

Salt and freshly ground pepper to taste
½ teaspoon ground cumin
8 ounces pasta spirals, fusilli or rotini (3 cups)
2 tablespoons butter

Heat 3 tablespoons oil in a large heavy skillet over medium heat. Add onion and bell pepper. Cook, stirring occasionally, about 12 minutes or until vegetables are very tender and onion is lightly browned. Transfer to a bowl.

Wipe skillet clean. Add remaining 3 tablespoons oil and heat over medium-high heat. Add livers and sprinkle with salt, pepper and cumin. Sauté briefly about 2½ minutes or until livers change color on all sides and are just tender.

Check by cutting into a large piece; it should look creamy-pink and no longer have the reddish color of uncooked liver. Do not overcook. Add livers to onion mixture; reserve skillet.

Bring a large pot of water to a boil; add salt, then pasta. Cook uncovered over high heat, stirring occasionally, 6 to 7 minutes or until tender but firm to the bite. Drain well.

Reheat onion-liver mixture gently in reserved skillet. Sprinkle with salt and pepper. Add pasta and butter to skillet. Heat over low heat, tossing, until butter is absorbed. Taste and adjust seasoning. Serve on heated plates.

Makes 3 main-course servings.

Vermicelli with Chicken in Peanut Sauce

Coconut Milk, see below
2 tablespoons dried shredded or
  grated unsweetened coconut
1 tablespoon vegetable oil
½ cup minced onion
4 medium garlic cloves, minced
½ teaspoon hot red-pepper flakes
  or hot-pepper sauce
1 pound boneless chicken
  thighs, skin removed, cut in
  about 1" x 1" x ½" pieces

Salt to taste
½ cup chunky peanut butter
2 tablespoons soy sauce
1 teaspoon brown sugar
1 teaspoon strained fresh lemon
  juice
1½ teaspoons grated peeled
  gingerroot
8 ounces vermicelli
⅓ cup minced green onions

Inspired by an Indonesian sauce used to accompany grilled meats, this easy, exotic-tasting sauce is based on a popular American ingredient—peanut butter. The sauce is luscious and creamy without the addition of any dairy products. Instead it makes use of a coconut milk made from unsweetened coconut, which is available at health-food stores and some supermarkets.

Prepare Coconut Milk; set aside. Toast 2 tablespoons coconut in a small skillet over medium heat until lightly browned, about 3 minutes. Transfer to a plate and reserve for garnish.

Heat oil in a medium saucepan over medium heat. Add onion and sauté about 7 minutes or until softened. Add garlic and sauté 30 seconds. Add Coconut Milk and red-pepper flakes (but not hot-pepper sauce). Bring to a boil. Add chicken and a pinch of salt. Reduce heat to medium and cook uncovered, stirring often, about 10 minutes or until just tender. (Coconut Milk often separates while chicken cooks but sauce will become smooth and creamy when peanut butter is added.) Remove chicken with a slotted spoon.

Remove pan from heat. Add peanut butter in about 4 portions to sauce, whisking after each addition. Stir in soy sauce, sugar, lemon juice, gingerroot and hot-pepper sauce, if using. Return chicken to sauce. Reheat over low heat; keep warm, uncovered, over low heat.

Bring a large pot of water to a boil; add salt, then pasta. Cook uncovered over high heat, separating strands occasionally with a fork, 6 to 7 minutes or until tender but firm to the bite. Drain well. Transfer to a large heated bowl.

Set aside about ½ cup sauce for serving separately. Toss remaining sauce with vermicelli. Add green onions and toss. Taste and adjust seasoning. Sprinkle with toasted coconut. Serve reserved sauce separately.

Makes 3 or 4 main-course or 6 first-course servings.

Coconut Milk

2 cups dried shredded or grated
  unsweetened coconut (about
  7 oz.)

1¾ cups hot water

Combine coconut and hot water in a food processor or blender. Process 30 seconds. Strain, pressing hard to extract as much liquid as possible; discard coconut.

You'll be surprised how delicious and beautiful this new, original dish is. The aromatic raspberry-vinegar sauce balances the sweetness of the berries and highlights their natural tartness. Snowpeas make a colorful accompaniment.

◆   *Photo on page 82.*

Chicken with Raspberries, Fettuccine & Raspberry Butter Sauce

RASPBERRY-VINEGAR BUTTER SAUCE

3/4 cup (6 oz.) cold unsalted butter, cut in 12 pieces
2 tablespoons minced shallots
3 tablespoons raspberry vinegar
1 tablespoon water
1/4 cup whipping cream
Salt and freshly ground pepper to taste

4 boneless chicken breast halves (1 to 1 1/4 lbs. total), skin removed

Salt and freshly ground pepper to taste
2 tablespoons vegetable oil
2 tablespoons butter
2 tablespoons thinly sliced or snipped fresh chives
9 to 10 ounces fresh fettuccine or egg noodles, homemade, page 178, or packaged, or 8 ounces dried
3/4 to 1 cup fresh raspberries
Whole chives, if desired

Raspberry-Vinegar Butter Sauce: Melt 1 tablespoon butter in a small heavy saucepan over low heat. Add shallots and cook about 2 minutes or until soft but not brown. Add vinegar and water. Simmer over medium heat until liquid is reduced to about 2 tablespoons. Stir in cream and a pinch of salt and pepper. Simmer, whisking occasionally, until mixture is reduced to about 3 tablespoons. Keep remaining butter in refrigerator until ready to use. (Sauce can be prepared to this point up to 4 hours ahead and kept, covered, at room temperature.)

Pat dry chicken breasts; sprinkle with salt and pepper. Heat oil and 1 tablespoon butter in a large heavy skillet over medium-high heat. Add chicken breasts in batches and sauté about 3 minutes on each side, or until golden brown. Transfer with a slotted spatula to an ovenproof platter and keep warm in a 200F (95C) oven.

Bring a large pot of water to a boil; add salt, then pasta. Cook uncovered over high heat, separating strands occasionally with a fork, 30 seconds to 2 minutes for fresh pasta or 2 to 5 minutes for dried or until tender but firm to the bite. Rinse with cold water and drain well. Transfer to a medium or large skillet. Add remaining 1 tablespoon butter.

To finish butter sauce: Set pan of shallot mixture over low heat and bring to a simmer, whisking. Add 2 pieces chilled butter and whisk quickly until just blended in. Whisk in remaining butter 1 piece at a time, lifting pan from heat occasionally to cool mixture and adding each new piece of butter before previous one is completely blended in. Butter should soften as it is added but sauce should not get hot enough to liquefy. Remove pan from heat as soon as last butter piece is incorporated. Taste and adjust seasoning. Keep sauce warm if necessary in an uncovered bowl set on a rack above hot but not simmering water over low heat, or in a thermos; try to serve as soon as possible.

Heat pasta over low heat, tossing; remove from heat. Add chives and 1/3 cup sauce to pasta; toss mixture. Taste and adjust seasoning.

To serve, make a bed of pasta on a serving platter and arrange chicken on top, discarding any liquid that drained from chicken. Spoon about 1 tablespoon sauce over each portion of chicken. Garnish with raspberries and whole chives, if desired; serve immediately. Serve remaining sauce separately.

Makes 4 main-course servings.

Fusilli with Citrus-Barbecued Chicken

The fresh citrus marinade for the chicken, accented with soy sauce and ginger, doubles as an easy sauce for the pasta spirals.

Citrus Marinade, see below
1¹/₂ pounds boneless chicken thighs or breasts, skin removed
1 large orange
1 pound fusilli, rotini or other pasta spirals
¹/₄ cup butter, room temperature
¹/₄ cup minced green onions

Prepare Citrus Marinade. Add chicken pieces to marinade and turn them over to coat. Rub marinade thoroughly into chicken. Cover chicken and refrigerate 2 to 24 hours, turning occasionally.

Use a serrated knife to cut skin and pith from orange. Separate sections by cutting on each side of membrane between them, inward to center; see photos page 173. Fold back membrane and cut to remove segment. Continue until all segments have been removed; discard membranes. Reserve segments for garnish.

Preheat broiler with rack about 6 inches from heat source; or prepare grill. Remove chicken from marinade. Transfer marinade to a small saucepan. Put chicken on hot broiler rack or grill. Broil or grill chicken, brushing once with marinade; turn after 4 minutes. Cook second side, brushing once with marinade, 2 to 3 minutes for breasts or 4 to 5 minutes for thighs or until tender when pierced in thickest part with a thin sharp knife and color inside is no longer pink. Transfer to a platter and keep warm.

Bring a large pot of water to a boil; add salt, then pasta. Cook uncovered over high heat, stirring occasionally, about 7 minutes or until tender but firm to the bite. Meanwhile, cut cooked chicken in bite-size pieces. Bring reserved marinade to a boil. Taste and adjust seasoning.

Drain pasta well. Transfer to a large heated bowl. Add marinade to pasta and toss. Add butter in pieces and toss. Add green onions and chicken; toss gently. Garnish with orange segments. Serve hot.
Makes 6 main-course servings.

Citrus Marinade

¹/₃ cup soy sauce
¹/₃ cup strained fresh orange juice
3 tablespoons strained fresh lemon juice
3 tablespoons vegetable oil
1 tablespoon plus 1 teaspoon honey
1 teaspoon finely grated orange zest
1 teaspoon finely grated lemon zest
2 medium shallots, minced
2 teaspoons grated peeled gingerroot
¹/₄ teaspoon ground cloves
¹/₄ teaspoon hot-pepper sauce

In a shallow dish, mix soy sauce, orange juice, lemon juice, oil, honey, grated orange and lemon zests, shallots, gingerroot, cloves and pepper sauce.

I always use unsalted butter because it is of finer quality, but you can use salted when the recipe does not specify otherwise.

COOKING TIP

The addition of fresh herbs and cream makes this quick and easy main course delightful even with canned tomato sauce. Pasta shells, called gnocchi or conchiglie by some Italian companies, are lovely in this dish because they catch a little of the sauce.

Pasta with Creamy Tomato Sauce, Chicken & Provençal Herbs

4 tablespoons butter
8 ounces boneless chicken breast, skin removed, cut in about ¹/₂-inch dice
Salt and freshly ground pepper to taste
¹/₂ cup tomato sauce, homemade, page 186, or packaged
3 tablespoons chopped fresh basil leaves or 1 tablespoon dried leaf, crumbled
2 tablespoons chopped fresh sage leaves or 2 teaspoons dried leaf, crumbled

1 tablespoon chopped fresh rosemary or 1 teaspoon dried, crumbled
¹/₄ cup whipping cream
8 ounces medium pasta shells (about 3¹/₂ cups), radiatore or rotelle
Fresh basil sprigs for garnish, if desired
Bowl of freshly grated Parmesan cheese (for serving)

Melt 2 tablespoons butter in a medium skillet over medium heat. Add chicken, salt and pepper. Sauté until chicken changes color, about 3 minutes. Transfer to a medium bowl. Add tomato sauce, basil, sage and rosemary to skillet; bring to a simmer. Stir in cream and return to a simmer. With sauce over low heat, return chicken to skillet and add remaining 2 tablespoons butter. Taste and adjust seasoning. (Sauce can be kept, covered, 1 day in refrigerator. Reheat over low heat before continuing.) Keep sauce warm over very low heat.

Bring a large pot of water to a boil; add salt, then pasta. Cook uncovered over high heat, stirring occasionally, 5 to 8 minutes or until tender but firm to the bite. Drain well. Transfer to a large heated serving bowl. Add sauce and toss. Taste and adjust seasoning. Garnish if desired with fresh basil sprigs. Serve with Parmesan cheese.

Makes 4 first-course or 2 or 3 main-course servings.

VARIATION
Quarter 8 ounces small mushrooms. Melt 2 tablespoons butter in a large skillet over medium heat. Add mushrooms and sprinkle with salt and pepper. Sauté about 5 minutes or until lightly browned. Add to pasta together with chicken mixture.

Butter-Baked Chicken with Pasta & Leeks

1 whole (3½-lb.) frying chicken, room temperature
Salt and freshly ground pepper to taste
2 tablespoons vegetable oil
2 tablespoons butter
2 large leeks (about 1 lb. total), white and light-green parts only, split lengthwise

3 tablespoons dry white wine
2 tablespoons snipped fresh dill
8 ounces radiatore (about 3 cups), pasta wheels or spirals

I love this dish; it uses only a few ingredients yet is superb. The chicken is very moist when cooked this way, and its juices impart to the pasta an intense chicken flavor. Because the sauce is not thick, it is good for showing off interesting pasta shapes, such as radiatore, wheels or bow ties.

Preheat oven to 400F (205C). Remove neck and giblets from chicken. Pull out fat from inside chicken on both sides near tail. Cut off tail and wing tips. Thoroughly pat chicken dry. Sprinkle evenly on all sides with salt and pepper.

Heat oil and butter in a heavy 4- to 5-quart oval enamel-lined cast-iron casserole over medium-high heat until butter melts. Set chicken in pan on its side so leg is in contact with fat. Cover with a large splatter screen and brown side of chicken, taking about 3 minutes. Using 2 wooden spoons to prevent tearing chicken skin and standing back to avoid splatters, turn chicken gently onto its breast and brown about 3 minutes. Turn chicken on other side and brown 3 minutes. Turn chicken on its back and brown 2 minutes. If fat begins to turn dark brown, reduce heat to medium; do not let fat burn.

Leave chicken on its back. Baste with pan juices. Cover and bake about 45 minutes or until juices run clear when thickest part of leg is pierced with a thin skewer; if juices are still pink, bake a few minutes longer and test again. (Chicken can be kept warm in casserole, covered, about 15 minutes.)

While chicken is cooking, soak leeks in cold water 15 minutes. Check between layers to be sure no sand remains and rinse thoroughly. Cut in thin crosswise slices.

When chicken is tender, transfer to a platter, reserving juices in casserole. Carve chicken. Cover chicken with foil and keep warm.

Add leeks to chicken juices in casserole and sprinkle with salt and pepper. Cover and cook over low heat, stirring occasionally, about 7 minutes or until just tender. Taste and adjust seasoning. Remove leeks using a slotted spoon.

Bring juices to a boil. Add wine and bring to a boil, stirring and scraping any browned juices from sides and bottom of casserole. Remove from heat. Stir dill and leeks into sauce. Taste sauce and adjust seasoning.

Bring a large pot of water to a boil; add salt, then pasta. Cook uncovered over high heat, stirring occasionally, about 9 minutes for radiatore or about 7 minutes for wheels or spirals or until tender but firm to the bite. Meanwhile, reheat sauce if necessary. Drain pasta well. Add to sauce and toss. Taste and adjust seasoning. Serve pasta alongside chicken.

Make 4 main-course servings.

Spicy Southwestern Turkey with Cocoa Pasta

Roasted jalapeños make this sauce hot, but the sweetness of the bell peppers and onions balances the flavors and makes the sauce a good partner for the savory cocoa pasta and a lively complement for the turkey. Using cocoa pasta might be surprising, but remember that spicy Mexican mole sauces for poultry often contain chocolate.

Roasted-Pepper Sauce, see below
1 pound boneless turkey breast (often called turkey tenderloin)
4 tablespoons olive oil
1 medium garlic clove, chopped
½ teaspoon ground cumin
2 tablespoons minced cilantro (fresh coriander) leaves

Salt and freshly ground pepper to taste
1 cup corn kernels, cooked
9 to 10 ounces fresh cocoa or egg fettuccine, homemade, page 182, or packaged, or 8 ounces dried

Prepare Roasted-Pepper Sauce; set aside. Cut turkey in bite-size cubes, about 1" x 1" x ½". Heat 3 tablespoons oil in a large heavy skillet over medium heat. Add ½ of turkey. Sauté about 3 minutes or until just tender. Remove with a slotted spoon. Repeat with remaining turkey. Return all of turkey to skillet. Add garlic, cumin and 1 tablespoon cilantro and sprinkle with salt and pepper. Heat over low heat, stirring, about 1 minute to blend flavors. Add to sauce and heat gently. Add corn. Taste and adjust seasoning. Keep warm over low heat.

Bring a large pot of water to a boil; add salt, then pasta. Cook uncovered over high heat, separating strands occasionally with a fork, 30 seconds to 2 minutes for fresh pasta or 2 to 5 minutes for dried or until tender but firm to the bite. Drain well. Transfer to a large bowl. Toss with remaining 1 tablespoon olive oil. Arrange around the edge of a serving platter. Heap turkey and sauce in center. Sprinkle with remaining cilantro and serve.
Makes 4 main-course servings.

Roasted-Pepper Sauce

1 green bell pepper
1 red bell pepper
3 jalapeño peppers
3 tablespoons olive oil
1 large onion, minced
1 pound ripe tomatoes, peeled, seeded, coarsely chopped, or 1 (28-oz.) can whole plum tomatoes, drained, coarsely chopped

2 medium garlic cloves, minced
3 tablespoons minced cilantro (fresh coriander) leaves
3 tablespoons minced fresh parsley leaves
2 teaspoons paprika
Red (cayenne) pepper to taste
½ teaspoon ground cumin
¼ teaspoon salt

Preheat broiler. Broil peppers about 2 inches from heat source, turning them often, until skins are blistery all over, about 5 minutes for jalapeño peppers and 15 to 25 minutes for bell peppers. Transfer to a plastic bag and close bag. Let stand about 10 minutes. Peel peppers using a paring knife. Halve lengthwise and discard seeds and ribs. Drain peppers in a colander 10 minutes. Cut bell peppers in ½-inch dice and jalapeños in about ¼-inch dice.

Heat oil in a large skillet over medium heat. Add onion and cook about 7 minutes or until softened. Add tomatoes, peppers, garlic, cilantro, parsley, paprika, red pepper, cumin and salt. Cook uncovered, stirring often, about 15 minutes or until mixture is thick. (Sauce can be kept, covered, 2 days in refrigerator. Reheat in covered saucepan over low heat.)

Spicy Southwestern Turkey with Cocoa Pasta

Remove charred peppers from the plastic bag and peel off skin using a paring knife.

Chili Pasta with Smoked Turkey

¾ cup frozen lima beans
¼ cup butter
6 tablespoons whipping cream
4 ounces sliced smoked turkey, cut in 2" x ⅜" strips
Salt and freshly ground pepper to taste
9 to 10 ounces fresh chili fettuccine, homemade, page 182, or packaged, or 8 ounces dried

3 tablespoons chopped green onions
3 to 4 tablespoons chopped cilantro (fresh coriander) or fresh parsley leaves
1 yellow or red bell pepper, roasted, see opposite, or from a jar, cut in ¼-inch strips

This dish illustrates how to use a spiced pasta to create a quick and delicious dish. Instead of chili pasta you can use homemade cumin pasta or cilantro pasta, page 182, or packaged "Cajun" pasta or any other type that is spicy. If you can't find a spicy pasta, you can substitute tomato pasta, but add ½ teaspoon cumin and 1 teaspoon chili powder or more to the sauce.

Cook lima beans uncovered in a medium saucepan of boiling salted water to generously cover over medium-high heat about 8 minutes or until just tender. Drain thoroughly.

Heat butter and cream in a small saucepan to a bare simmer. Add turkey, beans and a pinch of salt and pepper. Heat through over low heat.

Bring a large pot of water to a boil; add salt, then pasta. Cook uncovered over high heat, separating strands occasionally with a fork, 30 seconds to 2 minutes for fresh pasta or 2 to 5 minutes for dried or until tender but firm to the bite. Drain well. Transfer to a large heated bowl. Add turkey mixture and green onions; toss with pasta. Reserve 1 or 2 teaspoons cilantro or parsley and a few pepper strips for garnish. Add remaining peppers and cilantro or parsley to pasta and toss. Taste and adjust seasoning. Sprinkle reserved cilantro or parsley on top and garnish with pepper strips.

Makes 4 servings as a first course or light main course.

The tomato sauce accented with fresh tarragon and a touch of prosciutto adds zip to the vermicelli and turkey. A flavored pasta, such as garlic or lemon tagliarini, is fun to use once in a while instead of the vermicelli.

Vermicelli with Turkey, Tomatoes & Tarragon

Tomato-Tarragon Sauce, see below
1¼ pounds boneless turkey breast (often called turkey tenderloin)
2 medium zucchini
1 tablespoon butter
5 tablespoons olive oil or vegetable oil

Salt and freshly ground pepper to taste
1½ ounces thinly sliced prosciutto, cut in 1½" x ¼" strips
12 ounces vermicelli
Bowl of freshly grated Parmesan cheese (for serving)

Prepare Tomato-Tarragon Sauce; set aside. Cut boneless turkey in thin strips, about 1½" x ¼" x ¼". Cut zucchini in strips approximately same size as turkey. Heat butter and 2 tablespoons oil in a large heavy skillet over medium heat. Add ½ of turkey and sprinkle with salt and pepper. Sauté 3 minutes or until just tender. Using a slotted spoon, transfer to a bowl. Add 1 tablespoon oil to skillet and heat it. Sauté remaining turkey and remove to bowl. Add 1 tablespoon oil to skillet and heat it. Add zucchini and sauté over medium heat about 1 minute or until barely tender. Transfer to a plate.

Add prosciutto and turkey with any liquid that escaped from it to Tomato-Tarragon Sauce. Stir and keep warm over very low heat.

Bring a large pot of water to a boil; add salt, then pasta. Cook uncovered over high heat, separating strands occasionally with a fork, 6 to 7 minutes or until tender but firm to the bite. Drain well. Transfer to a large heated bowl. Toss with remaining 1 tablespoon oil, then with turkey mixture and zucchini. Taste and adjust seasoning. Serve with Parmesan cheese.
Makes 4 main-course servings.

Tomato-Tarragon Sauce

1 tablespoon olive oil or vegetable oil
1 tablespoon butter
1 large shallot, minced
3 pounds ripe tomatoes, peeled, seeded, chopped, or 3 (28-oz.) cans whole plum tomatoes, drained
¾ teaspoon fresh thyme leaves or ¼ teaspoon dried leaf, crumbled

1 bay leaf
Salt and freshly ground pepper to taste
3 tablespoons chopped fresh tarragon leaves or 1 tablespoon dried leaf, crumbled

Heat oil and butter in a large deep skillet or sauté pan over medium heat. Add shallot and sauté 1 minute. Add tomatoes, thyme, bay leaf, salt and pepper. Bring to a boil over high heat. Cook over medium heat, stirring often (and crushing canned tomatoes, if using), about 25 minutes or until tomatoes are soft and mixture is thick. Discard bay leaf. (Sauce can be kept, covered, 2 days in refrigerator. Bring to a simmer in skillet over low heat before continuing.) Add tarragon. Taste and adjust seasoning.

Note: Skinned boneless chicken breast can be substituted for turkey.

Tortellini with Walnut Sauce, Smoked Turkey & Spinach

Walnut Sauce, see below
2 pounds spinach, stems
    removed, leaves rinsed well
3 tablespoons butter
Salt and freshly ground pepper to
    taste
1 (9-oz.) package fresh or frozen
    cheese-filled tortellini

3 ounces sliced smoked turkey
    breast, cut in about 2" x ⅜"
    strips, room temperature
12 walnut halves, broken in 2
    pieces

The widespread availability of good-quality fresh tortellini makes it easy to create elegant dishes in no time. Here the tortellini are tossed with a quick walnut dressing and strips of smoked turkey, then served in a ring of bright-green spinach leaves to create an appetizer worthy of the most festive occasions.

Prepare Walnut Sauce; set aside. Add spinach to a large saucepan of enough boiling salted water to cover generously. Cook uncovered over high heat about 2 minutes or until wilted. Drain in a colander. Squeeze spinach gently to remove excess liquid but without breaking up leaves too much.

Melt butter in saucepan used to cook spinach. Add spinach, salt and pepper. Sauté over medium heat until hot.

Bring a large pot of water to a boil; add salt, then pasta. Cook uncovered over high heat, stirring occasionally, about 4 minutes or until tender but firm to the bite. Drain well. Transfer to a medium-size heated bowl.

Reserve a few turkey strips for garnish. Add remaining turkey and ½ cup Walnut Sauce to pasta; toss. Taste and adjust seasoning. Gently reheat spinach if necessary.

Spoon spinach in a ring onto each of 4 heated plates. Spoon tortellini mixture in center. Garnish with reserved turkey strips and walnuts. Serve remaining sauce separately.

Makes 4 first-course servings.

Walnut Sauce

¼ cup torn fresh basil leaves or 2
    teaspoons dried leaf, crumbled
1 cup walnut pieces (about
    3½ oz.)
3 tablespoons olive oil or
    walnut oil

2 tablespoons freshly grated
    Parmesan or romano cheese
½ cup whipping cream
Salt and freshly ground pepper to
    taste

Combine basil, walnuts, oil and cheese in a food processor. Process until finely chopped. With blades turning, gradually add whipping cream. Process until sauce is well blended. Season with salt and pepper. (Sauce can be kept, covered, 2 days in refrigerator. Bring to room temperature before using.)

The best quality canned tomatoes are whole plum tomatoes. When drained plum tomatoes are called for in a recipe, drain them thoroughly in a colander or strainer.

COOKING TIP

Stuffed Cornish Hens with Orzo, Raisins & Pecans

Orzo-Pecan-Raisin Stuffing, see below
4 medium (1¹/₄- to 1¹/₂-lb.) Cornish hens
¹/₂ teaspoon ground black pepper
1 teaspoon ground ginger

4 teaspoons soy sauce
2 teaspoons honey
2 tablespoons vegetable oil
Lime slices, if desired
Italian parsley sprigs

Prepare Orzo-Pecan-Raisin Stuffing; set aside to cool. Increase oven temperature to 400F (205C). Discard excess fat from hens. Mix pepper, ginger, soy sauce, honey and oil in a small bowl. Rub hens all over with honey mixture. Spoon ¹/₃ to ¹/₂ cup cooled stuffing into each hen, packing it in gently. Reserve remaining stuffing at room temperature.

Set hens in a roasting pan or shallow baking dish just large enough to contain them. Roast hens, basting every 10 to 15 minutes and adding 1 or 2 tablespoons hot water to pan juices if they brown, 45 minutes or until thickest part of drumstick is tender when pierced with a skewer and juices that run from drumstick are clear. If juices are pink, continue roasting hens a few minutes longer and check again.

Add 2 or 3 tablespoons pan juices to remaining stuffing mixture and reheat in a medium skillet over low heat, stirring gently with a fork, about 2 minutes. Serve in a separate heated dish.

To serve, spoon stuffing from hens onto a platter. Set hens around stuffing. Garnish with lime slices, if desired, and parsley sprigs.
Makes 4 main-course servings.

Orzo-Pecan-Raisin Stuffing

³/₄ cup pecan halves, broken in pieces
6 tablespoons butter
5 tablespoons minced peeled gingerroot
3 tablespoons chopped shallots
1¹/₂ cups orzo or riso (rice-shaped pasta) (about 12 oz.)

¹/₃ cup dark raisins
3 cups hot chicken stock or broth, homemade, page 187, or packaged
5 tablespoons minced fresh regular or Italian parsley leaves

Preheat oven to 350F (175C). Toast pecan pieces in oven about 4 minutes or until lightly browned. Transfer to a plate and let cool.

Set aside 2 tablespoons butter at room temperature. Melt remaining 4 tablespoons butter in a medium saucepan over medium heat. Add gingerroot and shallots. Sauté, stirring, 1 minute. Add orzo and cook over low heat, stirring, 3 minutes. Scatter raisins on top. Add stock or broth and bring to a boil. Cover and cook over low heat about 14 minutes or until barely tender.

Fluff mixture with a fork to break up any lumps in orzo. Add reserved 2 tablespoons butter, pecans and parsley; toss mixture to combine. Taste and adjust seasoning. Let stuffing cool.

Note: An easy way to carve hens is to cut each in half lengthwise with poultry shears.

PASTA WITH MEAT

Pasta with meat sauce has long been a favorite in both Europe and America, and for good reason—the pairing makes an ideal way to enjoy the rich flavor of meat without eating a large amount of it.

The finer cuts, such as beef rib-eye steaks and veal scaloppini, can either be sautéed or grilled and served on a bed of pasta, as in Veal Dijonnaise with Green Peppercorns & Tri-Colored Noodles, with the sauce as a flavoring for both meat and pasta. Alternatively, the meat can be cut in strips and tossed with the pasta and the sauce, as in Linguine with Steak & Double-Mushroom Madeira Sauce.

Braised meats and stews make sensational sauces for pasta because the long, slow simmering produces richly flavored juices as well as tender meats to serve with the pasta. Try, for example, such hearty main courses as Aromatic Macaroni and Beef Stew with Fennel, Marjoram & Mint, Rigatoni with Lamb & Peas, or Ruffled Pasta with Veal, Saffron & Ginger.

When you long for the comforting taste of pasta with a luscious meat sauce, Fettuccine with Old-Fashioned Italian Meat Sauce, made

Clockwise from top left: Lazy-Day Pasta with Smoked Sausage, Tomato Sauce & Corn, page 117; Pasta Shells with Mortadella, Dill Butter & Vegetables, page 116; Pasta Corkscrews with Bacon, Avocado & Tomato, page 116

with braised beef, red wine and porcini mushrooms, is a winner. Ground meat can also be used to make delicious renditions of "spaghetti sauce." These can be traditional, like the tomato- and thyme-scented meat sauce in Pasta with Bolognese Sauce & Sautéed Squash. Or they can use exotic flavorings, like Chinese plum sauce, which gives ground-beef sauce a new and delightful taste in Chinese Noodles with Beef, Ginger & Plum Sauce, page 148.

Sausages of all types, cold cuts like mortadella, and cured meats such as bacon or pancetta, the Italian bacon used in Classic Spaghetti Carbonara, page 61, lend great taste to pasta and are the basis for many quick pasta dishes.

Pasta shells are wonderful with ground-meat sauces because the meat lodges inside many of the shells. Capers, mushrooms and a generous amount of garlic give this "spaghetti sauce" its Mediterranean character.

Pasta Shells with Tunisian Beef & Artichoke Sauce

5 tablespoons olive oil
12 medium garlic cloves, minced
1 pound lean ground beef
1¹/₂ pounds ripe tomatoes, peeled, seeded, chopped, or 1 (28-oz.) can and 1 (14-oz.) can whole plum tomatoes, drained
1 bay leaf
Salt and freshly ground pepper to taste
¹/₄ cup tomato paste
¹/₄ cup water
8 ounces small mushrooms, quartered

1 (3¹/₄-oz.) jar capers, lightly rinsed, drained (5 tablespoons)
4 fresh artichokes or 16 frozen artichoke-heart pieces
1 lemon (if using fresh artichokes) or 1 teaspoon strained fresh lemon juice (if using frozen)
1 pound medium pasta shells, tricolored, tomato or plain
2 tablespoons chopped fresh parsley leaves

Heat 3 tablespoons oil in a large heavy casserole over low heat. Add 1 tablespoon garlic and cook over low heat 30 seconds, stirring. Add beef and sauté over medium heat, crumbling with a wooden spoon, until it changes color. Add tomatoes, bay leaf, salt and pepper. Bring to a boil, stirring (and crushing canned tomatoes, if using). Whisk tomato paste with water in a small bowl until smooth; add to tomato mixture. Bring to a boil. Simmer uncovered, stirring occasionally, over low heat, 30 minutes.

Add mushrooms and 3 tablespoons capers. Cover and simmer about 15 minutes or until mushrooms are tender and sauce is thick.

If using fresh artichokes, shape into artichoke hearts following directions on page 51. Prepare a medium saucepan of boiling salted water and squeeze in any juice remaining in lemon (if using fresh artichokes) or add 1 teaspoon lemon juice (if using frozen). Add fresh or frozen artichoke hearts to saucepan. Cover and simmer over low heat until tender when pierced with a knife, 15 to 20 minutes for fresh ones and about 7 minutes for frozen ones. Cool to lukewarm in liquid. Using a teaspoon, scoop out hairlike "choke" from center of each fresh artichoke heart. Return artichokes to liquid until ready to use. Drain, then cut each fresh artichoke into 8 pieces. If frozen artichoke pieces are large, cut in half after draining.

Discard bay leaf from beef sauce. Add remaining garlic and cook over low heat 2 minutes. Add artichokes and reheat. Taste and adjust seasoning; sauce should be quite highly seasoned to balance sharpness of capers. (Sauce can be kept, covered, up to 2 days in refrigerator. Reheat it, covered, over low heat.)

Bring a large pot of water to a boil; add salt, then pasta. Cook uncovered over high heat, stirring occasionally, 5 to 8 minutes or until tender but firm to the bite. Drain well. Transfer to a large heated bowl. Toss with remaining 2 tablespoons oil. Add sauce and 1 tablespoon capers; toss. Taste and adjust seasoning. Sprinkle with parsley and remaining 1 tablespoon capers.
Makes 6 main-course servings.

Chili-Topped Spaghetti

Chili, see below
1 pound spaghetti or corn pasta
3 tablespoons chopped cilantro (fresh coriander) or fresh parsley leaves, if desired

Bowl of grated Monterey Jack or cheddar cheese (for serving)

I like chili best as a rich sauce for pasta rather than on its own in a bowl. For a medium-spicy version I use two jalapeño peppers but if you like it really hot, use four. You can substitute corn pasta when it's available to emphasize the Southwest theme.

Prepare Chili; cover and keep warm. Bring a large pot of water to a boil; add salt, then pasta. Cook uncovered over high heat, separating strands occasionally with a fork, 8 to 9 minutes for spaghetti or until tender but firm to the bite.

Reserve 1 cup chili. Transfer pasta to a heated serving bowl and toss with remaining chili and 2 tablespoons cilantro or parsley, if desired. Spoon reserved chili on top. Sprinkle with remaining cilantro or parsley. Serve with cheese.
Makes 6 main-course servings.

Chili

3 tablespoons olive oil
1 large onion, chopped
2 to 4 fresh jalapeño peppers, if desired
1 pound ground beef, preferably "chili beef" or chuck
6 large garlic cloves, minced
3 tablespoons chili powder
2 tablespoons ground cumin, preferably fresh

1 tablespoon dried leaf oregano, crumbled
½ teaspoon hot red-pepper flakes or ¼ teaspoon red (cayenne) pepper or to taste
Salt and pepper to taste
1 (28-oz.) can whole plum tomatoes, undrained

Heat oil in a large casserole or saucepan over medium heat. Add onion and cook, stirring often, about 15 minutes or until very tender. Transfer to a bowl.

If using jalapeño peppers, wear gloves when handling them. Remove seeds and ribs; mince peppers.

Add beef to casserole and cook, stirring often, until it changes color, about 10 minutes. Return onion to casserole and add garlic, jalapeños, chili powder, cumin, oregano, hot-pepper flakes or red pepper and salt and pepper. Cook over low heat, stirring, about 3 minutes to coat meat with spices. Add tomatoes and bring to a boil, stirring and crushing tomatoes. Cook uncovered over low heat about 1 hour or until thick. Taste and adjust seasoning. If you would like it hot, add more red pepper. (Chili can be kept, covered, 2 days in refrigerator; or it can be frozen.)

In this country dish, prepared in various parts of the Mediterranean from Corsica to North Africa, the macaroni is cooked by an unusual technique—it simmers gently in the stew, thus absorbing the maximum amount of flavor from the broth. Small pasta shapes, such as elbow macaroni and pasta shells, are used because larger ones would not cook evenly. Seasonings vary slightly from place to place, but onion, garlic and tomatoes are always included and usually plenty of cheese as well. Instead of beef, sometimes lamb, pork or a mixture of meats is used.

Aromatic Macaroni & Beef Stew with Fennel, Marjoram & Mint

5 tablespoons olive oil
2 pounds beef chuck or stew meat, cut in ¾-inch cubes, patted dry
2 medium onions, halved, cut in thin slices
1 large fennel bulb (sometimes called anis), stalks removed, diced
8 large garlic cloves, minced
1 pound ripe tomatoes, peeled, seeded, coarsely chopped, or 1 (28-oz.) can whole plum tomatoes, drained, coarsely chopped
½ cup dry white wine
Salt and freshly ground black pepper
1 bay leaf

2 tablespoons chopped fresh marjoram leaves or 2 teaspoons dried leaf, crumbled
3 tablespoons chopped fresh mint leaves
About 1 quart hot water
1 pound small elbow macaroni
4 tablespoons chopped fresh parsley leaves
1½ cups freshly grated Parmesan cheese (about 4½ oz.), or 2 cups finely grated kashkaval or kefalotiri cheese (about 8 oz.) mixed with ½ cup grated Parmesan (about 1½ oz.)
Bowl of grated Parmesan, kashkaval or kefalotiri cheese, if desired (for serving)

Heat 3 tablespoons oil in a 4- to 5-quart wide heavy stainless steel or enameled casserole over medium-high heat. Add meat in batches and brown on all sides, removing with a slotted spoon as it browns. Add remaining 2 tablespoons oil to casserole. Add onions and fennel. Cook over medium-low heat about 10 minutes or until softened. Stir in 1 tablespoon minced garlic. Return meat to pan. Add tomatoes, wine, salt, pepper, bay leaf, marjoram and 2 tablespoons mint. Cover and cook over low heat 45 minutes. Add 2 cups hot water. Bring to a simmer. Cover and cook over low heat 30 minutes or until meat is tender when pierced with a knife. Discard bay leaf. (Stew can be kept, covered, 2 days in refrigerator. Reheat before continuing.)

Add 1½ cups hot water to casserole and bring to a boil. Add uncooked macaroni, remaining garlic and remaining 1 tablespoon mint. Push macaroni into liquid and cook uncovered over medium heat, stirring often to prevent sticking, about 9 minutes or until macaroni is just tender. If pan becomes dry while macaroni is cooking, add a little more boiling water. If mixture is a little too moist when macaroni is cooked, cover and let stand 5 minutes so macaroni absorbs excess liquid.

Stir in 2 tablespoons parsley. Set aside 1 or 2 tablespoons cheese for sprinkling. Stir in remaining cheese. Taste and adjust seasoning. Sprinkle with reserved cheese and remaining 2 tablespoons parsley. Serve from casserole with additional cheese.
Makes 5 or 6 main-course servings.

COOKING TIP

When tasting, think about whether the food will taste better if more salt, pepper or another of the flavorings in the dish is added. Add a little more of what is needed and taste again. Usually several tastings are needed until the seasoning is just right.

Linguine with Steak & Double-Mushroom Madeira Sauce

4 ounces fresh shiitake, oyster or chanterelle mushrooms
2 tablespoons vegetable oil
6 tablespoons butter
1 large shallot, minced
Salt and freshly ground pepper to taste
8 ounces button mushrooms, halved, cut in thin slices
½ cup Madeira
2 (8- or 9-oz.) rib-eye steaks, about 1 inch thick
9 to 10 ounces fresh linguine or 8 ounces dried
2 tablespoons minced fresh parsley leaves

There is little last-minute work involved in making this festive dish—the steak is grilled and the delectable Madeira-mushroom sauce can be prepared ahead. Before serving time they are gently heated together and tossed with linguine. This is an ideal way to enjoy the taste of good steak without eating a large amount—only two steaks are needed for four servings.

Remove stems of shiitake mushrooms but not of other mushrooms. Gently clean mushrooms with damp paper towels. Dry on paper towels. Halve shiitake caps and cut in thin slices. If oyster mushrooms or chanterelles are large, cut in bite-size pieces.

Heat 1 tablespoon oil and 2 tablespoons butter in a large heavy skillet over medium heat. Stir in shallot, then shiitake, oyster or chanterelle mushrooms, salt and pepper. Sauté, tossing often, about 4 minutes or until mushrooms are just tender. Remove from skillet. Add 3 tablespoons butter and melt over medium-high heat. Add button mushrooms, salt and pepper. Sauté until light brown, about 3 minutes. Return all mushrooms to skillet and reheat mixture until sizzling. Add ¼ cup Madeira and simmer over medium heat, stirring, until it is absorbed by mushrooms, about 3 minutes. Taste and adjust seasoning. Remove from heat.

Preheat broiler or grill with rack about 4 inches from heat source; or heat stove-top ridged grill over high heat. Pat steaks dry, sprinkle with salt and pepper and brush lightly with oil. Put 1 or both steaks on broiler rack or grill. Broil or grill about 2 minutes per side for rare meat or until steak is brown but does not resist when pressed. Transfer to a plate. Trim fat from steaks. Cut steaks crosswise in diagonal strips about ¼ inch wide and 2½ inches long.

Meanwhile, bring a large pot of water to a boil; add salt, then pasta. Cook uncovered over high heat, separating strands occasionally with a fork, about 2 minutes for fresh or 8 minutes for dried or until tender but firm to the bite. Drain well. Transfer to a large heated bowl. Toss with remaining 1 tablespoon butter.

Reheat mushroom mixture and add steak strips. Reheat gently. Add remaining ¼ cup Madeira. Gently toss over low heat about 1 minute. Add parsley. Spoon over pasta and toss. Taste, adjust seasoning and serve.
Makes 4 main-course servings.

Note: If exotic mushrooms are not available, increase amount of button mushrooms to 12 ounces and sauté in 2 batches.

Clockwise from top right: shiitake, oyster and chanterelle mushrooms.

If oyster mushrooms or chanterelles are large, cut in bite-size pieces. Halve shiitake caps and cut in thin slices.

Pasta with Bolognese Sauce & Sautéed Squash

Bolognese sauce is a rich and meaty pasta sauce in which tomato is only a background flavor. A basic sauce, it is used often in Italy with a wide variety of pastas including filled pastas such as ravioli. Here slices of the pretty, flower-shaped pattypan squash are a light, pleasant complement to the sauce and pasta. If two types of squash are not in season, use one type or substitute zucchini. Instead of squash other vegetables, such as cooked spinach or chard or even garbanzo beans, can be added.

Bolognese Sauce, see below
8 ounces dark or light-green pattypan squash
8 ounces yellow pattypan squash
3 tablespoons butter
Salt and freshly ground pepper to taste
1 pound cavatappi (spiral macaroni), orecchiette (pasta discs) or medium shells

2 tablespoons chopped fresh parsley leaves, preferably Italian parsley
Thyme sprigs, if desired
Bowl of freshly grated Parmesan cheese (for serving)

Prepare Bolognese Sauce; set aside. Halve green and yellow squashes into 2 semicircles. Put cut side down and cut in ¼-inch-thick slices. Melt 2 tablespoons butter in a large skillet over medium heat. Add ½ of squash; sprinkle with salt and pepper. Sauté, turning occasionally, about 5 minutes or until tender. Transfer to a plate. Add remaining 1 tablespoon butter to skillet; melt. Sauté remaining squash. Return squash to skillet; remove from heat.

Bring a large pot of water to a boil; add salt, then pasta. Cook uncovered over high heat, stirring occasionally, about 8 minutes for cavatappi, 10 minutes for orecchiette or 5 to 8 minutes for shells or until tender but firm to the bite. Meanwhile, reheat sauce in a covered saucepan over medium-low heat, stirring occasionally. Gently reheat squash.

Drain pasta well. Transfer to a large heated bowl. Add sauce and toss. Add squash and parsley; toss lightly. Taste and adjust seasoning. Garnish with thyme sprigs, if desired. Serve with Parmesan cheese.
Makes 4 main-course or 6 to 8 first-course servings.

Bolognese Sauce

¼ cup butter
1 medium onion, minced
½ medium carrot, chopped
1 celery stalk, chopped
12 ounces lean ground beef
12 ounces ripe tomatoes, peeled, seeded, or 1¼ cups chopped drained canned plum tomatoes
1 garlic clove, minced, if desired

1 bay leaf
2 teaspoons chopped fresh thyme leaves or ¾ teaspoon dried leaf, crumbled
Freshly grated nutmeg to taste
Salt and freshly ground pepper
2 to 3 tablespoons beef stock or water, if desired

Melt butter in a heavy medium casserole over medium heat. Add onion, carrot and celery. Cook, stirring, about 10 minutes or until onion is soft but not brown. Add beef and sauté over medium heat, crumbling with a fork, until it changes color.

Puree tomatoes in a food processor and add to casserole. Add garlic, bay leaf, thyme, nutmeg, salt and pepper and bring to a boil, stirring. Cover and cook over low heat, stirring from time to time, 45 minutes to 1 hour or until well flavored. Add stock or water if pan becomes dry. Discard bay leaf. (Sauce can be kept, covered, up to 2 days in refrigerator; or it can be frozen.)

Pasta with Bolognese Sauce & Sautéed Squash

Halve pattypan squashes into 2 semicircles. Put cut side down and cut in ¹/₄-inch-thick slices.

Fettuccine with Old-Fashioned Italian Meat Sauce

Traditional Meat Sauce, see below
8 ounces dried fettuccine, tagliatelle or ziti

3 tablespoons chopped fresh parsley leaves, preferably Italian parsley

Prepare Traditional Meat Sauce; keep warm. If using long ziti, break in 3-inch pieces. Bring a large pot of water to a boil; add salt then pasta. Cook uncovered over high heat, stirring occasionally, 4 to 5 minutes for fettuccine or tagliatelle or 9 minutes for ziti or until tender but firm to the bite. Meanwhile, cut meat from sauce in thin slices for serving alongside pasta.

Drain pasta well. Transfer to a large heated bowl. Toss pasta with 1 cup sauce and 2 tablespoons parsley. Sprinkle with remaining parsley. Serve remaining sauce separately for spooning over meat.
Makes 4 main-course servings.

Traditional Meat Sauce

4 tablespoons olive oil
1 large onion, diced
1 celery stalk, diced
1 small carrot, diced
1 (2-lb.) piece boneless beef chuck roast, patted dry, excess fat trimmed
2 medium garlic cloves, chopped
¹/₂ cup dry red wine
1 clove
4 large fresh thyme sprigs or 1 teaspoon dried leaf, crumbled
1 bay leaf

2 fresh marjoram sprigs or ¹/₂ teaspoon dried leaf, crumbled
8 ounces ripe tomatoes, diced or 1 (14-oz.) can whole plum tomatoes, drained, diced
About 1¹/₄ cups unsalted beef stock or broth, homemade, page 188, or packaged; or about 1 cup salted stock mixed with ¹/₄ cup water
¹/₂ ounce dried porcini mushrooms

This is bistro/trattoria-style cooking at its best. It is not for hurried days but rather for those times when you enjoy gently simmering a sauce to obtain the fabulous marriage of flavors that comes only from long cooking. The deep-brown sauce is essentially the braising juices of a piece of beef that is slowly cooked with red wine, porcini mushrooms, tomatoes and herbs. In traditional Italian cooking, the pasta tossed with the beef juices is an appetizer, while the beef is served as a main course, but you can certainly slice the beef and serve it American-style alongside the pasta. When prepared by the classic technique, in which the sauce is pureed in a food mill, it has a slightly richer taste and deeper color but I have also included an easier food-processor version of the sauce, which is slightly thicker.

Choose a heavy casserole or deep sauté pan that holds meat snugly. Heat 3 tablespoons oil in casserole over medium heat. Add onion, celery and carrot. Cook about 10 minutes or until onion is soft but not brown. Transfer vegetables with a slotted spoon to a bowl. Add remaining 1 tablespoon oil to casserole. Add meat and brown on all sides, taking about 10 minutes.

Return vegetables to casserole. Add garlic and wine. Tie clove, thyme, bay leaf and marjoram in a piece of cheesecloth; add to casserole. Bring to a boil and cook uncovered over medium heat, turning meat from time to time, until wine evaporates. Add tomatoes and enough beef stock, or stock mixed with water, to cover meat by about half. Bring to a simmer. Cover and cook over low heat, turning meat from time to time, 1¼ hours or until meat is very tender.

Soak mushrooms in enough hot water to cover 30 minutes. Remove mushrooms; rinse and coarsely chop. When meat is tender, remove from casserole. If serving meat with pasta, cover and keep warm.

Put sauce through a food mill. Transfer to a medium saucepan. Add mushrooms. Cover and cook 10 minutes. Taste; if sauce is not well flavored, cook uncovered about 5 minutes or until well flavored. If sauce is too thick, stir in 2 or 3 tablespoons more stock. (Sauce can be kept, covered, up to 2 days in refrigerator; or it can be frozen. If refrigerating or freezing meat, dice and mix with sauce.)

Notes: If a food mill is not available, puree sauce in a food processor. In this case, cook mushrooms separately in about ⅓ cup stock in a very small saucepan, covered, over low heat about 10 minutes or until tender; check and add more stock or water if pan gets dry. Stir mushroom mixture into pureed sauce. This method makes more sauce; toss 1½ cups sauce with pasta.

If porcini mushrooms are unavailable, use 4 ounces button mushrooms. Halve and slice; cook 10 minutes as in recipe, or in stock, as in note above.

Meat can be diced instead of sliced and mixed with the sauce and pasta.

Flavored with butter and a creamy dill sauce, this couscous becomes a bed for the sautéed veal scaloppini and their garnish of oval-shaped cucumber.

Veal with Couscous & Dill

1 long seedless European cucumber (about 10 oz.), peeled	**About ¼ cup all-purpose flour**
	2 tablespoons vegetable oil
1¼ pounds veal scaloppini, flattened to slightly over ⅛ inch thickness	**6 tablespoons butter**
	⅓ cup dry white wine
	1⅓ cups whipping cream
Salt and freshly ground pepper to taste	**1¼ cups water**
	1¼ cups couscous
	2 tablespoons snipped fresh dill

Quarter cucumber lengthwise and cut in 2-inch pieces. Trim each piece to an olive shape. Add cucumber pieces to a medium saucepan of enough boiling salted water to cover generously. Cook uncovered over high heat about 3 minutes or until crisp-tender. Drain well.

Sprinkle veal with salt and pepper on both sides. Dredge veal in flour, shaking off excess. Heat oil and 2 tablespoons butter in a large skillet over medium-high heat until hot. Add veal in batches and sauté 1½ minutes on first side and 1 minute on second, or until golden. Transfer veal with tongs to a platter and keep warm in a 300F (150C) oven.

Discard fat from skillet. Reheat skillet over low heat a few seconds. Add wine and boil over medium-high heat, scraping up brown bits clinging to bottom and sides. Stir in cream and cook sauce, stirring, until thick enough to coat a spoon. Add cucumbers and reheat briefly over low heat. Keep mixture warm, uncovered, over very low heat.

Cut 2 tablespoons butter in small pieces and reserve at room temperature. Cut remaining 2 tablespoons butter in small pieces. Put in a medium saucepan and add water to saucepan; bring to a boil. Stir in couscous and a pinch of salt and pepper; cover pan immediately and let couscous stand, off heat, 5 minutes.

Stir dill into sauce. Taste and adjust seasoning. Scatter reserved butter pieces over couscous. Cover and let couscous stand 1 minute. Drizzle 3 tablespoons dill sauce over couscous. Fluff couscous with a fork to break up any lumps, tossing until butter and sauce are blended in. Taste couscous and adjust seasoning.

To serve, divide couscous and veal among 4 heated plates and coat veal with some of sauce and cucumbers. Serve remaining sauce separately.
Makes 4 main-course servings.

Note: Flattened skinless boneless chicken breasts can be substituted for veal.

Vermicelli with Veal & Lemon Sauce

Here the popular combination of veal scaloppini and lemon is used to make a luscious pasta dish with a creamy lemon sauce. If fine veal is not available, enjoy this delicious sauce with thin, boneless chicken breasts.

Lemon Sauce, see below
3 tablespoons butter
¾ to 1 pound veal scaloppini, about ⅛ inch thick, patted dry
Salt and freshly ground pepper to taste
1 medium carrot, cut in julienne strips (about 1½" x ⅛" x ⅛")
1 medium leek, white and light-green parts only, cut in julienne strips
1 medium zucchini, cut in julienne strips
8 ounces vermicelli
¼ cup whipping cream
1 tablespoon strained fresh lemon juice
1 tablespoon chopped fresh parsley leaves
Bowl of freshly grated Parmesan cheese (for serving)

Prepare Lemon Sauce; set aside. Melt 2 tablespoons butter in a large skillet over medium-high heat. Add veal, salt and pepper. Sauté about 1 minute on each side, or until color has changed on both sides. Remove veal. Cut in thin strips, about size of vegetable strips.

Add 1 tablespoon butter to skillet and melt over low heat. Add carrot and leek strips. Cook about 10 minutes or until carrots are tender. Add zucchini and cook 1 minute. Remove from heat. Stir in veal and any liquid that escaped from it.

Bring a large pot of water to a boil; add salt, then vermicelli. Cook uncovered over high heat, separating strands occasionally with a fork, 6 to 7 minutes or until tender but firm to the bite. Meanwhile, reheat sauce.

Drain pasta well. Transfer to a large heated bowl. Reheat veal and vegetable mixture. Add ¼ cup cream and bring to a simmer. Add to pasta and toss.

Remove sauce from heat and stir in lemon juice. Add to pasta and toss. Taste and adjust seasoning. Sprinkle with parsley. Serve with Parmesan cheese.
Makes 3 or 4 main-course servings.

Lemon Sauce

2 tablespoons butter
1 medium garlic clove, minced
1 tablespoon finely grated lemon zest
1 cup whipping cream
¾ teaspoon chopped fresh thyme leaves or ¼ teaspoon dried leaf, crumbled
Salt and freshly ground pepper to taste

Melt butter in a small saucepan over low heat. Add garlic and lemon zest. Cook, stirring, 1 minute. Add cream and bring to a simmer over high heat. Cook over medium heat, stirring, about 5 minutes or until thick enough to lightly coat a spoon. Add thyme and a pinch of salt and pepper.

Ligurian Veal with Zucchini & Fusilli

In a classic recipe from Liguria on the Italian Riviera, a delicate veal and vegetable stew is flavored with ripe tomatoes which are added toward the end of the cooking time and contribute a fresh taste. In our version the stew is tossed with corkscrew-shaped fusilli.

1½ pounds boneless veal shoulder or veal stew meat, cut in 1" x 1" x ½" pieces
½ cup olive oil
2 medium onions, chopped
1 medium carrot, finely diced
3 celery stalks, finely diced
6 large garlic cloves, minced
⅓ cup dry white wine
½ cup veal stock or chicken stock, homemade, page 187 or 188, or packaged
Salt and freshly ground pepper to taste

1½ pounds ripe tomatoes, peeled, seeded, finely chopped
1 pound small zucchini, cut in ¼-inch slices crosswise
2 tablespoons chopped fresh basil leaves or 2 teaspoons dried leaf, crumbled
12 ounces fusilli or other spiral-shaped pasta
1 tablespoon chopped fresh basil or parsley leaves for garnish
Basil sprig, if desired
Bowl of freshly grated Parmesan cheese (for serving)

Pat veal dry. Heat ¼ cup oil in a heavy wide casserole over medium-high heat. Add about ⅓ of veal and lightly brown. Transfer with a slotted spoon to a plate. Repeat with remaining veal in 2 batches. Pour browning oil into a small bowl and reserve.

Heat remaining ¼ cup oil in casserole over low heat. Add onions, carrot and celery. Cook, stirring, about 10 minutes or until onions are soft but not brown. Add 1 tablespoon garlic and cook 1 minute, stirring.

Return veal to casserole with any juices that have accumulated on plate; add reserved oil. Bring to a simmer. Add wine and bring to a boil. Simmer uncovered over medium heat, stirring often, about 7 minutes or until most of liquid has evaporated. Add stock, salt and pepper to taste. Bring to a boil. Cover and simmer over low heat about 50 minutes or until veal is nearly tender. While veal is simmering, put chopped tomatoes in a strainer to drain off excess liquid.

When veal is nearly tender, sprinkle tomatoes over ingredients in casserole and stir gently. Cover and cook over low heat about 15 minutes or until veal is tender when pierced with a knife. Transfer meat to a plate with a slotted spoon.

Add zucchini and remaining garlic to casserole. Boil uncovered over high heat, stirring, 2 minutes or until zucchini are barely tender; they will continue to cook when mixture is reheated. Return meat and any juices on plate to casserole. (Stew can be kept covered, 1 day in refrigerator. Reheat in casserole, covered, over low heat.) Add basil; taste and adjust seasoning.

Bring a large pot of water to a boil; add salt, then pasta. Cook uncovered over high heat, stirring occasionally, about 7 minutes or until tender but firm to the bite. Drain well. Add pasta to casserole and toss lightly with veal mixture.

Serve from casserole or from a heated serving dish. Sprinkle with more basil or parsley for garnish. Add a basil sprig, if desired. Serve with Parmesan cheese. Makes 4 to 6 main-course servings.

This aromatic veal-and-vegetable sauce is prepared in the manner of the Moroccan type of stew called a tajine. In Morocco it is often served with couscous but it is also delicious when tossed with mafalda, or ruffled pasta, or other wide pasta shapes.

Ruffled Pasta with Veal, Saffron & Ginger

2 tablespoons vegetable oil
3 tablespoons butter
1 medium onion, finely chopped
1½ pounds boneless veal stew meat, excess fat trimmed, cut in ¾-inch pieces, patted dry
8 medium garlic cloves, minced
2 tablespoons minced peeled gingerroot
Salt and freshly ground pepper to taste
6 tablespoons minced cilantro (fresh coriander) leaves
2 pounds ripe tomatoes, peeled, seeded, chopped, or 2 (28-oz.) cans whole plum tomatoes, drained, chopped

⅔ cup brown veal or chicken stock, homemade, page 187 or 188, or packaged
¼ teaspoon saffron threads, crushed
8 ounces green beans, ends removed, broken in 3 pieces
1 small cauliflower, divided in small flowerets
2 tablespoons tomato paste
1 cup pitted black olives, drained
12 ounces ruffled flat pasta (mafalda) or mezza lasagna
2 tablespoons minced fresh parsley leaves

Heat 2 tablespoons oil and 1 tablespoon butter in a large heavy casserole over medium heat. Add onion and cook over low heat, stirring, about 7 minutes or until softened. Add veal, garlic, gingerroot, salt, pepper and 3 tablespoons cilantro. Cook over low heat, stirring, 5 minutes to coat veal with seasonings. Stir in tomatoes and bring to a boil. Add ⅓ cup stock and saffron; bring to a boil, stirring. Cover and cook over low heat, stirring occasionally, about 50 minutes or until veal is tender when pierced with a knife.

Add green beans to a large saucepan of enough boiling salted water to cover generously. Cook uncovered over high heat 2 minutes. Add cauliflower and boil 2 minutes; vegetables should not yet be tender. Drain vegetables, rinse with cold water and drain well.

When veal is tender, remove with a slotted spoon to a large plate. Add cauliflower and green beans to casserole. Cover and cook over high heat, stirring occasionally, about 5 minutes or until vegetables are just tender. Add tomato paste and remaining ⅓ cup stock; bring to a simmer. Return veal to casserole and add olives. Heat over low heat 1 to 2 minutes. (Veal stew can be kept, covered, 1 day in refrigerator. Reheat it, covered, over low heat.)

Bring a large pot of water to a boil; add salt, then pasta. Cook uncovered over high heat, separating strands occasionally with a large fork or tongs, about 11 minutes or until tender but firm to the bite. Drain well. Transfer to a large heated bowl. Toss with remaining 2 tablespoons butter.

Remove sauce from heat and stir in remaining 3 tablespoons cilantro. Taste and adjust seasoning. Toss pasta gently with about ⅔ of stew. Taste again and adjust seasoning. Sprinkle with parsley. Spoon more of stew over each serving. Serve rest of stew separately.
Makes 4 main-course servings.

Note: Pappardelle or very wide noodles can be substituted for the pasta.

Green & White Fettuccine with Veal, Spinach & Morel Sauce

1 ounce dried morels (about ¾ cup)
1 pound spinach, stems removed, leaves torn in bite-size pieces, rinsed well
5 tablespoons butter, room temperature
2 medium shallots, minced
⅓ cup dry white wine
1 cup chicken stock, homemade, page 187, or packaged
Salt and freshly ground pepper to taste

1¼ cups whipping cream
12 ounces veal scaloppini, about ⅛ inch thick, patted dry
¼ cup Madeira
5 ounces fresh spinach fettuccine or noodles, homemade, page 180, or packaged, or 4 ounces dried
5 ounces fresh egg fettuccine or noodles, homemade, page 178, or packaged, or 4 ounces dried

Morel mushrooms and Madeira give a fabulous flavor to the rich creamy French sauce. Other dried mushrooms, such as porcini, can be substituted, but morels have a unique character and a distinctive shape and, although expensive, are worth looking for. They can be found in gourmet or specialty shops and some fine supermarkets. Lightly cooked spinach leaves add color and freshness while complementing the spinach noodles.

Soak morels in hot water to cover 30 minutes or until soft. Remove morels, reserving liquid. Rinse and drain well. Halve any large morels.

Cook spinach leaves in a large pan of boiling salted water just until wilted, about 1 minute. Drain, rinse with cold water and drain well. Gently squeeze out excess water.

Melt 1 tablespoon butter in a medium saucepan over low heat. Add shallots and cook about 2 minutes or until softened. Add white wine and bring to a boil, stirring. Add stock, morels, salt and pepper. If morel soaking liquid is not sandy, add 3 tablespoons to morel mixture. Bring to a boil and simmer over medium heat about 10 minutes or until liquid is reduced to about ¾ cup. Stir in cream and bring to a boil. Simmer sauce, stirring occasionally, over medium heat about 7 minutes or until thick enough to lightly coat a spoon. Taste and adjust seasoning. (Sauce can be kept, covered, 1 day in refrigerator.)

Melt 2 tablespoons butter in a large skillet over medium-high heat. Add veal, salt and pepper. Sauté about 1 minute on each side or until veal changes color on outer surface; inside will still be pink but veal will finish cooking later. Transfer to a plate. Add Madeira to skillet and bring to a simmer, stirring in any brown bits. Pour Madeira into morel sauce.

Cut veal in strips about ¼ inch wide and 2 to 3 inches long. Add veal and juices from plate to sauce. Simmer 2 to 3 minutes or until veal is just tender and sauce lightly coats a spoon. Stir in spinach.

Bring 2 pots or large saucepans of water to a boil and add salt. Add spinach pasta to one and egg pasta to the other and cook uncovered over high heat, separating strands occasionally with a fork, 30 seconds to 2 minutes for fresh or 2 to 5 minutes for dried or until tender but firm to the bite. While pasta is cooking, reheat sauce uncovered over medium heat, stirring.

Drain pasta well. Transfer both to a large heated bowl. Toss with remaining 2 tablespoons butter. To serve, toss pasta with sauce and transfer to a heated platter or plates.

Makes 3 or 4 main-course servings.

Notes: If pasta is fresh and both types were made on the same day, they can be cooked together.

If in doubt about whether both types of pasta will cook in the same time, but you prefer to use 1 pot, cook the first batch of pasta slightly less than usual and rinse with cold water; then cook the second batch and just before draining, return first batch to the pot for a second so it becomes reheated from boiling water, then drain together.

Sometimes you can buy a package of mixed green and white noodles; they might be labeled "paglia e fieno" or "straw and hay," the Italian name for a dish made with both colors of noodles.

Dijonnaise refers to the sauce made with Dijon mustard. It is a classic partner for meat and is also great with pasta. Here the pasta is served in the French style: veal scaloppini are placed on a bed of noodles and both are coated with sauce.

Veal Dijonnaise with Green Peppercorns & Tri-Colored Noodles

6 to 8 tablespoons butter
2 shallots, minced
1/2 cup dry white wine
1 cup whipping cream
1 1/4 pounds veal scaloppini, patted dry
Salt and freshly ground pepper to taste
1 tablespoon vegetable oil

1 pound fresh tri-colored or spinach noodles or fettuccine, homemade, pages 180 and 181, or packaged, or 12 ounces dried
2 tablespoons Dijon mustard or mustard with green peppercorns
2 teaspoons green peppercorns, rinsed, drained

Melt 1 tablespoon butter in a heavy medium saucepan over low heat. Add shallots and cook, stirring, about 2 minutes or until softened. Add 1/4 cup wine and simmer, stirring often, until reduced to about 2 tablespoons. Stir in cream and cook over medium heat, stirring often, about 7 minutes or until sauce is thick enough to coat a spoon.

Sprinkle veal with salt and pepper. Heat oil and 3 tablespoons butter in a heavy large skillet over medium-high heat. Add veal and sauté about 2 minutes per side or until no longer pink. Transfer to a platter. Cover and keep warm.

Discard fat from skillet. Add remaining 1/4 cup wine and boil, stirring and scraping up brown pieces, until reduced to about 2 tablespoons. Pour into sauce. Reserve skillet.

Bring a large pot of water to a boil; add salt, then pasta. Cook uncovered over high heat, separating strands occasionally with a fork, 30 seconds to 2 minutes for fresh or 2 to 5 minutes for dried or until tender but firm to the bite. Drain well. Transfer to skillet. Add remaining 2 to 4 tablespoons butter and season lightly with salt and pepper. Reheat if necessary over low heat.

Reheat sauce over low heat and whisk in mustard. Taste and adjust seasoning. Add 2 or 3 tablespoons sauce to pasta and toss.

Transfer pasta to a heated platter or plates and set veal on top. Coat veal with remaining mustard sauce and sprinkle with green peppercorns. Serve immediately.

Makes 4 or 5 main-course servings.

Ground lamb makes a fine and flavorful meat sauce for linguine, spaghetti or other pasta. The enticing topping of toasted nuts makes the dish look festive.

Linguine with Lamb, Pine Nuts & Pistachios

1/2 cup shelled raw or roasted pistachios (about 2 oz.)
3 tablespoons butter
1/3 cup pine nuts (about 1 1/2 oz.)
Salt and freshly ground pepper to taste
1 medium onion, minced
3/4 pound ground lean lamb
3 medium garlic cloves, minced
1/8 teaspoon ground allspice
Pinch of ground cinnamon

1 pound ripe tomatoes, peeled, seeded, chopped, or 1 (28-oz.) can whole plum tomatoes, drained, chopped
3 tablespoons tomato paste
1/4 cup chopped fresh mint or cilantro (fresh coriander) leaves
12 ounces to 1 pound dried linguine

If using raw pistachios, rub off skin if desired, so color will be bright green; not all of skin will come off. Melt 1 tablespoon butter in a medium skillet over medium heat. Add pine nuts, raw pistachios (but not roasted ones) and a pinch of salt. Sauté until pine nuts are lightly browned, about 3 minutes. Transfer to a plate and set aside.

Melt remaining 2 tablespoons butter in medium skillet over medium-low heat. Add onion and cook, stirring, about 7 minutes or until softened. Add lamb, garlic, allspice and cinnamon. Cook over medium heat, stirring often, about 10 minutes or until meat changes color. Add tomatoes, salt and pepper. Cover and cook 10 minutes. Add tomato paste and stir until blended. Cook 10 minutes or until sauce is thick. (Sauce can be kept, covered, 2 days in refrigerator. Reheat before continuing.) Add mint or cilantro. Taste and adjust seasoning.

Bring a large pot of water to a boil; add salt, then pasta. Cook uncovered over high heat, separating strands occasionally with a fork, about 8 minutes or until tender but firm to the bite. Meanwhile, reheat sauce over medium heat, stirring.

Drain pasta well. Transfer to a heated serving bowl. Add about ½ of sauce and toss. Taste and adjust seasoning. Spoon remaining sauce across top center of pasta. Sprinkle pine nuts and pistachios over sauce or serve separately.
Makes 4 main-course servings.

Note: Nut mixture can be replaced by ⅔ cup pine nuts or slivered almonds.

Rigatoni with Lamb & Peas

2 tablespoons olive oil
1 pound boneless lamb shoulder, trimmed of excess fat, cut in ¾-inch pieces, patted dry
4 large garlic cloves, chopped
1 tablespoon minced fresh rosemary leaves, or 1 teaspoon dried leaf, crumbled
1½ pounds ripe tomatoes, peeled, seeded, chopped, or 1 (28-oz.) and 1 (14-oz.) can whole plum tomatoes, drained

Salt and freshly ground pepper to taste
⅓ cup water
2 pounds fresh peas, shelled, or 2 cups frozen peas
1 pound rigatoni

Rigatoni is best with robust sauces like this fragrant Mediterranean stew in which cubes of lamb and tomatoes cook together slowly with rosemary and garlic. Penne, or diagonal-cut macaroni, can be substituted for the rigatoni.

In a wide heavy stainless steel or enameled casserole, heat oil over medium-high heat. Add lamb in batches and brown on all sides. Transfer with a slotted spoon to a plate.

Pour out all but about 1 tablespoon oil. Add garlic and rosemary to casserole. Cook over medium-low heat, stirring, 30 seconds. Stir in tomatoes. Return lamb to casserole with any juices that have accumulated on plate. Add salt, pepper and water. Bring to a boil, stirring. Cover and simmer over low heat, stirring occasionally (and crushing canned tomatoes, if using), about 1 hour or until meat is very tender when pierced with a sharp knife. (Stew can be kept, covered, 2 days in refrigerator. Reheat, covered, over low heat.)

Add peas to casserole. Cover and simmer 3 to 5 minutes or until peas are tender. Taste and adjust seasoning.

Bring a large pot of water to a boil; add salt, then pasta. Cook uncovered over high heat, stirring occasionally, about 10 minutes or until tender but firm to the bite. Drain well.

Reheat stew if necessary. Spoon about 1 cup stew into a bowl for serving separately. Add drained pasta to casserole and toss with stew. Taste and adjust seasoning. Serve, accompanied by bowl of stew.
Makes 4 main-course servings.

Perfect for brunch, this colorful dish is light, flavorful and very easy to prepare. It is also good with Cajun, chili or cilantro pasta.

◆   *Photo on page 100.*

Pasta Corkscrews with Bacon, Avocado & Tomato

6 bacon slices (about 4 oz. total)
1 small ripe avocado
8 ounces corkscrew-shaped or spiral pasta, such as fusilli or rotelle (about 3¹/₃ cups)
2 or 3 tablespoons olive oil, preferably extra virgin, or butter at room temperature
²/₃ cup finely grated provolone cheese, preferably imported (about 2 oz.)
2 tablespoons chopped fresh basil leaves or 2 teaspoons dried leaf, crumbled
1 large ripe tomato, halved, seeded, cut in small dice
Freshly ground pepper to taste
Bowl of grated provolone cheese (for serving)

Put bacon in a dry medium skillet and fry over medium heat, turning often, until crisp. Drain on paper towels. Crumble bacon. Halve, pit and peel avocado. Cut ¹/₂ of avocado in small dice. Slice other ¹/₂ in thin slices and divide among 4 plates.

Bring a large pot of water to a boil; add salt, then pasta. Cook uncovered over high heat, stirring occasionally, about 7 minutes or until tender but firm to the bite. Drain well. Transfer to a heated bowl. Toss with olive oil or butter.

Set aside about 2 tablespoons grated cheese. Add basil, remaining cheese, tomato, diced avocado and crumbled bacon to pasta; toss. Season with freshly ground pepper. Transfer to a serving dish and sprinkle with reserved cheese. Spoon next to avocado slices on plates and serve with more cheese.
Makes 4 servings as a light main course.

This simple, colorful recipe is one of my favorites for a quick meal. You can replace the mortadella by other sliced meats, such as salami, ham or smoked turkey. Dill and a large proportion of vegetables give it a refreshing taste and look.

◆   *Photo on page 100.*

Pasta Shells with Mortadella, Dill Butter & Vegetables

Dill Butter, opposite
8 thin slices mortadella (about 6 oz. total)
2 medium-size yellow zucchini or crookneck squash
2 pounds fresh peas, shelled, or 2 cups frozen peas
Salt and freshly ground pepper to taste
2 tablespoons vegetable oil
1 pound medium pasta shells
2 medium carrots, peeled, coarsely grated
2 tablespoons snipped fresh dill
Dill sprig, if desired
Bowl of freshly grated Parmesan cheese (for serving), if desired

Prepare Dill Butter; put ¹/₂ cup in a large bowl and let stand at room temperature. Set aside remaining ¹/₄ cup flavored butter. Cut mortadella slices in half, then in ¹/₂-inch-wide strips. Halve squash lengthwise, except for thin part of crookneck squash; cut squash in ¹/₈-inch-thick slices.

Add peas to a medium saucepan of enough boiling salted water to cover generously. Cook uncovered over high heat about 3 minutes for fresh or about 1 minute for frozen or until barely tender. Drain, rinse with cold water and drain thoroughly.

Heat oil in a large skillet over medium heat. Add enough squash to make 1 layer; sprinkle with salt and pepper. Sauté, turning once or twice, about 3 minutes or until crisp-tender. Transfer to a plate. Cover and keep warm. Repeat with remaining squash. Reserve skillet.

Meanwhile, bring a large pot of water to a boil; add salt, then pasta. Cook uncovered over high heat, stirring occasionally, 5 to 8 minutes or until tender but firm to the bite. Drain well. Transfer to bowl of Dill Butter and toss.

Add remaining Dill Butter and carrots to skillet from cooking squash. Sauté over medium heat 2 minutes. Add peas and heat over low heat, stirring occasionally, about 2 minutes or until heated through. Stir in mortadella strips and heat a few seconds until hot.

Add sautéed squash, mortadella mixture and 1 tablespoon dill to pasta and toss. Taste and adjust seasoning. Sprinkle with remaining dill. Garnish with dill sprig, if desired. Serve with Parmesan cheese, if desired.

Makes 4 or 5 main-course servings.

Dill Butter

¾ cup (6 oz.) butter, softened
6 tablespoons snipped fresh dill

Salt and freshly ground pepper to taste

Beat butter in a medium bowl until smooth. Add dill, salt and pepper. Beat until well blended. (Flavored butter can be kept, covered, 2 days in refrigerator. Bring to room temperature before using.)

Lazy-Day Pasta with Smoked Sausage, Tomato Sauce & Corn

Easy Tomato Sauce, see below
8 ounces smoked sausage, such as Polish Kielbasa
1 pound cavatelli or other small pasta shells or spiral macaroni
3 cups frozen corn kernels
¼ cup olive oil, preferably extra virgin

1 cup thin strips of roasted red bell pepper from a jar, patted dry
Chopped fresh thyme leaves, if desired
Bowl of grated Parmesan or romano cheese (for serving)

For a quick and delicious lunch or supper made with ingredients likely to be in the kitchen, try this hearty dish of pasta shells tossed with slices of sausage, a quick tomato sauce and roasted peppers from a jar.

◆ *Photo on page 100.*

Prepare Easy Tomato Sauce; set aside. Bring to a simmer in a medium saucepan enough water to cover sausage. Add sausage and simmer 10 minutes. Remove from pan; discard skin. Cut sausage in ¼-inch slices and halve each slice, if desired. Reheat tomato sauce over low heat. Add sausage and keep warm over low heat.

Bring a large pot of water to a boil; add salt, then pasta. Cook uncovered over high heat, stirring occasionally, about 5 minutes or until nearly tender. Add corn and cook about 2 minutes or until pasta is tender but still firm to the bite. Drain pasta and corn together.

Transfer to a heated serving bowl. Add olive oil and peppers; toss. Add sausage slices and sauce; toss. (Sauce can also be served on top of pasta mixture on individual plates.) Taste and adjust seasoning. Garnish with chopped thyme, if desired. Serve with cheese.

Makes 4 main-course servings.

Easy Tomato Sauce

3 tablespoons olive oil
1 (28-oz.) can whole plum tomatoes, drained
4 teaspoons dried leaf thyme, crumbled

Salt and freshly ground pepper to taste

Heat oil in a large skillet. Add tomatoes, thyme, salt and pepper. Cook over medium-high heat, crushing tomatoes and stirring often, until thick, about 15 minutes.

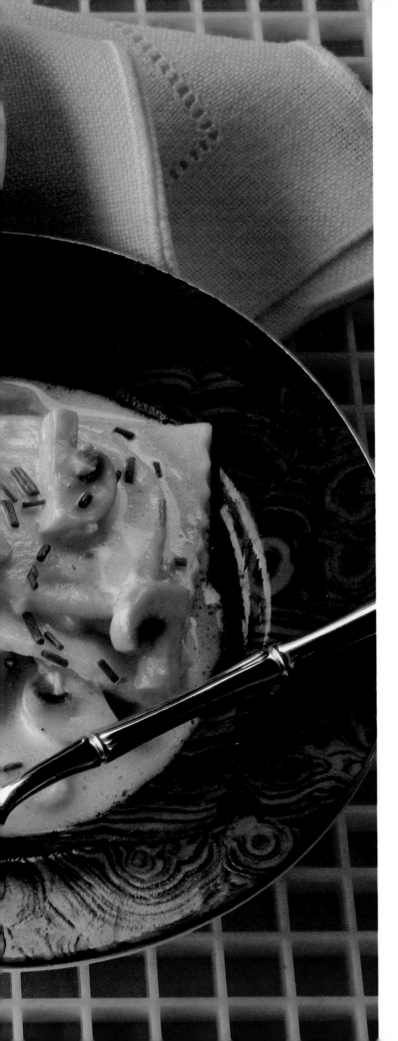

STUFFED & BAKED PASTA

From delicate tortellini in a creamy sauce to hearty many-layered lasagne, stuffed and baked pastas include the most elaborate and elegant of pasta creations. Eating the pasta together with a filling and a sauce gives a special taste sensation and makes stuffed and layered pastas favorites among pasta dishes.

STUFFED PASTA

In the past few years, ravioli and other stuffed pastas have obtained a place of honor on the best of tables. Luxurious ingredients, such as shellfish, duck and even truffles and foie gras sometimes replace traditional fillings.

Ravioli, the simplest type of stuffed pasta to make, are formed by lining up mounds of filling in rows on a sheet of pasta dough, covering the filling with a second sheet and cutting between the mounds to make squares; there is no need to fold or hand-shape each one individually.

Agnolotti are formed by cutting the dough in circles and folding it in half over the filling to make half-moon shapes.

Clockwise from the top: Agnolotti with Sun-Dried-Tomato Sauce, page 128; Ravioli with Mushroom Sauce & Chives, page 127; Tortelloni with Herb Butter, page 124

119

Cappelletti, tortellini and tortelloni begin as squares or circles. After they are folded in half, their ends are joined to give them distinctive shapes that resemble small hats or rings.

Canneloni are made of large squares of dough that are rolled like cigars around the filling and then baked. They can also be made from packaged canneloni tubes or from diagonal-cut *manicotti* tubes. Jumbo pasta shells can also be stuffed, as in the delicious Turkey Salad with Pistou Dressing in Jumbo Shells, page 20.

The only piece of special equipment needed to make stuffed pasta easily is a pasta machine, although a ravioli cutter or fluted pastry wheel is useful if you want to give stuffed pasta an attractive edge.

The dough for making stuffed pasta is the same basic dough used to make noodles. Flavored doughs are also good and can add intriguing flavor interest, as in Chili Tortelloni with Cheese Filling.

Fillings for stuffed pastas can be delicate or zesty and are easy to prepare. Even with the increasing availability of good-quality fresh stuffed pasta at the markets, homemade ravioli and other stuffed pastas are more exciting and creative because the fillings can be flavored with non-traditional ingredients such as jalapeño chiles, Roquefort cheese or whatever you like.

Most filling ingredients are cooked before being put in the dough because the cooking time of the pasta dough is very brief. Only a few mixtures, such as Lemony Scallop Filling, cook so quickly that there is no need to precook them.

In Italy, custom dictates that stuffed pasta be served as a first course, yet it can make a wonderful main course for a light meal. Stuffed pasta is good as an addition to chicken soup or even as a side dish. For example, in southern France ravioli often accompany flavorful meat stews and the meat juices act as a sauce.

To show homemade stuffed pastas to their best advantage, serve them with a light sauce, or with melted butter and a sprinkling of grated Parmesan cheese. A fresh tomato sauce is delicious with meat or cheese ravioli, but my personal preferences with seafood or mushroom ravioli are butter sauces like Basil Butter Sauce, page 126, or cream-based sauces such as Mushroom Sauce, page 127, or Sun-Dried-Tomato Cream Sauce, page 128.

BAKED PASTA

From layered lasagne to old-fashioned macaroni and cheese, baked pasta dishes have long been popular in America, both for parties and for casual family suppers. Most, like Macaroni Moussaka and Lasagne with Rich Meat Sauce & Fontina Cheese, are hearty and constitute a whole meal-in-one-dish. Others, like Noodle Kugel with Sautéed Mushrooms, are satisfying side dishes. Elegant Layered Spinach, Pasta & Parmesan Soufflé is fun to prepare and serve, with its golden soufflé topping on a bed of spinach and pasta shells, and can be either a first course or main dish.

Basic Ravioli

Choice of Fillings, page 122
Basic Egg Pasta dough, page 178
Tomato sauce or other favorite
sauce, chicken soup, Herb
Butter, page 124, or ½ cup
(4 oz.) butter

Salt and freshly ground pepper
Bowl of freshly grated Parmesan
cheese, preferably imported, if
desired

Ravioli is the easiest of stuffed pasta to make and is wonderful served with sauces or flavored butters, or simply with melted butter and grated cheese, or in homemade chicken soup.

Prepare Filling; set aside. Make pasta dough. Generously flour 2 or 3 trays or baking sheets and a large surface on which you can cut dough. Turn smooth rollers of pasta machine to widest setting. Cut dough in 4 pieces; leave 3 pieces wrapped. Flatten 1 piece of dough into approximately a 4-inch square and lightly flour. Run through rollers of machine. Fold from each end so ends just meet in center, press seams together and flatten again slightly. Run dough through rollers again. Repeat folding and rolling, lightly flouring only when necessary to prevent it from sticking, until smooth and velvety, about 7 more times. If dough is less than 3½ inches wide, fold and roll 1 or 2 more times so it will be wider. (This helps ensure final sheet of dough will be wide enough to make 2 rows of ravioli.) Turn dial of pasta machine 1 notch to adjust to next narrower setting. Without folding piece of dough, run it through machine. Repeat on each narrower setting, dusting with flour as necessary, until dough is ¹⁄₁₆ inch thick (generally this is on next to narrowest setting of machine).

Loosely cover mounds of filling with second dough sheet. Press down around filling to seal dough on 3 sides and to force out air through open end of dough; press to seal fourth side.

Lay dough sheet on floured surface. Cut dough in half. Spoon filling onto 1 sheet of dough by teaspoonfuls about 1 inch in from edges and spacing centers of mounds about 2 inches apart. Cover loosely with second dough sheet. Seal between lengthwise rows of ravioli by pressing on dough. Press down around filling to seal dough on 3 sides and to force out air through open end of dough; last press to seal fourth side.

With a fluted pastry wheel, ravioli cutter-sealer or sharp heavy knife, cut dough in about 2-inch squares between and around mounds of filling. Set on floured tray in 1 layer. Check each ravioli to be sure edges are well sealed. Flour work surface again. Repeat with remaining dough and filling, making ravioli with 1 piece of dough at a time. (Ravioli can be kept, covered with a floured kitchen towel, up to 4 hours in refrigerator; after 1 hour, turn ravioli over carefully so they do not stick. Or they can be frozen on a floured baking sheet, put in a plastic bag when solid and kept up to 2 weeks. Do not thaw before cooking.)

With a fluted pastry wheel, ravioli cutter-sealer or sharp heavy knife, cut dough in about 2-inch squares between and around mounds of filling.

To serve, either prepare sauce, soup or flavored butter; or melt butter in a heavy small saucepan over low heat and season lightly with salt and pepper. Keep warm.

Butter a large baking sheet. Bring a large pot of water to a boil over high heat and add salt. Add ½ of ravioli and stir gently to prevent sticking. Return to a boil. Reduce heat to medium-high and simmer uncovered until pasta is just tender but firm to the bite, about 4 minutes (frozen ravioli usually require about 2 more minutes). Remove with a large slotted skimmer or slotted spoon. Drain gently but thoroughly. Transfer to buttered baking sheet. Cover and keep warm in a 200F (95C) oven while cooking remaining ravioli.

Drain again if necessary and transfer to heated plates or bowls. Serve with sauce, in soup or with flavored or plain melted butter. If desired, serve with Parmesan cheese.

Makes about 32 ravioli, 5 or 6 first-course or 3 main-course servings.

Fillings For Ravioli

All the fillings given here can be used to prepare agnolotti, tortellini, tortelloni and cappelletti as well as ravioli. They can also be used in ravioli made of flavored pasta dough, or in won-ton wrappers, as on page 124.

Mushroom Filling

Ravioli with this filling are great with Mushroom Sauce, page 127, or thyme butter, page 124.

8 ounces mushrooms
2 tablespoons butter
2 tablespoons minced shallots
2 teaspoons minced garlic
Salt and freshly ground pepper to
  taste

¹/₄ cup whipping cream
1¹/₂ teaspoons chopped fresh
  thyme leaves or ¹/₂ teaspoon
  dried leaf, crumbled
1 large egg yolk

Clean mushrooms; pat dry thoroughly. Cut in quarters. Chop very finely in a food processor using on/off motion.

Melt butter in a large skillet over low heat. Add shallots and cook, stirring, 1 minute. Add garlic and stir. Add mushrooms, salt and pepper. Cook, stirring often, over medium-high heat, until most of liquid that escapes from mushrooms has evaporated and mixture is very dry, about 4 minutes. Reduce heat to medium. Stir in cream and cook, stirring, until absorbed, about 2 minutes. Stir in thyme. Transfer mixture to a medium bowl and cool to room temperature. Beat in egg yolk. Taste and adjust seasoning. Cover and refrigerate 30 minutes before using. (Filling can be kept 1 day.)
Makes scant 1 cup.

Roquefort & Onion Filling

Ravioli made with this filling should have a simple accompaniment, such as plain melted butter or parsley butter, page 124.

2 tablespoons butter
1 medium onion, minced
¹/₂ cup Roquefort cheese (3 oz.),
  room temperature, finely
  mashed

6 tablespoons ricotta cheese
1 large egg yolk
1 tablespoon unseasoned dry
  bread crumbs
Freshly ground pepper to taste

Melt butter in a medium skillet over medium-low heat. Add onion and cook, stirring occasionally, about 10 minutes or until soft and dry but not brown. Transfer to a medium bowl. Cool about 5 minutes. Thoroughly mix in Roquefort. Add ricotta and egg yolk; beat well. Stir in bread crumbs. Season with pepper. Cover and refrigerate 30 minutes before using. (Filling can be kept 1 day.)
Makes scant 1 cup.

Lemony Scallop Filling

Oregano butter, page 124, is good with this light pasta filling.

6 ounces scallops, rinsed,
  thoroughly patted dry
1 tablespoon softened butter
1 large egg yolk
³/₄ teaspoon dried leaf oregano,
  crumbled
3 tablespoons whipping cream

1 teaspoon finely grated lemon
  zest
2 tablespoons unseasoned dry
  bread crumbs
¹/₄ teaspoon salt
Pinch of red (cayenne) pepper

Remove small white muscle at side of scallops. Puree scallops in a food processor until smooth. Add butter, egg yolk and oregano; process until blended. With blade turning, pour in cream. Transfer mixture to a medium bowl. Add lemon zest, bread crumbs, salt and red pepper. Taste and adjust seasoning. Cover and refrigerate 30 minutes before using. (Filling can be kept 4 hours.)
Makes scant 1 cup.

Chicken Filling with Chiles & Cilantro

2 tablespoons butter
1 or 2 jalapeño peppers, minced
5 ounces boneless skinless
    chicken breast, cut in about
    $^1/_2$-inch dice
1 ounce prosciutto (2 slices),
    diced

1 ounce mortadella (2 slices),
    diced
4 teaspoons chopped cilantro
    (fresh coriander) leaves
1 large egg yolk
Salt and freshly ground pepper, if
    desired

Melt butter in a medium skillet over medium heat. Stir in peppers and chicken. Cook, stirring, about 3 minutes or until chicken is barely tender; do not let peppers brown. Transfer mixture immediately to a medium bowl. Cool to room temperature.

Transfer cooled chicken mixture to a food processor. Add prosciutto and mortadella. Grind together until fairly fine and well blended. Transfer to a bowl. Stir in cilantro and egg yolk. Taste and adjust seasoning. Cover and refrigerate 30 minutes before using. (Filling can be kept 1 day.)
Makes scant 1 cup.

Ravioli made with this spicy stuffing are excellent with cilantro or parsley butter, page 124, or with Tomato-Cream Sauce, page 186.

Meat Filling with Rosemary & Sage

2 tablespoons butter
5 teaspoons olive oil
$^1/_2$ large onion, minced ($^2/_3$ cup)
2 medium garlic cloves, minced
2 teaspoons minced fresh
    rosemary leaves or $^1/_2$ teaspoon
    dried, crumbled
4 teaspoons minced fresh sage
    leaves or $1^1/_4$ teaspoons dried
    leaf, crumbled
$^1/_3$ cup ground veal (about 2 oz.)
$^1/_4$ cup ground pork shoulder
    (about $1^1/_2$ oz.)

$^1/_4$ cup ground beef sirloin
    (about $1^1/_2$ oz.)
Salt and freshly ground pepper to
    taste
3 tablespoons dry white wine
$^1/_4$ cup freshly grated Parmesan
    cheese, preferably imported
1 large egg yolk
3 tablespoons unseasoned dry
    bread crumbs

Heat butter and oil in a medium skillet over medium-low heat. Add onion and cook, stirring often, about 5 minutes or until softened. Add garlic, rosemary and sage. Increase heat to medium and add veal, pork, beef, salt and pepper. Cook, stirring to separate clumps of ground meat and to blend meat with onion mixture, until meat changes color, about 5 minutes. Add wine and bring to a boil. Reduce heat to medium-low and simmer until wine is absorbed, about 5 minutes.

Transfer mixture to a medium bowl. Cool to room temperature. Stir in Parmesan cheese, egg yolk and bread crumbs. Taste and adjust seasoning. Cover and refrigerate 30 minutes before using. (Filling can be kept 1 day.)
Makes about 1 cup.

Sage butter, page 124, is a good accompaniment for ravioli with this filling.

Ravioli are more economical to make than agnolotti, tortelloni or tortellini because some dough is wasted when making circles.

COOKING TIP

Herb Butter

Serve this with ravioli, tortelloni or other stuffed pastas. For a quick and easy dish, toss it with cooked packaged tortelloni as in the photo.

◆ Photo on page 118.

½ cup (4 oz.) butter
1 tablespoon minced fresh herbs (parsley, basil, chives, tarragon, oregano, sage or thyme) or 1½ teaspoons dried leaf oregano or thyme, crumbled

Salt and freshly ground pepper to taste

Melt butter in a heavy small saucepan over low heat. Stir in herbs. Season with salt and pepper. Serve warm.
Makes about ½ cup.

Easy Spinach-Filled Ravioli Made with Won-Ton Wrappers

Won-ton wrappers are available at many supermarkets, sometimes in the produce section. They make ravioli preparation simple and quick because there is no need to prepare pasta dough. These make large ravioli; if you prefer smaller stuffed pastas, make cappelletti as in the variation, opposite. When the pasta is cooked, the bright-green spinach filling shows through. A quickly made brown sage butter moistens the ravioli, but if you like, you can serve them instead with Fresh Tomato Sauce, page 186, Mushroom Sauce, page 127, or Sun-Dried-Tomato Cream Sauce, page 128.

Spinach Filling, opposite
About 38 won-ton wrappers, thawed if frozen
6 tablespoons butter, cut in pieces, room temperature

2 tablespoons chopped fresh sage leaves
Bowl of freshly grated Parmesan cheese (for serving)

Prepare Spinach Filling; set aside. Generously flour 2 or 3 trays or baking sheets. While shaping ravioli, cover remaining won-ton wrappers with plastic wrap or a dampened towel or keep package closed to prevent them from drying out. Put 1 won-ton wrapper on a work surface and mound 1 level tablespoon Spinach Filling in center. Moisten wrapper all around filling and all over edges with a little water. Place another wrapper over filling and pinch edges together, pressing out excess air and sealing well. Continue with remaining won-ton wrappers and filling. Transfer to floured tray. (Ravioli can be kept, covered loosely with plastic wrap, 1 day in refrigerator.)

Butter a large baking sheet. Bring a large pot of water to a boil; add salt, then ⅓ to ½ of ravioli. Reduce heat to medium-high so water simmers and cook, stirring occasionally, about 2 minutes or until tender but firm to the bite. Remove with a large slotted skimmer or slotted spoon. Drain gently but thoroughly. Transfer to buttered baking sheet. Cover and keep warm in a 200F (95C) oven while cooking remaining ravioli.

Heat butter in a small heavy saucepan over medium heat until butter browns lightly and has a nutty aroma. Pour into a small bowl. Stir in sage. Drain ravioli again if necessary and transfer to a heated shallow serving bowl. Immediately pour sage butter over pasta; toss gently. Serve with Parmesan cheese.
Makes about 19 large ravioli, 3 main-course or 5 or 6 first-course servings.

Easy Spinach-Filled Ravioli Made with Won-Ton Wrappers

Put 1 won-ton wrapper on a work surface and mound 1 level tablespoon of filling in center. Moisten wrapper all around filling and all over edges with a little water. Place another wrapper over filling and pinch edges together, pressing out excess air and sealing well.

Spinach Filling

1¹/₂ pounds spinach, stems removed, leaves rinsed well or 1 (10-oz.) package frozen leaf spinach
2 tablespoons butter
1 medium shallot, minced
Salt and freshly ground pepper to taste

¹/₂ cup ricotta cheese (4 oz.)
¹/₂ cup freshly grated Parmesan cheese (1¹/₂ oz.)
1 large egg yolk
Freshly grated nutmeg to taste

Add spinach to a large saucepan of enough boiling salted water to cover generously. Cook uncovered over high heat about 2 minutes or until wilted. Drain, rinse with cold water and drain well. Squeeze out as much liquid as possible. Chop spinach.

Melt butter in a medium skillet. Add shallot and cook over low heat about 2 minutes or until tender. Add spinach and a pinch of salt and pepper. Cook 2 minutes. Transfer to a medium bowl and cool. Stir in ricotta, Parmesan, egg yolk and nutmeg. Taste and adjust seasoning. (Filling can be kept, covered, 1 day in refrigerator.)

Makes 1¹/₂ cups.

VARIATION

Spinach-Filled Cappelletti: Put 1 won-ton wrapper on a work surface and mound 1¹/₂ teaspoons of filling in center. Moisten 2 adjoining edges with water. Fold in half to make a triangle, sticking other 2 edges to moistened ones. Stick 2 ends at base of triangle together by first moistening 1 end with a little water and sticking other end to it.

Makes 38 cappelletti.

This dish was inspired by a wonderful ravioli of langoustines I enjoyed at Jamin, considered by many to be the best restaurant in Paris. Here I am using shrimp, which is more available, and instead of the foie-gras-flavored sauce used at the restaurant, I paired the ravioli with a luscious butter sauce flecked with fresh basil. Cooks who are developing the modern Italian style of cuisine called nuova cucina also use these French butter sauces with stuffed pastas. At a fine seafood restaurant in Rome, for example, I recently enjoyed scallop-stuffed ravioli with a fresh-sage butter sauce.

Shrimp & Swiss-Chard Ravioli with Basil Butter Sauce

Shrimp & Chard Filling, opposite
12 ounces Basic Egg Pasta dough, page 178
1 cup Fresh Tomato Sauce, page 186, if desired

BASIL BUTTER SAUCE
3 tablespoons minced shallots
3 tablespoons dry white wine
3 tablespoons water
1/4 cup whipping cream
Salt and freshly ground white pepper to taste

1 cup plus 2 tablespoons (9 oz.) cold unsalted butter, cut in 20 pieces
3 tablespoons minced fresh basil leaves or 1 tablespoon dried leaf, crumbled
2 teaspoons strained fresh lemon juice

Small fresh basil sprigs for garnish, if desired

Prepare Shrimp & Chard Filling; set aside chard and refrigerate shrimp. Make pasta dough. Generously flour 2 or 3 trays or baking sheets and a large surface on which you can cut dough. Cut dough in 6 pieces; leave 5 pieces wrapped. Roll 1 piece of dough until thin, see page 178. Turn dial of pasta machine to lowest notch (in which rollers are closest together) and feed piece of dough through rollers.

Lay dough sheet on floured surface. Trim any uneven edges and any "tail" so piece of dough is of uniform width. Measure length of rolled dough and cut it in 2 pieces crosswise so 1 piece is about 1 inch longer than other. Set aside longer piece. Set mounds of 1/2 teaspoon Swiss chard in 2 rows on short piece, spacing them about 1 inch from edges and with their centers about 2 inches apart. Top each mound of chard with a shrimp piece. Brush dough around filling lightly with beaten egg. Set longer piece of dough on top and press it firmly to bottom piece around mounds of filling, using the side of your hand. With a sharp heavy knife or fluted pastry wheel, cut dough in approximately 2-inch squares, between rows of filling. Arrange ravioli on floured tray in 1 layer. Repeat with remaining dough and filling. (Ravioli can be kept, uncovered, 2 hours in refrigerator.) Prepare Fresh Tomato Sauce.

Basil Butter Sauce: Combine shallots, wine and water in a small heavy saucepan. Simmer over medium heat until liquid is reduced to about 3 tablespoons. Stir in cream and a pinch of salt and white pepper. Simmer, whisking occasionally, until liquid is reduced to about 3 tablespoons. Keep butter pieces in refrigerator until ready to use. (Sauce can be prepared to this point up to 4 hours ahead and kept, covered, at room temperature.)

Butter a large baking sheet. Bring a large pot of water to a boil over high heat and add salt. Add 1/2 of ravioli and stir gently to prevent sticking. Reduce heat to medium-high and simmer uncovered about 4 minutes, or until shrimp are just tender; taste one to check. Remove with a large slotted skimmer or slotted spoon. Drain gently but thoroughly. Transfer to buttered baking sheet. Cover and keep warm in a 200F (95C) oven while cooking remaining ravioli. Heat tomato sauce.

To finish butter sauce: Set pan of shallot mixture over low heat and bring to a simmer, whisking. Add 2 pieces chilled butter and whisk quickly until just blended in. Whisk in remaining butter 1 piece at a time, lifting pan from heat occasionally to cool mixture and adding each new piece of butter before previous one is completely blended in. Butter should soften as it is added but sauce should not get hot enough to liquefy. Remove pan from heat and stir in basil and lemon juice. Taste and adjust seasoning. Keep sauce warm if necessary in an uncovered bowl set on a rack above hot but not simmering water over low heat, or in a thermos; try to serve as soon as possible.

To serve, arrange 6 or 7 ravioli for a first course or 12 to 14 for a main course on unheated plates and coat lightly with Basil Butter Sauce. Garnish the center of each plate with a spoonful of tomato sauce, if desired, and with a small basil sprig. Serve any remaining butter sauce separately.
Makes 50 to 60 ravioli, 8 to 10 first-course or 4 main-course servings.

Shrimp & Chard Filling

2 pounds Swiss chard, ribs
 discarded, leaves rinsed well
2 tablespoons butter
Salt and freshly ground pepper to
 taste

1 egg, beaten
4 ounces small shrimp, shelled,
 deveined, rinsed, patted dry
1 teaspoon olive oil

Add chard to a large saucepan of enough boiling salted water to cover generously. Cook uncovered over high heat about 3 minutes or until tender. Drain, rinse with cold water and drain well. Squeeze out as much liquid as possible. Chop chard fine. Melt butter in a medium saucepan. Add chard, salt and pepper. Cook over medium heat 1 minute or until butter is absorbed. Transfer chard to a bowl and let cool. Gradually add about 1 tablespoon beaten egg to chard, adding just enough so chard is moistened. Reserve remaining egg. Taste chard and add salt and pepper if necessary.

Cut each shrimp in 3 pieces crosswise. In a small bowl, combine shrimp with olive oil and a pinch of salt and pepper; toss. Refrigerate 15 minutes.

Ravioli with Mushroom Sauce & Chives

Mushroom Sauce, see below
8 or 9 ounces ravioli or agnolotti
 stuffed with mushrooms,
 homemade, page 121, or
 packaged, fresh or frozen

1 to 1¹/₂ tablespoons snipped
 fresh chives

A creamy mushroom sauce and a sprinkling of chives is a perfect complement for homemade ravioli with Mushroom Filling, or Lemony Scallop Filling, page 122. For a quick and easy dish, serve this sauce with packaged fresh or frozen ravioli or agnolotti, choosing those with delicate fillings of mushrooms, spinach, cheese or chicken. In Pesaro on Italy's Adriatic coast, I tasted ravioli with a similar mushroom sauce to which a few strips of prosciutto were added at the last minute.

◆ *Photo on page 118.*

Prepare Mushroom Sauce. Cook ravioli or agnolotti according to recipe or to package directions. Meanwhile, reheat sauce. Drain pasta gently but thoroughly. Transfer to heated plates. Spoon sauce over ravioli or agnolotti and sprinkle with chives.
Makes 4 or 5 first-course servings.

Mushroom Sauce

6 ounces small mushrooms
1 tablespoon vegetable oil
1 tablespoon butter
Salt and freshly ground pepper to
 taste

³/₄ cup dry white wine
1 large shallot, minced
³/₄ cup chicken stock or broth
3 medium garlic cloves, minced
1¹/₂ cups whipping cream

Halve mushrooms, place cut side down and cut in thin slices. Heat oil and butter in a large skillet or sauté pan over medium heat. Add mushrooms, salt and pepper. Sauté about 5 minutes or until lightly browned. Transfer to a bowl.

Add wine and shallot to skillet; bring to a boil. Add stock and boil 2 minutes. Add garlic and cream; bring to a boil. Return mushrooms to pan and simmer over medium heat, stirring, until sauce is thick enough to coat a spoon, about 7 minutes. Taste and adjust seasoning. (Sauce can be kept, covered, 1 day in refrigerator.)

This easy sauce came about when I was looking for something to do with the dry-packed version of sun-dried tomatoes, those that are not packed in oil. Because they reminded me of dried mushrooms, I treated them in a similar way. I was delighted with the result—a creamy sauce that retained the pungent character of the tomatoes. The festive sauce is perfect for an elegant first course with either homemade or purchased ravioli, agnolotti or tortellini.

✦ *Photo on page 118.*

Ravioli with Sun-Dried-Tomato Cream Sauce

Sun-Dried-Tomato Cream Sauce, see below
8 or 9 ounces fresh or frozen ravioli or agnolotti, with ricotta cheese or meat filling, homemade, page 121, or packaged
2 tablespoons chopped fresh basil leaves or 2 teaspoons dried leaf, crumbled

2 tablespoons chopped fresh parsley leaves (if using dried basil)
Salt and freshly ground pepper to taste

Prepare Sun-Dried-Tomato Cream Sauce; set aside. Cook ravioli or agnolotti according to recipe or package directions. Meanwhile, reheat sauce. Drain pasta gently but thoroughly. Add basil to sauce and, if desired, parsley. Taste and adjust seasoning. To serve, spoon a little sauce onto heated plates, top with a few ravioli or agnolotti and spoon a little sauce over them.
Makes 4 first-course servings.

Sun-Dried-Tomato Cream Sauce

2 tablespoons butter
1 garlic clove, minced
1 cup chicken stock or broth, homemade, page 187, or packaged

1/2 cup dry-packed sun-dried tomatoes
1 cup whipping cream

Melt butter in a small saucepan over low heat. Add garlic and cook 30 seconds. Add stock and tomatoes; bring to a boil. Simmer, uncovered, over medium heat about 10 minutes or until tomatoes are tender. Remove tomatoes. Cut small tomatoes in quarters, large ones in 1/2-inch pieces. Return to saucepan. Add cream and bring to a boil, stirring. Simmer over medium heat until sauce is thick enough to lightly coat a spoon. (Sauce can be kept, covered, 1 day in refrigerator.)

Fresh ginger, garlic and cumin give the meat filling an intriguing flavor. To complement the spiciness, these tortellini are served with a lightly seasoned cream sauce. Instead of being made as ring-shaped tortellini, they can be formed as cappelletti, in which case they have little points and resemble hats. You can also make half-moon-shaped agnolotti.

Tortellini with Spicy Meat Filling

Spicy Meat Filling, opposite
12 ounces Basic Egg Pasta dough, page 178
Light Cream Sauce, opposite
2 tablespoons butter

2 tablespoons minced fresh parsley leaves
1/2 small ripe tomato, diced (for garnish), if desired

Prepare Spicy Meat Filling; cover and refrigerate. Make pasta dough and shape tortellini exactly like tortelloni, page 130, but use a 2-inch plain cookie cutter or glass to cut dough in circles and use 1/2 teaspoon Spicy Meat Filling in each. (Tortellini can be kept, covered with a floured kitchen towel, up to 4 hours in refrigerator; after 1 hour, turn tortellini over carefully so they will not stick. Or they can be frozen on floured baking sheet, put in a plastic bag when solid and kept up to 2 weeks. Do not thaw before cooking.)

Prepare Light Cream Sauce; set aside. Butter a large baking sheet. Bring a large pot of water to a boil over high heat and add salt. Add ½ of tortellini and stir gently to prevent sticking. Return to a boil. Reduce heat to medium-high and simmer uncovered until pasta is just tender but firm to bite, about 4 minutes (frozen tortellini usually require about 2 more minutes). Remove with a large slotted skimmer or slotted spoon. Drain gently but thoroughly. Transfer to buttered baking sheet. Cover and keep warm in a 200F (95C) oven while cooking remaining tortellini.

Just before serving, bring sauce to a simmer. Set over low heat and stir in butter by tablespoons. Remove from heat and add parsley. Taste and adjust seasoning. Transfer tortellini to a heated serving bowl and gently toss with sauce. Serve, including some sauce with each serving. Sprinkle each portion with diced tomato, if desired.

Makes 3 main-course or 5 or 6 first-course servings.

Spicy Meat Filling

2 tablespoons vegetable oil
½ large onion, minced (⅔ cup)
⅔ cup ground beef chuck
**   (about 4 oz.)**
2 teaspoons ground cumin
Salt and freshly ground pepper to
**   taste**
¼ teaspoon ground turmeric
¼ teaspoon red (cayenne)
**   pepper**

1 tablespoon minced peeled
**   gingerroot**
2 medium garlic cloves, minced
3 tablespoons chicken stock or
**   broth**
1 large egg yolk
2 tablespoons unseasoned dry
**   bread crumbs**

Heat oil in a medium skillet over medium-low heat. Add onion and cook, stirring often, about 5 minutes or until softened. Add beef, cumin and a pinch of salt and pepper. Cook over medium heat, stirring to separate clumps of ground meat and to blend meat with onion mixture, until meat changes color, about 5 minutes. Add turmeric, red pepper, gingerroot and garlic. Stir over low heat 30 seconds.

Add stock and bring to a boil. Simmer over medium-low heat until stock is absorbed, about 5 minutes. Transfer to a medium bowl. Cool to room temperature. Stir in egg yolk and bread crumbs. Taste and adjust seasoning. Cover and refrigerate 15 minutes. (Filling can be kept 1 day.)

Makes 1⅓ cups.

Light Cream Sauce

1 cup whipping cream
¼ teaspoon ground cumin
½ teaspoon paprika

Salt and freshly ground pepper to
**   taste**

Bring cream to a boil in a medium saucepan. Simmer about 5 minutes over medium heat or until thick enough to coat a spoon. Whisk in cumin, paprika, salt and pepper; set aside.

VARIATIONS

Agnolotti with Spicy Meat Filling: Cut dough sheet in circles with a 2-inch plain cookie cutter or glass. Put ½ teaspoon filling in center of each circle and fold in half to make half-moon shape. Seal edges. If necessary, moisten them first with a little water.

Cappelletti with Spicy Meat Filling: Cut dough in 2-inch squares with a knife. Put ½ teaspoon filling in center of each. Continue as for tortelloni, folding each square in 2 to make a triangle. Make a crease by folding edges of triangle upward, then bring ends around filling as for tortelloni.

A traditional ricotta-Parmesan filling gains new excitement when enclosed in a chili-flavored pasta dough to make these tortelloni. Of course, you can use the filling inside plain pasta dough or in won-ton wrappers as on page 124.

Chili Tortelloni with Cheese Filling

Ricotta-Parmesan Filling, see below
Chili Pasta dough, page 182
3 tablespoons melted butter

2 tablespoons freshly grated Parmesan cheese
Bowl of freshly grated Parmesan cheese (for serving)

Prepare Ricotta-Parmesan Filling; cover and refrigerate. Make pasta dough. Generously flour 2 or 3 trays or baking sheets and a large surface on which you can cut dough. Cut dough in 4 pieces; leave 3 pieces wrapped. Roll 1 part to $\frac{1}{16}$ inch thick, following instructions on page 178. Do not dry sheet.

Lay dough sheet on a floured surface. Cut in circles with a 3-inch plain cookie cutter or glass. Put 1 teaspoon Ricotta-Parmesan Filling in center of each circle and fold in half. Seal edges. If necessary, moisten edges first with a little water. Fold round edge up slightly. Bring pointed ends together around filling, curving folded-up edge around filling to form a ring. Press 1 end over other to seal, moistening edges if necessary.

Set tortelloni on floured tray in 1 layer. Check tortelloni to be sure edges are well sealed. Flour work surface again. Continue with remaining dough, rolling and filling 1 sheet at a time. (Tortelloni can be kept, covered with a floured kitchen towel, up to 4 hours in refrigerator; after 1 hour, turn tortelloni over carefully so they will not stick. Or they can be frozen on floured baking sheet, put in a plastic bag when solid and kept up to 2 weeks. Do not thaw before cooking.)

Butter a large baking sheet. Bring a large pot of water to a boil over high heat and add salt. Add $\frac{1}{2}$ of tortelloni and stir gently to prevent sticking. Return to a boil. Reduce heat to medium-high and simmer uncovered until pasta is just tender but firm to the bite, about 4 minutes (frozen tortelloni usually require about 2 more minutes). Remove with a large slotted skimmer or slotted spoon. Drain gently but thoroughly. Transfer to buttered baking sheet. Cover and keep warm in a 200F (95C) oven while cooking remaining tortelloni.

Transfer to a heated serving dish. Toss with melted butter and 2 tablespoons Parmesan cheese. Serve with more Parmesan.
Makes 32 tortelloni, 4 or 5 first-course or 2 or 3 main-course servings.

Cut dough sheet in circles with a 3-inch plain cookie cutter or glass. Put 1 teaspoon filling in center of each circle and fold in half. Seal edges, moistening first with a little water if necessary.

To shape, fold round edge up slightly. Bring pointed ends together around filling, curving folded-up edge around filling to form a ring. Press 1 end over the other to seal, moistening edges if necessary.

Ricotta-Parmesan Filling

1 large egg yolk
$\frac{2}{3}$ cup ricotta cheese (about 5 oz.)
$\frac{1}{2}$ cup freshly grated Parmesan cheese ($1\frac{1}{2}$ oz.)
$\frac{1}{4}$ cup chopped fresh parsley leaves

Salt and freshly ground pepper to taste
Red (cayenne) pepper to taste
Freshly grated nutmeg to taste

Beat egg yolk in a medium bowl. Stir in ricotta until blended. Stir in Parmesan, parsley, salt, pepper, red pepper and nutmeg. Cover and refrigerate until ready to use. (Filling can be kept 1 day.)
Makes generous $\frac{3}{4}$ cup.

Eggplant & Feta-Filled Canneloni

Eggplant-Feta Filling, see below
16 dried canneloni tubes
2 to 2½ cups smooth tomato sauce, homemade, page 187, or packaged

2 teaspoons dried leaf oregano, if desired
Freshly ground pepper to taste
4 to 5 tablespoons freshly grated Parmesan cheese

Packaged canneloni tubes are just fine for the rustic filling of sautéed eggplant and feta cheese accented with garlic and green onions. The usual way to prepare canneloni is to precook the pasta tubes before filling, so the pasta cooks evenly and is tender. An easier way is to fill them raw and bake them directly in the tomato sauce, as in the variation, below. I have allowed extra canneloni tubes in case any tear during cooking.

Prepare Eggplant-Feta Filling; set aside. Butter 2 (8-inch) square baking dishes or a large shallow baking dish. For serving canneloni as soon as they are ready, preheat oven to 400F (205C).

Bring a large pot of water to a boil; add salt, then canneloni tubes. Cook uncovered over high heat, stirring occasionally, about 7 minutes or until partially cooked. Transfer carefully to a bowl of cold water to keep them from sticking to each other. Before filling, drain well and put on a plate.

Fill canneloni using a pastry bag without a tip, by holding each tube upright and piping filling inside until full. Or, use a teaspoon to fill each canneloni with about 3½ tablespoons filling.

Arrange filled canneloni in 1 layer in buttered dish or dishes. Season tomato sauce with oregano, if desired, and pepper. Spoon sauce evenly over canneloni. Sprinkle with Parmesan cheese. (Canneloni can be prepared to this point and kept, covered, up to 1 day in refrigerator. Bring to room temperature and preheat oven before continuing.)

Bake canneloni in preheated oven about 15 minutes or until filling is hot and cheese is melted. Brown in broiler, 1 to 1½ minutes. Serve immediately from baking dishes.
Makes 12 canneloni, 4 main-course servings.

Eggplant-Feta Filling

2 medium eggplants (about 2 lbs. total), peeled
Salt and freshly ground pepper to taste
About ¾ cup plus 2 teaspoons olive oil
4 medium garlic cloves, minced

½ cup ricotta cheese
1 cup finely crumbled feta cheese (about 4 oz.)
1 teaspoon dried leaf oregano, crumbled
6 tablespoons minced green onions, green and white parts

Cut eggplant in ⅜-inch slices crosswise. Sprinkle lightly but evenly with salt on both sides. Divide slices between 2 colanders or large strainers. Put a bowl with a weight on top of each and leave to drain 30 minutes. Pat slices dry with several changes of paper towels.

Heat 3 tablespoons oil in a large heavy skillet over medium heat. Add enough eggplant slices to make 1 layer; add quickly so first slices won't absorb all of oil. Sauté about 2½ minutes per side or until tender when pierced with a fork. Transfer to a plate. Add 2 tablespoons oil to skillet and heat. Continue sautéing remaining eggplant in batches, adding oil as needed.

Add 2 teaspoons oil to skillet and reduce heat to low. Add garlic and cook, stirring, 5 seconds. Immediately pour garlic mixture into a small bowl.

Chop eggplant with a knife. Transfer to a large bowl. Add ricotta, feta, garlic, oregano, green onions and pepper; mix very well. Taste and adjust seasoning.

VARIATION
For a quick way to use packaged canneloni, fill tubes without cooking first. Use a pastry bag or spoon to fill. Increase amount of tomato sauce to 3 cups; sauce should be relatively thin. Put filled canneloni in buttered baking dishes and cover with tomato sauce. Cover and bake at 400F (205C) 25 minutes. Uncover, sprinkle with cheese and bake 25 minutes longer.

This dish takes some time but the spectacular result is worth it. The recipe is adapted from "La Cuisine du Poisson," the seafood cookbook I authored in France with Chef Fernand Chambrette. The delicate filling of shrimp and salmon in a seafood sauce deserves to be enclosed in homemade canneloni.

Creamy Seafood Canneloni

Seafood Filling, see below
Basic Egg Pasta dough, page 178
1¹/₂ cups whipping cream
Salt to taste

Freshly grated nutmeg to taste
Red (cayenne) pepper to taste
²/₃ cup finely grated Gruyère cheese (about 2 oz.)

Prepare Seafood Filling; set aside. Make pasta dough, page 178. Follow instructions through rolling pasta until ¹/₁₆ inch thick. Hang sheets of dough on a pasta rack or on the back of a towel-covered chair and let dry 20 to 30 minutes. Lightly flour a work surface and 2 or 3 baking sheets or trays. On floured surface, cut dough in pieces about 4¹/₂ inches long with a sharp heavy knife; trim ends. Let dry in 1 layer on baking sheets or trays 10 minutes.

For serving canneloni as soon as they are ready, preheat oven to 400F (205C). Generously butter several gratin dishes or other shallow baking dishes.

Bring a large pot of water to a boil and add salt. Cook pasta pieces in pot, a few at a time, 1 minute or until flexible. Transfer gently with a slotted spoon to a large bowl of cold water. Remove, 1 at a time, and spread out in 1 layer on towels to drain. Transfer gently to a work surface.

Spoon ¹/₄ cup Seafood Filling near 1 long side of each pasta piece. Spread in a strip nearly to short sides, leaving about ¹/₂ inch of pasta uncovered along each short side. Roll up each piece gently in a cigar shape to make canneloni. Arrange filled canneloni in 1 layer in prepared baking dishes. (Canneloni can be prepared to this point and kept, covered, up to 1 day in refrigerator. Bring to room temperature before continuing.)

Simmer cream in a large sauté pan, stirring often, until cream is reduced to about 1 cup. Season with salt, nutmeg and red pepper. Pour cream evenly over canneloni and sprinkle with Gruyère cheese. Bake canneloni in preheated oven 10 minutes. Broil until lightly browned, about 1¹/₂ minutes. Serve immediately from baking dishes. Garnish as desired.

Makes 16 canneloni, 8 first-course or 4 or 5 main-course servings.

Seafood Filling

12 ounces medium shrimp, shelled, reserving shells, deveined, halved crosswise
1 cup fish stock, homemade, page 188, or packaged, or clam juice
¹/₂ cup dry white wine
1 pound salmon fillet
Salt and freshly ground pepper to taste

About ²/₃ cup milk
3 tablespoons butter
¹/₄ cup all-purpose flour
Freshly grated nutmeg to taste
Red (cayenne) pepper to taste
2 large egg yolks
¹/₄ cup whipping cream

Combine reserved shrimp shells, fish stock or clam juice and wine in a medium saucepan. Bring to a boil. Cover and simmer 10 minutes. Strain liquid into a bowl, pressing hard on shells. Return liquid to saucepan.

Remove skin from salmon with a sharp flexible knife. Run your fingers over salmon to check for bones. Remove any bones with tweezers, a pastry crimper, or a small sharp knife. Cut salmon in approximately ³/₄-inch cubes.

Add salmon, salt and pepper to strained shrimp stock. Bring to a simmer. Cover and poach salmon over low heat 2 minutes. Transfer salmon to a bowl with a slotted spoon. Add shrimp to liquid. Cover and poach 2 minutes. Transfer to bowl with slotted spoon. Measure liquid and add enough milk to obtain 2 cups; set aside.

Creamy Seafood Canneloni

Spoon ¼ cup filling near 1 long side of each pasta piece. Spread in a strip nearly to short sides. Roll up each piece gently in a cigar shape to make canneloni.

Melt butter in a heavy medium saucepan over low heat. Whisk in flour and cook, whisking, 2 minutes or until foaming but not browned. Remove from heat. Whisk in reserved 2 cups liquid. Bring to a boil, whisking. Add salt, pepper, nutmeg and red pepper. Simmer sauce over low heat, whisking often, 3 minutes. Remove from heat. Whisk egg yolks with cream in a small bowl until blended. Gradually whisk about ¼ cup sauce into egg-yolk mixture. Whisk this mixture into remaining sauce and heat over low heat, whisking, about 2 minutes or until slightly thickened; do not let sauce boil. Drain any liquid from seafood. Gently fold seafood into sauce. Taste and adjust seasoning. Rub surface of mixture with a small piece of butter to prevent a skin from forming.

The sheets of fresh pasta dough required for fresh lasagne, canneloni and stuffed pastas can be purchased from some pasta shops.

COOKING TIP

Macaroni Moussaka

Meat Sauce, see below
About ¾ cup olive oil
1 large eggplant (about 1½ lbs.), cut in ¼-inch slices crosswise
½ cup pine nuts
½ cup chopped fresh parsley leaves

4 large garlic cloves, minced
1 pound large elbow macaroni
Béchamel Sauce, see below
½ cup freshly grated Parmesan cheese (about 1½ oz.)
⅓ cup freshly grated Parmesan cheese (for sprinkling)

Prepare Meat Sauce. While it is cooking heat 3 tablespoons oil in a large skillet over medium-high heat. Add enough eggplant slices to make 1 layer; add quickly so first slices won't absorb all of oil. Sauté about 2 minutes per side or until tender when pierced with a fork. Transfer to paper towels. Add 2 tablespoons oil to skillet and heat. Continue sautéing remaining eggplant in batches, adding oil as needed. Transfer to paper towels.

Add pine nuts to Meat Sauce and cook 2 minutes longer. Add parsley and garlic. Transfer to a large bowl.

Bring a large pot of water to a boil; add salt, then pasta. Cook uncovered over high heat, stirring occasionally, about 6 minutes or until nearly tender but firmer than usual, since pasta will be baked. Drain, rinse with cold water and drain well. Add to bowl of Meat Sauce and toss. Stir in ½ cup grated Parmesan cheese. Taste and adjust seasoning.

Prepare Béchamel Sauce. Preheat oven to 350F (175C). Butter a 13" x 9" x 2" baking dish. Put enough eggplant slices in dish to make 1 layer. Cover with about ½ of macaroni-meat mixture. Cover with another layer of eggplant. Spread remaining meat mixture on top. Cover with a layer of remaining eggplant.

Reheat Béchamel Sauce until flowing. Pour sauce over top layer and spread evenly with a spatula. Sprinkle with ⅓ cup Parmesan cheese. (Dish can be kept, covered, 1 day in refrigerator. Bring to room temperature before continuing.)

Bake in preheated oven about 35 minutes or until golden. Let stand about 10 minutes before serving. Serve from baking dish.
Makes 6 to 8 main-course servings.

Meat Sauce

3 tablespoons olive oil
1 large onion, minced
1¼ pounds ground lamb or ground beef
Salt and freshly ground pepper to taste

2 pounds ripe tomatoes, peeled, seeded, chopped, or 2 (28-oz.) cans whole plum tomatoes, drained, chopped

Heat oil in a large skillet over medium-low heat. Add onion and cook about 10 minutes or until tender. Add meat and cook over medium heat, crumbling with a fork, until it changes color, about 7 minutes. Add salt, pepper and tomatoes. Cook, stirring occasionally, 35 minutes or until mixture is quite dry.

Béchamel Sauce

3 tablespoons butter
3 tablespoons all-purpose flour
2 cups milk

Salt and white pepper to taste
Freshly grated nutmeg to taste

Melt butter in a heavy medium saucepan over low heat. Whisk in flour and cook, whisking, 2 minutes or until foaming but not browned. Remove from heat. Whisk in milk. Cook over medium-high heat, whisking constantly, until sauce thickens and comes to a boil. Add a pinch of salt, white pepper and nutmeg. Simmer sauce over low heat, whisking often, 10 minutes. Taste and adjust seasoning.

Layered Spinach, Pasta & Parmesan Soufflé

This dramatic looking dish is composed of a bright-green layer of spinach pasta shells mixed with spinach, topped by a golden, light, cheese soufflé. Use a glass soufflé dish so the colors show through.

SPINACH-PASTA LAYER
4 ounces medium spinach pasta shells (1½ cups)
3 pounds fresh spinach, stems removed, leaves rinsed well, or 2 (10-ounce) packages frozen leaf spinach
1 tablespoon butter
½ cup whipping cream
5 tablespoons freshly grated Parmesan cheese
Salt and freshly ground pepper to taste
Freshly grated nutmeg to taste

PARMESAN-SOUFFLÉ LAYER
2 tablespoons butter
2 tablespoons all-purpose flour
¾ cup milk
Salt and freshly ground white pepper to taste
3 large egg yolks
Freshly grated nutmeg to taste
⅓ cup freshly grated Parmesan cheese
5 large egg whites

Preheat oven to 400F (205C). Generously butter a 6-cup soufflé dish. Have a heatproof platter ready near oven.

SPINACH-PASTA LAYER
Bring a large pot of water to a boil; add salt, then pasta. Cook uncovered over high heat, stirring occasionally, about 5 minutes or until nearly tender but firmer than usual, because pasta will be baked. Drain, rinse with cold water and drain well.

Add spinach to a large saucepan of enough boiling salted water to cover generously. Cook uncovered over high heat about 2 minutes or until wilted. Drain, rinse with cold water and drain well. Squeeze out as much liquid as possible. Chop spinach.

Melt butter in pan used to cook spinach. Add spinach and toss briefly over medium heat. Add ⅓ cup cream and bring to a simmer. Transfer to a medium bowl. Add cooked pasta and remaining cream; toss well. Add Parmesan cheese and mix. Season with salt, pepper and nutmeg. (Mixture can be kept, covered tightly, up to 1 day in refrigerator. Reheat to lukewarm in a medium saucepan before using.) Transfer to prepared dish. Spread evenly but lightly.

PARMESAN-SOUFFLÉ LAYER
Melt butter in a small heavy saucepan over low heat. Whisk in flour and cook, whisking constantly, 2 minutes or until foaming but not browned. Remove from heat. Whisk in milk. Bring to a boil over medium-high heat, whisking. Add a small pinch of salt and pepper. Simmer over low heat, whisking often, 5 minutes.

Remove mixture from heat and vigorously whisk in egg yolks, 1 at a time. Cook over low heat, whisking constantly, about 3 minutes or until thickened; do not overcook or let mixture boil or yolks may curdle. Add nutmeg. Taste and adjust seasoning. (Mixture can be kept, covered, up to 8 hours in refrigerator. Reheat in a small saucepan over low heat, whisking, until just warm. Remove from heat.) Stir in Parmesan cheese.

Beat egg whites in a large dry bowl until stiff but not dry. Quickly fold about ¼ of whites into cheese mixture. Spoon mixture over remaining whites and fold in lightly but quickly, just until blended.

Transfer mixture to prepared soufflé dish and smooth top. Bake in preheated oven about 20 minutes or until puffed and browned; when you gently move oven rack, soufflé should shake very slightly in center. Set soufflé dish on platter and serve immediately.
Makes 3 or 4 servings as a light main course.

Pasta Gratin with Porcini Mushrooms

1 ounce dried porcini mushrooms
2 cups whipping cream
Salt and freshly ground pepper to taste
1½ teaspoons chopped fresh thyme leaves or ½ teaspoon dried leaf, crumbled
2 medium garlic cloves, minced
8 ounces cavatelli (about 2 cups) or medium plain or colored pasta shells (about 3 cups)

2 cups shredded imported asiago, Gruyère or Swiss cheese (about 7 oz.)
Freshly grated nutmeg to taste
Red (cayenne) pepper to taste
3 tablespoons chopped fresh parsley leaves, preferably Italian

Soak porcini mushrooms in hot water to cover 30 minutes. Remove and rinse. Discard any hard portions. Pat dry. Cut in dice.

Bring cream to a simmer in a wide medium saucepan. Add porcini, salt and pepper. Bring to a boil and simmer over medium-low heat about 9 minutes or until mixture is reduced to 2 cups. Stir in thyme and garlic. Transfer to a large bowl. Cool to room temperature.

Preheat oven to 400F (205C). Bring a large pot of water to a boil; add salt, then pasta. Cook uncovered over high heat, stirring occasionally, about 8 minutes for cavatelli or 5 to 7 minutes for shells or until nearly tender but firmer than usual, because pasta will be baked. Drain well.

Set aside ½ cup cheese. Add nutmeg and red pepper to porcini mixture. Add pasta, parsley and remaining cheese; toss mixture. Taste and adjust seasoning; mixture should be well flavored with salt, pepper and nutmeg.

Butter a shallow 4½- to 5-cup baking dish. Transfer pasta mixture to dish and sprinkle with reserved cheese. (Pasta can be kept, covered, 1 day in refrigerator. Bring to room temperature before continuing.)

Bake about 10 minutes or until pasta absorbs cream. If top is not brown, broil 1 to 2 minutes or until lightly browned. Serve from baking dish.
Makes 4 main-course or 6 side-dish servings.

COOKING TIP

Although homemade stock or broth, pages 187 and 188, is best, often there is no time to prepare it. It is now possible to buy frozen stocks and stock concentrates that are close to homemade. Of the canned varieties, generally the unsalted is better. If using a salted canned broth labeled "concentrated" or "double-strength," bring it to regular strength by adding the amount of water specified on the can (usually an equal amount) before measuring it for recipes.

Pasta "Cassoulet"

Laden with meats, sausage and bacon, aromatic with herbs and garlic, this pasta version of the well-known dish is quicker to make than the traditional cassoulet of southwest France, which pairs the meats with cooked white beans. It makes a great dish for winter.

1½ pounds boneless lamb shoulder or lamb for stew or 2 to 2½ pounds lamb with bone
8 ounces bacon, preferably thick-sliced, cut crosswise in ½-inch-wide strips
1 pound pork shoulder, excess fat trimmed, cut in 1-inch cubes
1 large onion, chopped
3 garlic cloves, chopped
1½ pounds ripe tomatoes, peeled, seeded, chopped or 1 (28-oz.) can and 1 (14-oz.) can whole plum tomatoes, drained, chopped
1 cup beef or chicken stock or broth, homemade, page 187 or 188, or packaged

1 cup water
Salt and freshly ground pepper to taste
1 large fresh thyme sprig or 1 teaspoon dried leaf, crumbled
1 bay leaf
5 parsley stems
1 tablespoon chopped fresh basil leaves or 1 teaspoon dried leaf, crumbled
8 ounces smoked Polish Kielbasa sausage or other smoked sausages

PASTA AND TOPPING
1 pound rigatoni
2 medium garlic cloves, minced
2 teaspoons chopped fresh thyme leaves or ¾ teaspoon dried leaf, crumbled

4 tablespoons olive oil
Salt and freshly ground pepper to taste
¼ cup unseasoned dry bread crumbs

Trim excess fat from lamb and remove any bones. Cut meat in 1-inch cubes. Cook bacon in a large heavy casserole over medium heat until lightly browned. Remove with a slotted spoon and drain on paper towels. Pour off fat into a bowl; return 2 tablespoons fat to casserole. Add lamb cubes in 2 batches and brown on all sides over medium-high heat. Transfer to a bowl. Add pork cubes to casserole and brown. Transfer to bowl. Add 2 tablespoons fat to casserole. Add onion and cook over low heat 5 minutes. Add garlic and cook 30 seconds. Stir in tomatoes and cook 2 minutes.

Return lamb and pork to casserole. Add stock or broth, water and a little salt and pepper. Tie thyme, bay leaf and parsley in a piece of cheesecloth; add to casserole. Bring to a boil. Cover and simmer 45 minutes to 1 hour or until meats are tender when pierced with a knife. Discard herb bag. With a slotted spoon, transfer meat to a bowl. Boil cooking liquid until reduced to 2½ cups. Add basil. Taste and adjust seasoning. Return lamb and pork to sauce.

Put sausage in a medium saucepan. Cover with water; bring just to a simmer. Cook over low heat 10 minutes. Drain, remove skin; cut in ½-inch slices.

PASTA AND TOPPING
Bring a large pot of water to a boil; add salt, then pasta. Cook uncovered over high heat, stirring occasionally, about 10 minutes or until nearly tender but firmer than usual, because pasta will be baked. Drain, rinse with cold water and drain well. Transfer to a large bowl. Add garlic, thyme and 3 tablespoons olive oil; toss to combine. Season with salt and pepper.

Preheat oven to 400F (205C). Oil a 10-cup gratin dish or other heavy baking dish. Put ½ of pasta in gratin dish. With a slotted spoon, arrange lamb and pork on pasta. Top with sausage slices and bacon. Spoon remaining pasta on top. Ladle sauce over pasta. (Dish can be prepared ahead up to this point, covered and kept up to 3 days in refrigerator. If any cooking liquid remains, reserve and add to refrigerated cassoulet before baking to compensate for slight drying in refrigerator. Bring to room temperature before continuing.)

Sprinkle cassoulet with bread crumbs, then with remaining 1 tablespoon oil. Bake 30 to 40 minutes or until hot and golden brown. Serve from baking dish. Makes 6 to 8 main-course servings.

Lasagne with Rich Meat Sauce & Fontina Cheese

Tomato-Meat Sauce, see below
Ricotta Layer, see below
12 ounces dried lasagne noodles
1 pound fontina cheese,
**   shredded (about 4 cups)**

1/3 cup freshly grated Parmesan
**   cheese**

Prepare Tomato-Meat Sauce and Ricotta Layer; set aside. Bring a large pot of water to a boil; add salt, then lasagne noodles. Cook uncovered over high heat, stirring occasionally, about 7 minutes or until flexible but not yet tender. Put in a large bowl of cold water so they don't stick to each other. Before using, put them in 1 layer on towels and pat dry.

Preheat oven to 375F (190C). Butter a 13" x 9" x 2" baking dish. Spoon 1 cup Tomato-Meat Sauce on bottom of dish and spread evenly with a spatula. Top with 1 layer lasagne noodles, cutting some to fit in an even layer. Sprinkle with 1½ cups fontina.

Top with another layer of noodles. Top with all of ricotta mixture by spoonfuls; carefully spread in an even layer. Top with another layer of noodles, then with 1 cup meat sauce. Sprinkle with 1½ cups fontina.

Top with another layer of noodles. Spoon remaining meat sauce over top. Sprinkle evenly with remaining fontina, then with remaining Parmesan. (Lasagne can be kept, covered, 1 day in refrigerator. Bring to room temperature before continuing.)

Bake 30 to 40 minutes or until bubbling and lightly browned. Let stand 5 minutes in a warm place so juices are reabsorbed. Cut in squares and serve. Makes 6 to 8 main-course servings.

Tomato-Meat Sauce

3 tablespoons olive oil
1 medium onion, minced
½ medium carrot, chopped
1 celery stalk, chopped
12 ounces lean ground beef
2 pounds ripe tomatoes, peeled,
**   seeded, chopped or 2 (28-oz.)**
**   cans whole plum tomatoes,**
**   drained well**

3 garlic cloves, minced
1 bay leaf
¾ teaspoon dried leaf oregano,
**   crumbled**
¼ to ½ teaspoon hot red-pepper
**   flakes, if desired**
Salt and freshly ground pepper to
**   taste**
3 tablespoons tomato paste

Heat oil in a heavy medium casserole over medium heat. Add onion, carrot and celery. Cook, stirring, about 10 minutes or until onion is soft but not brown. Add beef; sauté over medium heat, crumbling with a fork, until color changes.

Add tomatoes, garlic, bay leaf, oregano, pepper flakes, salt and pepper. Bring to a boil, stirring. Cover and cook over low heat, stirring from time to time (and crushing canned tomatoes, if using), 45 minutes. Discard bay leaf. Stir in tomato paste. Increase heat to medium and simmer uncovered 15 minutes, stirring often, until thick. Taste and adjust seasoning. (Sauce can be kept, covered, up to 2 days in refrigerator; or it can be frozen.)
Makes 3½ cups.

Ricotta Layer

2 cups ricotta cheese
**   (about 1 lb.)**
2 large egg yolks
½ cup freshly grated Parmesan
**   cheese (1½ oz.)**

¼ cup minced fresh parsley
**   leaves**
Freshly grated nutmeg to taste
Salt and freshly ground pepper to
**   taste**

Mix ricotta, egg yolks, Parmesan, parsley, nutmeg, salt and pepper in a bowl. Taste and adjust seasoning; mixture should be flavored generously with nutmeg.

Creamy Macaroni with Four Cheeses

Spiced Cream Sauce, see below
2 cups elbow macaroni (about 8 oz.), regular or whole-wheat
1 cup shredded Swiss or Gruyère cheese (about 3 oz.)
1 cup shredded sharp cheddar cheese (about 3 oz.)

1 cup shredded provolone cheese (about 3 oz.)
2 tablespoons finely grated Parmesan cheese

When available, use tri-colored macaroni or sesame spirals to prepare this glorious macaroni and cheese. Instead of using four cheeses, you can substitute 3 cups of any one of the three shredded cheeses and pair it with the Parmesan.

Prepare Spiced Cream Sauce; set aside. Preheat oven to 375F (190C). Bring a large pot of water to a boil; add salt, then pasta. Cook uncovered over high heat, stirring occasionally, about 6 minutes or until nearly tender but firmer than usual, since pasta will be baked. Drain, rinse with cold water and drain well. Transfer to a large bowl.

Lightly butter a 6- to 7-cup baking dish. Add Spiced Cream Sauce to macaroni and stir. Add Swiss or Gruyère, cheddar and provolone cheeses. Taste and adjust seasoning. Spoon into buttered baking dish. Sprinkle with Parmesan. (Dish can be prepared 2 days ahead to this point and kept, covered, in refrigerator.)

Bake in preheated oven 20 to 30 minutes or until bubbling. Brown under broiler 1 to 2 minutes. Serve from baking dish.
Makes 4 to 6 main-course servings.

Spiced Cream Sauce

1 fresh or 1 canned roasted jalapeño pepper, if desired
¼ cup butter
⅓ cup minced onion
¼ cup all-purpose flour
2 cups milk

Salt and freshly ground white pepper to taste
Freshly grated nutmeg to taste
½ cup whipping cream
Red (cayenne) pepper to taste

If using fresh jalapeño pepper, wear gloves when handling it; remove seeds and ribs. Mince fresh or canned pepper. Melt butter in a heavy medium saucepan over low heat. Add onion and jalapeño pepper. Cook, stirring occasionally, 5 minutes. Remove from heat and stir in flour. Cook over low heat, stirring constantly, 2 minutes. Remove from heat. Whisk in milk. Cook over medium-high heat, whisking until sauce thickens and comes to a boil. Add a pinch of salt, white pepper and nutmeg. Simmer over low heat, whisking often, 5 minutes. Whisk in cream and bring to a boil. Add red pepper. Taste and adjust seasoning.

For the best flavor in Parmesan, buy a piece of Parmigiano-Reggiano cheese and grate it yourself a short time before using. The next best is to purchase grated imported Parmesan in a fine store where cheese is grated often, especially cheese shops or stores which specialize in Italian products. Freshly grated imported cheese is also available in good supermarkets, but should be in the refrigerated section. Avoid grated cheese that is stored at room temperature. If you want to "grate" Parmesan in a food processor, it should be treated differently from most other cheeses—chop it with the metal blade rather than grating with the grating disc.

COOKING TIP

Mediterranean Vegetable Lasagne

1 eggplant (about 1 lb.), peeled
About 11 tablespoons olive oil
1 pound zucchini, sliced ³/₈ inch thick
1 tablespoon butter
8 ounces mushrooms, halved, sliced thin
Salt and freshly ground pepper to taste
2 garlic cloves, minced
Cream Sauce with Herbs, see page 142

12 ounces dried lasagne noodles
3 cups tomato sauce, homemade, page 186, or good-quality packaged
3¹/₂ cups shredded mozzarella cheese (about 12 oz.)
1 cup freshly grated Parmesan cheese (about 3 oz.)
3 plum tomatoes, peeled, sliced

Halve eggplant lengthwise; slice crosswise ³/₈ inch thick. Heat 3 tablespoons oil in a large skillet over medium-high heat. Add enough eggplant slices to make 1 layer; add quickly so first slices won't absorb all of oil. Sauté about 2¹/₂ minutes per side or until tender when pierced with a fork. Transfer to paper towels. Add 2 tablespoons oil to skillet and heat. Continue sautéing remaining eggplant in batches, adding oil as needed. Transfer to paper towels.

Heat 2 tablespoons oil in skillet over medium-high heat. Add enough zucchini slices to make 1 layer. Sauté 1 minute per side. Transfer to paper towels. Continue sautéing remaining zucchini, adding oil as necessary.

Melt 1 tablespoon butter in large skillet over medium heat. Add mushrooms, salt and pepper. Sauté about 5 minutes or until tender. Add garlic and sauté 30 seconds longer. Transfer to a bowl.

Prepare Cream Sauce with Herbs; set aside. Bring a large pot of water to a boil; add salt, then lasagne noodles. Cook uncovered over high heat, stirring occasionally, about 7 minutes or until flexible but not yet tender. Put in a large bowl of cold water so they don't stick to each other. Before using, put them in 1 layer on towels.

If tomato sauce is thin, simmer until thick. Preheat oven to 375F (190C). Butter a 13" x 9" x 2" or large oval baking dish. Pat lasagne dry.

Spoon ²/₃ cup cream sauce on bottom of baking dish and spread evenly with a spatula. Top with 1 layer lasagne noodles, cutting some to fit in an even layer. Top with all eggplant; sprinkle lightly with salt and pepper. Spoon 1¹/₂ cups tomato sauce over eggplant. Sprinkle with 1¹/₄ cups mozzarella, then with ¹/₃ cup Parmesan.

Top with another layer of noodles. Add ²/₃ cup cream sauce and spread carefully on noodles with spatula. Top with all of zucchini and sprinkle lightly with salt and pepper. Spoon remaining tomato sauce over zucchini. Sprinkle with 1¹/₄ cups mozzarella, then ¹/₃ cup Parmesan.

Top with another layer of noodles. Add remaining cream sauce and carefully spread it smooth. Scatter mushrooms over top. Sprinkle with remaining mozzarella. Arrange tomato slices over center. Sprinkle remaining Parmesan over all. (Lasagne can be kept, covered, 1 day in refrigerator. Bring to room temperature before continuing.)

Bake lasagne in preheated oven 30 to 40 minutes or until bubbling and lightly browned. Let stand 15 minutes in a warm place so juices are reabsorbed. Cut in squares and serve.

Makes 6 main-course servings.

Cream Sauce with Herbs

¼ cup butter
¼ cup all-purpose flour
2 cups milk
Salt and freshly ground white
   pepper to taste
Freshly grated nutmeg to taste
½ cup whipping cream

1½ teaspoons chopped fresh
   thyme leaves or ½ teaspoon
   dried leaf, crumbled
2 tablespoons chopped fresh
   basil leaves or 2 teaspoons
   dried leaf, crumbled

Melt butter in a heavy medium saucepan over low heat. Whisk in flour and cook, whisking, 2 minutes or until foaming but not browned. Remove from heat. Whisk in milk. Cook over medium-high heat, whisking constantly, until mixture thickens and comes to a boil. Add a pinch of salt, white pepper and nutmeg. Simmer sauce over low heat, whisking often, 10 minutes. Whisk in cream and bring to a simmer. Stir in thyme and basil. Taste and adjust seasoning.

Note: Extra lasagne noodles are allowed because a few will break or stick together during cooking.

My mother taught me to prepare several versions of this dish. It makes a great accompaniment for roast chicken. The sour-cream kugel in the variation, below, is a delicious side dish with broiled fish, or can be served with a green salad.

Noodle Kugel with Sautéed Mushrooms

8 ounces medium egg noodles
5 tablespoons vegetable oil or
   butter
1 large onion, minced
8 ounces small mushrooms,
   quartered if small, halved and
   sliced if large

Salt and freshly ground pepper to
   taste
¾ teaspoon paprika
2 large eggs, beaten
3 tablespoons chopped fresh
   parsley leaves, if desired

Preheat oven to 350F (175C). Bring a large pot of water to a boil; add salt, then pasta. Cook uncovered over high heat, stirring occasionally, about 4 minutes or until nearly tender but firmer than usual, because the noodles will be baked. Drain, rinse with cold water and drain well. Transfer to a large bowl.

Heat 3 tablespoons oil or butter in a large skillet over medium-low heat. Add onion and sauté about 12 minutes or until very tender. Add 1 tablespoon oil or butter and heat. Add mushrooms, salt, pepper and ¼ teaspoon paprika. Sauté about 12 minutes or until mushrooms are tender and onions are browned.

Add mushroom mixture, eggs and parsley to noodles; mix well. Taste and adjust seasoning. Butter or oil a 6-cup baking dish. Spoon in noodle and mushroom mixture. Sprinkle with remaining 1 tablespoon oil or butter, then with remaining ½ teaspoon paprika. Bake 30 minutes or until set. Serve from baking dish.

Makes 4 or 5 side-dish servings.

VARIATION

Noodle Kugel with Mushrooms & Sour Cream: Stir 1 cup sour cream into noodle mixture before baking.

Pasta & Cheese Timbales with Roasted-Pepper Sauce

Molding pasta as timbales has long been popular in Italy. Often Italian pasta timbales contain béchamel sauce but this simpler version does not. It is served with a vibrant red sauce of roasted bell peppers.

6 ounces small pasta shells
  (about 2 cups)
1/3 cup plus 1 tablespoon ricotta
  cheese
3/4 cup whipping cream
3 large eggs
2 1/4 cups grated asiago or
  Gruyère cheese (about 6 oz.)
1/3 cup chopped fresh parsley
  leaves
1/3 cup chopped green onions
1 1/2 tablespoons chopped fresh
  thyme leaves or 1 1/2 teaspoons
  dried leaf, crumbled

Freshly grated nutmeg to taste
Salt and freshly ground pepper to
  taste
Unseasoned dry bread crumbs
  for coating ramekins
Roasted-Red-Pepper Sauce, see
  below
1/4 cup butter, cut in 4 pieces,
  chilled

Preheat oven to 375F (190C). Bring a large pot of water to a boil; add salt, then pasta. Cook uncovered over high heat, stirring occasionally, about 5 minutes or until nearly tender but firmer than usual, because pasta will be baked. Drain, rinse with cold water and drain well.

Mix ricotta with cream in a medium bowl. Stir in eggs. Stir in grated cheese, parsley, green onions, thyme and pasta. Season with nutmeg, salt and pepper.

Butter 4 (1- to 1 1/4-cup) ramekins. Line base of each with a round of foil or waxed paper. Butter foil or paper. Coat bases and sides of ramekins with bread crumbs.

Fill ramekins with pasta mixture. Put in a roasting pan. Add enough boiling water to pan to come halfway up sides of ramekins. Set a sheet of buttered foil over ramekins. Bake about 1 hour or until firm when touched on top; top will feel oily but batter should not stick to your finger. Meanwhile, prepare Roasted-Red-Pepper Sauce; set aside.

Remove timbales from water and let stand about 5 minutes. Run a thin-bladed knife carefully around each timbale. Unmold by inverting on heated plates and, holding mold with plate, tapping together on towel-lined surface. Carefully lift mold straight up.

Just before serving, bring sauce to a simmer. Reduce heat to low. Stir in cold butter, 1 piece at a time. Remove from heat as soon as butter is absorbed.

Spoon a little sauce around base of timbales and more sauce over timbales to half cover them. Serve any remaining sauce separately.
Makes 4 main-course servings.

Roasted-Red-Pepper Sauce

2 red bell peppers
2 medium shallots, minced
1 1/2 teaspoons fresh thyme leaves
  or 1/2 teaspoon dried leaf,
  crumbled

1/2 cup dry white wine
1 cup chicken stock or broth,
  homemade, page 187, or
  packaged

Preheat broiler. Broil bell peppers about 2 inches from heat source, turning about every 5 minutes with tongs, until pepper skin is blistered and charred, 15 to 25 minutes. Transfer to a plastic bag and close bag. Let stand 10 minutes. Peel using a paring knife, see photo page 95. Halve peppers and discard seeds and ribs. Drain well and pat dry. Puree in a food processor until smooth.

Combine shallots, thyme and wine in a medium saucepan; bring to a boil. Boil about 2 minutes. Add 1/2 cup stock and boil until liquid is reduced to about 1/2 cup. Stir in pepper puree and remaining 1/2 cup stock. (Sauce can be prepared 1 day ahead and kept, covered, in refrigerator.)

EXOTIC PASTA

This chapter is designed to give ideas for using the pastas found in supermarkets in the Oriental and "gourmet" sections. It is not necessary to know Oriental cooking techniques in order to use these noodles and they can add great variety to Western menus.

When I visited the Orient on a culinary study trip, I was fascinated by the fresh-noodle stands at the markets. There was a wide selection of fresh Chinese noodles that in the West I had seen only packaged in their dried form. Won-ton and other wrappers were also displayed. I enjoyed the pasta in delicious yet simple soups which owed their excellence to the pure flavor of good chicken stock, or tossed with very fresh seafood or crunchy vegetables. In recent years more types of Oriental pastas, and even fresh Chinese noodles, have become increasingly available in this country.

MAJOR TYPES OF ORIENTAL NOODLES AND HOW TO USE THEM
Western pastas are made primarily of wheat flour, while Asian pastas are also made of rice flour, bean starch and other flours. Even when made of wheat flour, Oriental noodles possess

Chinese Noodles with Oriental Vegetables, page 150, and Couscous with Red Pepper, Walnuts & Fresh Herbs, page 155

145

a different taste and texture from Western ones. They are generally described as Chinese or Japanese but are also used in Thai, Vietnamese and other Asian cuisines.

Oriental wheat-flour noodles come in several types and are cooked and used much like Western noodles. The most delicious are fresh Chinese egg noodles which are available in cities with a large Chinatown. In many supermarkets there are now fresh Chinese noodles, which are quite good.

Dried Chinese wheat noodles are made either without egg or with some egg and are sometimes labeled *Chinese spaghetti*. A similar type of thin, bright-yellow, Japanese wheat noodle is often labeled *Japanese-style alimentary paste* or *chuka soba*.

Udon are straight, white, chewy, Japanese wheat noodles in varying widths, from thin ones that resemble linguine to much thicker ones. Still another type of Japanese wheat noodle is *somen*. These very thin, delicate, white noodles are sometimes labeled *Oriental vermicelli* but look more like white angel-hair pasta.

Japanese buckwheat noodles, made of a mixture of wheat flour, buckwheat flour and Japanese yam flour, are beige and shaped like linguine. They have plenty of character and are good when paired with flavorful ingredients as in Buckwheat Noodles with Prosciutto, Mushrooms & Cilantro. Like wheat noodles, buckwheat noodles can be cooked in the same way as Western pasta.

Rice sticks, rice vermicelli and *rice noodles (mai fun)* are white, usually very thin and come in skeins. They often resemble spaghettini although some are flat like linguine. They can be prepared by several cooking techniques. The most unusual and most fun is deep frying because they puff up beautifully in seconds. Rice noodles can also be cooked in boiling liquid like other noodles, or cooked directly in a sauce, but they are usually soaked in warm water before being cooked by these methods.

Bean threads or *cellophane noodles (sai fun)* are made from mung beans and resemble thin rice noodles when dry, although very thin bean threads may look almost translucent. When cooked, bean threads become transparent and are therefore sometimes called *silver noodles*. This intriguing quality, and their ability to absorb flavors, makes them interesting to use. Like rice noodles, bean threads usually require soaking before cooking and can be cooked by the same techniques.

Oriental wheat noodles, rice noodles and bean threads are also delicious in soup, such as Chicken Soup with Rice Noodles, Spinach & Chinese Mushrooms, page 163, and Delicate Chicken Soup with Bean Threads, page 162.

Fresh won-ton wrappers, made of wheat flour, are another type of widely available Oriental pasta. In addition to traditional won tons, they are great for easy-to-make ravioli, page 124.

Our recipes are not classic Chinese, Japanese or Thai noodle dishes, but rather use Oriental and Western flavorings to illustrate some delicious ways to use Oriental noodles.

COUSCOUS

Although many people think couscous is a grain because of its tiny particles, it is actually a pasta. Like Italian dried pastas, it is made of durum wheat semolina. The light, delicate texture of couscous bears a certain resemblance to that of rice and other grains.

I first learned to prepare couscous from a Tunisian woman when I lived in Israel. In the traditional manner, she lightly moistened the couscous, placed it in a special small-holed steamer called a *couscoussier,* and steamed the couscous several times above a simmering meat stew. After each steaming she removed the couscous and rubbed it carefully between her fingers to be sure the grains were separate. Watching her was fascinating but the steaming procedure was very time-consuming.

My next introduction to couscous was in Paris, where it was cooked by a French chef. He prepared a fragrant stew to accompany the couscous but seemed to ignore the couscous itself. Just before serving time, I was astonished to see him pour hot chicken stock over the couscous and toss in a pat of butter. The couscous was ready in just a few minutes.

Like the traditional technique for cooking couscous, the quick method is essentially steaming. Boiling water, stock or milk is poured over the couscous in a saucepan or skillet and the pan is covered tightly. The steam that is created tenderizes the grains, which absorb the liquid and expand.

Couscous is the most famous specialty of the cuisine of the Maghreb countries of Morocco, Algeria and Tunisia, but is also widespread in France. Like pasta, couscous is a wonderful partner for seafood, poultry and meat, whether they are broiled, roasted, sautéed, or served in sauce, as in Moroccan Chicken with Almonds & Couscous. It can be tossed with these foods for a main course or a first course or served alongside them as an accompaniment. Combined with vegetables, nuts or cheeses, it can be the basis for a vegetarian meal. With the addition of vinaigrette and fresh vegetables, couscous becomes a salad as in Couscous Salad with Tomatoes, Pine Nuts & Mint, page 36. It can even be made into desserts, such as Couscous with Strawberries & Cream, page 172.

Couscous is available at specialty food stores, natural foods shops, Middle Eastern stores and many supermarkets. Instructions for how to prepare quick couscous vary among the different brands and some are labeled "precooked," but with all of them the quick-steam method used in the couscous recipes in this chapter produces light, fluffy couscous.

1. Bean threads (sai fun), 2. Couscous, 3. Fresh Chinese wheat noodles, 4. Chinese spaghetti, 5. Buckwheat noodles, 6. Chuka soba, 7. Won-ton wrappers, 8. Rice sticks (mai fun), 9. Udon, 10. Somen

Japanese Noodles with Napa Cabbage, Shiitake Mushrooms & Sesame Oil

1 ounce dried shiitake
  mushrooms
About ¹/₂ head or 1¹/₂ pounds
  Napa cabbage (also called
  Chinese cabbage)
3 tablespoons vegetable oil
2 medium garlic cloves, minced
1 tablespoon minced peeled
  gingerroot
2 tablespoons soy sauce

¹/₂ cup chicken stock or broth
1 (10-oz.) package thin dried
  udon, or linguine-shaped
  Japanese wheat noodles
1 tablespoon Oriental sesame oil
2 tablespoons plus 1 teaspoon
  chopped green onions
¹/₂ teaspoon Oriental chili oil or
  Tabasco sauce, or more if
  desired

In a medium bowl, soak mushrooms in hot water to cover 30 minutes. Remove from water. Rinse and squeeze gently to remove excess water. Cut off and discard stems; quarter caps.

Cut off and discard 2¹/₂ inches of base of cabbage. Finely shred enough cabbage to obtain 6 cups.

Heat vegetable oil in a wok, large skillet or deep sauté pan over medium-high heat. Add garlic and gingerroot. Cook, stirring, a few seconds. Add cabbage and mushrooms. Cook, tossing, until cabbage wilts, about 2 minutes. Add soy sauce and chicken stock; bring to a boil. Remove from heat and cover.

Bring a large pot of water to a boil; add salt, then noodles. Cook uncovered over high heat, stirring often with chopsticks or a fork, about 9 minutes or until tender but firm to the bite. Drain well. Transfer to a large heated serving bowl. Toss with sesame oil.

Reheat sauce to simmer. Add to noodles and toss. Add 2 tablespoons chopped green onions and chili oil to taste. Sprinkle with remaining 1 teaspoon green onion and serve.
Makes 4 side-dish servings.

Chinese Noodles with Beef, Ginger & Plum Sauce

8 ounces ground beef
7 tablespoons vegetable oil
5 tablespoons soy sauce
8 ounces snow peas, ends and
  strings removed, cut in half
  crosswise
1¹/₂ cups sliced peeled celery
3 tablespoons minced peeled
  gingerroot

¹/₂ cup chicken stock or broth
1 pound fresh or 12 ounces dried
  Chinese or Japanese egg or
  wheat noodles (sometimes
  called Chinese spaghetti) or
  regular spaghetti
3 tablespoons plum sauce
¹/₄ cup chopped green onions

Combine beef, 1 tablespoon oil and 1 tablespoon soy sauce in a medium bowl; mix well and set aside.

Add snow peas to a large saucepan of enough boiling salted water to cover generously. Cook uncovered over high heat 1 minute. Drain, rinse with cold water and drain well.

Heat a wok or large skillet. Add 4 tablespoons oil and heat over medium heat. Add celery and sauté about 3 minutes or until crisp-tender. Remove with a slotted spoon. Add gingerroot and stir, then add beef mixture. Sauté over medium heat, crumbling with a fork, about 4 minutes or until beef changes color.

Add stock or broth and remaining 4 tablespoons soy sauce; bring to a simmer. Return celery to skillet. (Sauce can be kept, covered, up to 1 day in refrigerator, although celery will be less crisp; refrigerate snow peas separately.)

If using fresh Chinese noodles, spread on a plate and fluff to separate. Bring a large pot of water to a boil; add salt, then noodles. Cook uncovered over high heat, stirring often with chopsticks or a fork, 2 to 5 minutes for fresh noodles or 7 to 8 minutes for dried or until tender but firm to the bite. Drain, rinse with cold water and drain well. Transfer to a large heated serving bowl. Toss with remaining 2 tablespoons oil.

Reheat beef sauce if necessary. Add plum sauce, snow peas and green onions. Heat a few seconds. Remove from heat, add to noodles and toss. Serve hot. Makes 4 main-course servings.

Spicy Somen with Steak Strips, Chiles & Mint

4 green onions
8 ounces good-quality boneless steak, such as rib-eye, excess fat trimmed
6 ounces somen (very thin white Japanese wheat noodles)
9 tablespoons vegetable oil
1 medium onion, halved lengthwise, cut in thin slices, separated in half-rings

2 serrano chiles, halved lengthwise
4 garlic cloves, minced
1/2 cup beef broth
2 tablespoons soy sauce
2 tablespoons oyster sauce
1 cup whole fresh mint leaves

This hot and spicy pasta is inspired by a dish I often enjoy at a Thai restaurant in Santa Monica, where it is made with wide rice noodles. I have substituted the more available Japanese somen, very thin, white noodles made of wheat. If you've never cooked these noodles, you are in for a pleasant surprise. They give the dish a creamy quality that is a perfect foil for its spiciness.

Chop white and light-green parts of green onions. Cut dark-green part in 3-inch pieces. Cut steak in 3" x 1/4" x 1/4" strips.

Bring a large pot of water to a boil; add salt, then noodles. Cook uncovered over high heat, stirring often with chopsticks or a fork, about 1 1/2 minutes or until just tender. Drain well. Transfer to a large bowl. Toss with 1 tablespoon oil.

Heat 3 tablespoons oil in a large skillet or wok over medium heat. Add sliced onion and chiles. Sauté, stirring, about 7 minutes or until onion browns lightly; it may still be a bit crunchy. Transfer to a medium bowl.

Add 2 tablespoons oil to skillet and heat over high heat. Add steak and sauté until it changes color, about 1 minute; do not overcook. Add to onions.

Add remaining 3 tablespoons oil to skillet and heat over medium-low heat. Add garlic and all of green onions. Sauté 30 seconds. Add noodles and heat through. Add broth, soy sauce and oyster sauce; heat through. Add sautéed steak, onion slices, chiles and mint leaves. Toss 30 seconds over low heat. Serve on heated plates. Chiles can be removed or left in for garnish. They are extremely hot.
Makes 2 or 3 main-course servings.

Oriental wheat noodles are usually more starchy than Western-style noodles and therefore require thinner sauces.

COOKING TIP

Chinese Noodles with Oriental Vegetables

Even if you have not done any Chinese cooking, do not hesitate to try this dish, which is popular in many Chinese restaurants. It is colorful and delicious, and although the list of ingredients might appear long, it is quick and easy to cook. If using baby corn, use the type that is canned in water and salt, and not corn pickled with vinegar. When available, use fresh baby corn and blanch briefly in boiling water.

◆ *Photo on page 144.*

1 ounce dried shiitake mushrooms (about 10 large)
2 medium carrots
6 ounces fresh water chestnuts or 1 (8-oz.) can whole water chestnuts
12 ounces bok choy
1 pound fresh Chinese noodles or 12 ounces dried Chinese noodles or Japanese chuka soba (yellow wheat noodles)
7 tablespoons peanut oil or vegetable oil
Rice-Wine Sauce, see below
3 large garlic cloves, minced
1 tablespoon minced peeled gingerroot

2 ounces snow peas, ends and strings removed (½ cup)
⅓ cup sliced green onions, green part only
1 (8-oz.) can bamboo shoots, drained, rinsed
8 ears rinsed canned or cooked frozen baby corn, if desired
1 (3- to 3½-oz.) package enoki mushrooms, bases trimmed off, rinsed well
2 teaspoons Oriental sesame oil
Salt and freshly ground pepper, if desired
2 tablespoons coarsely chopped cilantro (fresh coriander) leaves, if desired

In a medium bowl, soak mushrooms in hot water to cover 30 minutes. Remove from water. Rinse and squeeze gently to remove excess water. Cut off and discard stems; quarter caps.

Peel carrots. Put in a medium saucepan and add water to cover. Bring to a simmer and cook over medium heat 5 minutes. Drain, rinse with cold water and drain well. Cut in thin crosswise slices.

Peel fresh water chestnuts, if using. Add to a medium saucepan of boiling water to generously cover. Cook 3 minutes. Drain, rinse with cold water and drain well. Cut in thin slices. If using canned water chestnuts, rinse and drain; cut each chestnut in half to make rounds.

Separate bok choy leaves from stalks; reserve stalks for other uses. Tear leaves in bite-size pieces.

If using fresh Chinese noodles, spread on a plate and fluff to separate. Bring a large pot of water to a boil; add salt, then noodles. Cook uncovered over high heat, stirring often with chopsticks or a fork, 2 to 5 minutes for fresh noodles or 3 to 8 minutes for dried or until tender but firm to the bite. Drain, rinse with cold water and drain well. Transfer to a large bowl. Toss with 2 tablespoons oil.

Prepare Rice-Wine Sauce; set aside. (Ingredients can be prepared ahead up to this point and kept about 2 hours at room temperature.)

Heat a wok, a large deep skillet or a sauté pan. Add 4 tablespoons oil and heat over medium-high heat. Add garlic and gingerroot. Stir-fry about 10 seconds. Add carrots and cook 1 minute, then add snow peas and cook 1 minute. Add dried mushrooms, green onions, water chestnuts, bamboo shoots, baby corn, if desired, and enoki mushrooms. Cook, tossing, 1 minute. Add bok choy leaves and cook 30 seconds. Add ¼ cup sauce and bring to a boil, stirring. Cook until leaves wilt. Transfer mixture to a bowl. Wipe pan dry.

Add remaining 1 tablespoon oil to pan and heat over medium-high heat. Add noodles and sauté 30 seconds. Add remaining sauce and toss over heat until noodles are coated and hot. Remove from heat. Sprinkle with sesame oil and toss. Taste and add salt and pepper if desired. To serve, put pasta on hot plates and spoon vegetables on top. Sprinkle with cilantro, if desired.

Makes 4 main-course or 6 first-course or side-dish servings.

Rice-Wine Sauce

¼ cup soy sauce
3 tablespoons rice wine or dry sherry
½ teaspoon sugar

¼ teaspoon hot red-pepper flakes
¾ cup chicken stock or broth, homemade, page 187, or packaged

Combine ingredients in a medium bowl and mix well.

Oriental Noodle & Vegetable Salad with Peanut-Butter Dressing

This colorful dish is an American adaptation of a Chinese cold noodle dish with a sesame-paste dressing. Fresh crunchy vegetables and a tasty peanut-butter dressing with soy sauce, ginger and chili oil make it delightful.

1 pound fresh Chinese egg or wheat noodles or fresh linguine or 12 ounces dried
2 tablespoons Oriental sesame oil
8 ounces green beans, ends removed, broken in 2 or 3 pieces
4 ounces white mushrooms
1 teaspoon strained fresh lemon juice

3 ounces bean sprouts, ends removed
1 medium zucchini, cut in thin strips, or 4-inch piece cucumber, cut in thin slices
1 medium carrot, coarsely grated
Peanut-Butter Dressing, see below
2 to 4 tablespoons chicken stock or broth, if desired

If using fresh Chinese noodles, spread on a plate and fluff to separate. Bring a large pot of water to a boil; add salt, then pasta. Cook uncovered over high heat, stirring often with chopsticks or a fork, 2 to 5 minutes for fresh noodles or 7 to 8 minutes for dried or until tender but firm to the bite. Drain, rinse with cold water and drain well. Transfer to a large bowl; toss with sesame oil.

Add green beans to a large saucepan of enough boiling salted water to cover generously. Cook uncovered over high heat about 5 minutes or until crisp-tender. Drain, rinse with cold water and drain well. Add to noodles.

Halve mushrooms and cut in thin slices. Sprinkle with lemon juice, toss and add to noodles. Reserve a few bean sprouts and zucchini strips and a little grated carrot for garnish. Add remaining bean sprouts, zucchini (but not cucumber) and carrot to noodle mixture.

Prepare Peanut-Butter Dressing and toss with noodle mixture. If mixture is too thick, add stock by spoonfuls until salad is moist. Taste and add more soy sauce or chili oil if desired.

Garnish with reserved vegetables. If using cucumber, arrange slices around edge of serving bowl. (Salad can be kept, covered, 8 hours in refrigerator. Bring to room temperature before serving.)
Makes 4 to 6 first-course servings.

Peanut-Butter Dressing

1/2 cup creamy peanut butter
1/2 cup warm chicken stock or broth
3 tablespoons Oriental sesame oil
3 tablespoons soy sauce, or more if desired
1 tablespoon rice vinegar

1 teaspoon Oriental chili oil or Tabasco sauce, or more if desired
1 tablespoon minced garlic
1 tablespoon minced peeled gingerroot
1 teaspoon sugar

Combine ingredients in a food processor and process until well blended.

Turkey & Asparagus Salad with Deep-Fried Rice Noodles

12 ounces fresh asparagus or 1 (8-oz.) package frozen spears, thawed
3 cups chicken stock or broth, homemade, page 187, or packaged
1 pound boneless turkey breast (turkey tenderloin), about 1 inch thick
Salt
Oriental Vinaigrette, see below

½ cup raw or toasted cashews
3 ounces thin rice noodles, rice sticks or rice vermicelli
About 3 cups vegetable oil (for frying)
¼ cup minced green onions
½ cup coarsely grated carrot
1 or 2 heads Boston lettuce or butter lettuce
1 or 2 heads radicchio, if desired

Peel fresh asparagus. Discard tough bases. Cut 2-inch tips from fresh or frozen asparagus. Cut stalks in ¼-inch diagonal slices. Add tips and slices to a medium saucepan of enough boiling salted water to cover generously. Cook uncovered over high heat about 2 minutes or until crisp-tender. Rinse and drain well.

Bring stock or broth to a simmer in a medium skillet. Add turkey breast. Cover and cook over very low heat about 10 minutes. To check if turkey is done, cut into thickest part; meat should be whitish and have lost its raw pink color. Remove from stock and cool. (Stock can be reused.) Shred turkey by pulling it apart.

Prepare Oriental Vinaigrette. Add turkey to vinaigrette and toss. (Salad can be prepared 1 day ahead to this point and kept, covered, in refrigerator.)

If using raw cashews, preheat oven to 350F (175C). Toast cashews in oven, stirring occasionally, about 8 minutes or until golden. Transfer to a plate and reserve at room temperature.

Hold rice noodles inside a paper bag so they won't scatter and break in about 3-inch pieces. Prepare paper towels and a large slotted spoon. Pour enough oil into a medium sauté pan so it is 1 inch deep. Heat over medium-high heat; when oil is hot enough, a rice noodle added should puff in a few seconds. Add about ⅛ of rice noodles. They will puff in a few seconds. Immediately remove with slotted spoon and transfer to paper towels. Repeat with remaining rice noodles in small batches.

Transfer turkey mixture to a large bowl. Add asparagus, green onions and carrot. Toss to combine. On 4 or 6 plates, make a bed of lettuce leaves, or set 2 radicchio leaves alternating with 2 green lettuce leaves. Leave a space in center.

Lightly crush enough fried noodles to make 1 quart. Just before serving, add these noodles to turkey salad and toss lightly. Using remaining fried noodles, make a bed of noodles on each plate and spoon turkey salad over noodles. Sprinkle toasted cashews on top.

Makes 4 main-course or 6 first-course servings.

Oriental Vinaigrette

2 tablespoons plus 1 teaspoon rice vinegar
¼ cup vegetable oil
2 tablespoons Oriental sesame oil
1 tablespoon soy sauce

1 teaspoon sugar
2 teaspoons finely grated peeled gingerroot
½ teaspoon Oriental chili oil or Tabasco, or to taste

Combine ingredients in a medium bowl and whisk until sugar dissolves.

Note: Salad is still good next day, although noodles are no longer crunchy.

Turkey & Asparagus Salad with Deep-Fried Rice Noodles

Add about ¹/₈ of rice noodles at a time to hot oil in pan. Noodles will puff in a few seconds. Immediately remove with a slotted spoon and transfer to paper towels.

Buckwheat Noodles with Prosciutto, Mushrooms & Cilantro

Japanese buckwheat noodles can be found in the Oriental sections of some supermarkets. They are good with assertive ingredients like the garlic, cilantro and prosciutto here. If buckwheat noodles are not available, use spaghetti or whole-wheat noodles. Smoked turkey or ham can be substituted for the prosciutto. The cilantro can be replaced by parsley.

4 tablespoons olive oil
2 teaspoons finely minced peeled gingerroot
8 ounces mushrooms, halved, sliced thin
Salt and freshly ground pepper to taste
4 large garlic cloves, minced

8 or 9 ounces Japanese buckwheat noodles
4 ounces ripe tomatoes, peeled, seeded, diced
2 ounces thinly sliced prosciutto, cut in 3" x ¼" strips
4 tablespoons chopped cilantro (fresh coriander) leaves

Heat 2 tablespoons olive oil in a large skillet over medium-high heat. Add gingerroot and mushrooms. Sprinkle with salt and pepper. Sauté 5 minutes or until mushrooms are tender and lightly browned. Add garlic and sauté 30 seconds. Remove from heat.

Bring a large pot of water to a boil; add salt, then noodles. Cook uncovered over high heat, stirring often with chopsticks or a fork, 3 to 4 minutes or until tender but firm to the bite. Drain well. Transfer to a heated serving bowl.

Add mushroom mixture and remaining 2 tablespoons olive oil; toss. Add tomatoes, prosciutto and 3 tablespoons cilantro; toss again. Sprinkle with remaining 1 tablespoon cilantro and serve hot.

Makes 4 first-course servings.

Oriental rice noodles are wonderful with Western-style dishes. The thin rice noodles soften very quickly and require only brief soaking before being heated in the aromatic butter.

Shrimp with Rice Noodles & Spiced Butter

Spiced Butter, see below
1 jalapeño pepper, if desired
7 ounces thin dried rice noodles, rice sticks or rice vermicelli
2 large garlic cloves, minced
1 pound medium or large shrimp, shelled, deveined if desired, rinsed, patted dry

¹/₂ cup minced green onions
¹/₄ cup bottled clam juice
¹/₂ cup whipping cream
Red (cayenne) pepper to taste
1 tablespoon minced fresh parsley leaves

Prepare Spiced Butter; set aside. Wearing gloves, halve jalapeño pepper, if using, and remove seeds and ribs; mince pepper. Wash hands, cutting board and any utensils that came in contact with jalapeño pepper, with soap and hot water.

Put noodles in a large bowl. Cover generously with hot water and soak 10 minutes. Drain well.

Melt 4 tablespoons Spiced Butter in a large deep skillet or sauté pan over medium heat. Add garlic and jalapeño pepper and stir, then add shrimp. Sauté, tossing often, 1¹/₂ to 2 minutes or until shrimp are pink. Transfer to a platter.

Add remaining Spiced Butter to skillet. Add rice noodles and sauté over medium heat about 2 minutes. Add green onions and sauté about 1 minute. Add clam juice and heat until absorbed. Add cream and heat until absorbed and noodles are tender but slightly firm to bite.

Return shrimp to skillet and toss lightly over low heat. Add red pepper; taste and adjust seasoning. Transfer to a heated serving dish or to heated plates and sprinkle with parsley.
Makes 4 main-course servings.

Spiced Butter

¹/₂ cup (4 oz.) butter, softened
2 teaspoons ground cumin
¹/₂ teaspoon turmeric

1 teaspoon ground coriander
Salt and freshly ground pepper to taste

Combine ingredients in a medium bowl and mix well.

This light, delicate dish is based on a recipe I learned at the Wei Chuan Cooking School in Taipei during a fabulous course in Chinese cuisine directed by Nina Simonds, one of America's top teachers of Chinese cooking. For a colorful entree, use snow crab.

Rice Noodles with Crab & Bok Choy

7 ounces very thin rice noodles or rice vermicelli
1 pound fresh crabmeat
1¹/₂ pounds bok choy
6 tablespoons vegetable oil
1 tablespoon minced garlic
1 tablespoon plus 1 teaspoon minced peeled gingerroot
²/₃ cup minced green onions
3 tablespoons rice wine or dry sherry

1 cup chicken stock or broth, homemade, page 187, or packaged
Salt and freshly ground pepper to taste
¹/₂ cup very thin carrot strips (¹/₂ medium)
1 (15-oz.) can straw mushrooms, drained
1 tablespoon soy sauce
2 tablespoons Oriental sesame oil

Put noodles in a large bowl. Cover generously with hot water and soak 10 minutes. Drain well. Pick through crabmeat and discard any pieces of shell or cartilage. Dice any large pieces.

Keeping bok choy leaves and stalks separate as you cut, cut each crosswise in strips about ¼ inch wide. Bring a large pan of water to a boil, add salt and bok choy stalks. Boil about 2 minutes or until crisp-tender. Add leaves and cook 1 minute. Drain, rinse with cold water and drain well.

Heat a wok or large deep skillet over high heat. Add 3 tablespoons oil and heat. Add garlic, gingerroot and ⅓ cup green onions; stir-fry about 10 seconds. Add crab and wine; heat about 30 seconds. Add ¼ cup chicken broth; bring to a simmer. Pour mixture into a medium bowl.

Add 2 tablespoons oil to wok and heat over medium heat. Add bok choy. Sprinkle with salt and pepper; toss over heat a few seconds. Transfer to bowl of crab mixture.

Add remaining 1 tablespoon oil to wok and heat. Add carrot and remaining ⅓ cup green onions; stir-fry about 30 seconds. Add ¾ cup chicken broth and mushrooms; bring to a boil. Add rice noodles and simmer over medium-high heat about 2 minutes or until just tender and broth is absorbed. Add soy sauce and toss.

Add crab mixture and toss over low heat. Remove from heat. Add sesame oil and toss. Taste and adjust seasoning. Serve on heated plates.
Makes 4 or 5 main-course servings.

Couscous with Red Pepper, Walnuts & Fresh Herbs

2 teaspoons vegetable oil
Salt and freshly ground pepper to taste
½ cup walnut pieces
1 small red bell pepper, seeds and ribs discarded, cut in 2" x ¼" strips
¼ cup olive oil
1 cup couscous

1 cup boiling water
1 teaspoon strained fresh lemon juice
3 tablespoons minced fresh parsley leaves
3 tablespoons coarsely chopped fresh basil leaves
8 small fresh basil leaves, for garnish, if desired

Heat vegetable oil in a small skillet over medium heat. Add walnuts and a pinch of salt. Sauté, stirring often, about 2 minutes or until lightly browned. Transfer to a plate.

Set aside a few pepper strips for garnish, if desired. Heat 2 tablespoons olive oil in a large skillet over medium-low heat. Add remaining pepper strips and cook, stirring often, about 5 minutes or until softened. Add couscous and a pinch of salt and pepper; stir mixture with a fork until blended. Remove skillet from heat and shake to spread couscous in an even layer. Pour boiling water evenly over couscous, immediately cover skillet tightly and let stand 5 minutes.

Fluff mixture with a fork to break up any lumps in couscous. Drizzle lemon juice and remaining 2 tablespoons olive oil over mixture. Add parsley, chopped basil and walnuts; toss. Taste and adjust seasoning. Transfer to a serving dish or to plates. Garnish with basil leaves, if desired. Serve couscous hot or at room temperature.
Makes 4 first-course or side-dish servings.

In perfectly made couscous, each grain is tender but not mushy and is separate from the others. The North African cooks' technique of rubbing couscous between their fingers and tossing it is useful to remember if the grains begin to clump, although fluffing cooked couscous with a fork is usually enough. For this colorful dish, couscous is sautéed with red peppers and then steamed. Accented with sautéed walnuts and fresh basil, it makes a lovely appetizer or accompaniment for roast chicken.
◆ *Photo on page 144.*

It is best to use a fork for stirring ingredients into couscous to avoid crushing the grains and causing them to stick together.

COOKING TIP

155

Moroccan Chicken with Almonds & Couscous

Buttery couscous is served with chicken in a rich sweet-and-savory sauce of prunes, honey and cinnamon. Sautéed almonds provide the final touch to this spectacular dish.

Large pinch of saffron threads
   (about ¹/₈ teaspoon)
¹/₄ cup hot water
1 (3- to 3¹/₂-lb.) chicken (with
   giblets), cut in 4 serving pieces,
   patted dry
¹/₂ teaspoon salt
¹/₄ teaspoon freshly ground
   pepper
2 medium onions, minced
3 tablespoons butter

1 (2-inch) cinnamon stick
³/₄ cup water
2 tablespoons vegetable oil
1 cup whole blanched almonds
   (5 oz.) (see Note below)
1¹/₂ cups moist pitted prunes
   (8 oz.)
2 tablespoons mild honey
Freshly grated nutmeg to taste
Couscous, see below

Add saffron to ¹/₄ cup hot water in a cup and let stand 20 minutes. Combine chicken pieces, back, neck, gizzard, wing tips, salt, pepper, onions and butter in a heavy stainless steel or enameled casserole. Cover and cook over low heat, turning chicken pieces over occasionally, 15 minutes.

Add saffron mixture, cinnamon stick and ³/₄ cup water, pushing cinnamon stick into liquid. Bring to a boil. Cover and simmer over low heat, turning chicken pieces over from time to time, about 25 minutes or until breast pieces are tender when pierced with a knife. Transfer breast pieces with tongs to a plate. Cook remaining pieces, covered, over low heat, about 10 minutes or until very tender. Transfer leg pieces to plate, leaving as much of chopped onion as possible in casserole. Discard neck, gizzard, wing tips and back.

Heat oil in a large skillet over medium-high heat. Add almonds and sauté, tossing often with a slotted spoon, about 5 minutes or until lightly browned. Transfer to paper towels. Sprinkle lightly with salt.

Add prunes to chicken cooking liquid. Cook, uncovered, over medium heat 15 to 20 minutes or until just tender. Add honey and cook, stirring gently to avoid breaking up prunes, about 5 minutes or until sauce thickens. Add nutmeg; taste and adjust seasoning. Discard cinnamon stick. With a slotted spoon, transfer prunes to a heated bowl, leaving as much of chopped onions as possible in casserole. Cover prunes to keep warm.

Return chicken pieces to casserole and turn to coat with sauce. Cover and reheat over low heat 5 minutes. (Chicken can be kept, covered, 2 days in refrigerator; refrigerate prunes separately. Cover almonds and keep at room temperature. Reheat chicken in sauce over low heat, covered. Remove chicken, then reheat prunes in sauce.)

Prepare Couscous; mound on a heated platter. Arrange chicken around couscous and spoon sauce and about ²/₃ of prunes over chicken. Garnish with about ¹/₃ of almonds. Serve remaining prunes and almonds in separate dishes.
Makes 4 servings.

Couscous

4 tablespoons butter
1¹/₄ cups water
1¹/₄ cups couscous

Salt and freshly ground pepper to
   taste

Cut 2 tablespoons butter in small pieces and put in a medium saucepan. Add water and bring to a boil. Stir in couscous and a pinch of salt and pepper; cover pan immediately and let couscous stand, off heat, 5 minutes. Cut remaining 2 tablespoons butter in small pieces and scatter over couscous. Cover and let couscous stand 1 minute. Fluff couscous with a fork to break up any lumps, tossing until butter is absorbed. Taste couscous and adjust seasoning.

Note: To blanch almonds with skins, add to a pan of boiling water and boil 10 seconds; drain. Press end of each almond to remove it from skin. Dry peeled almonds thoroughly on paper towels before using.

Thai Chicken with Bean Threads & Ginger Julienne

4 large dried shiitake mushrooms
1¼ pounds boneless chicken thighs, skin removed
Pinch of red (cayenne) pepper
2 tablespoons soy sauce
6 large garlic cloves, minced
1 (2-oz.) piece gingerroot (about 2½" x 1½" x 1¼"), peeled
7 to 8 ounces bean threads, broken in 4-inch lengths
½ cup thin carrot slices

Oyster-Clam Sauce, see below
¼ cup peanut oil or vegetable oil
1 medium onion, halved, sliced thin
5 medium-size green onions, cut in 2-inch lengths
1½ cups chicken stock or broth, homemade, page 187, or packaged
2 tablespoons chopped cilantro (fresh coriander) leaves

At home I call this aromatic Thai sauté "Chicken Somchit Singchalee," for my close friend from Bangkok who gave me fascinating lessons in Thai cooking when we were both studying French cooking in Paris. The ginger strips provide plenty of zest but if you would like the heat of chiles, add 1 to 3 chopped seeded serrano, jalapeño or other hot chiles at the same time as the garlic. Or accompany the dish with a chili sauce, preferably from Thailand, China or Japan, but even Mexican chili sauce, Louisiana hot sauce or Tabasco will be fine. Thai cooks would add 1 or 2 tablespoons bottled fish sauce (nam pla) instead of the clam juice. If you prefer, substitute fresh basil or mint for the cilantro.

In a small bowl, soak mushrooms in hot water to cover 30 minutes. Remove from water. Rinse and squeeze gently to remove excess water. Cut off and discard stems. Cut caps in strips ¼ inch wide.

Trim fat from chicken. Cut chicken in wide strips of about 3" x ½" x ½". Put in a medium bowl. Add red pepper, soy sauce, and 2 teaspoons minced garlic; mix well. Let stand to marinate about 20 minutes.

Cut gingerroot in ⅛-inch-thick strips; you will have about ⅔ cup strips. Soak in a small bowl of cold water about 15 minutes. Drain and pat dry.

Put bean threads in a large bowl. Cover generously with warm water (or boiling water, if specified on package) and soak 10 minutes. Drain well.

Put carrot slices in a small saucepan and add water to cover; bring to a boil. Simmer over medium heat about 3 minutes or until crisp-tender. Drain well.

Prepare Oyster-Clam Sauce; set aside. Heat oil in a large skillet or wok over medium-high heat. Add sliced onion and remaining minced garlic. Sauté about 3 minutes or until onion is crisp-tender. Add chicken mixture and sauté, tossing often, about 5 minutes or until chicken is tender. Add green onions, carrots, mushrooms, gingerroot and sauce; bring to a boil, tossing. Transfer to a bowl. Reserve skillet.

Add stock to skillet and bring to a boil. Add bean threads and cook about 5 minutes or until translucent. Return chicken mixture to pan and toss over low heat 1 minute. Transfer to a heated bowl. Add 1 tablespoon cilantro and toss. Sprinkle with remaining 1 tablespoon cilantro. Serve immediately.
Makes 4 main-course servings.

Oyster-Clam Sauce

3 tablespoons bottled clam juice
1 tablespoon oyster sauce
3 tablespoons soy sauce
¼ teaspoon hot red-pepper flakes

Combine ingredients in a small bowl.

Note: Boneless skinless chicken breasts can be substituted for thighs. Reduce sautéing time to about 3 minutes.

The longer couscous remains covered after steaming, the softer it becomes. For this reason, if couscous is to be served hot, it should be cooked at the last minute.

COOKING TIP

PASTA IN SOUP

Among the two basic ways for serving pasta—in broth and with sauce—the first deserves more attention than it usually gets. It is hard to find a better comfort food than a bowl of homemade chicken soup with noodles. Besides, soup provides a lovely way to enjoy pasta that is relatively low in fat. Soups with pasta make fine first courses but many are satisfying enough to be served as light meals.

Generally, small pasta shapes are best for soups for the simple reason that they are easy to eat with a spoon. Still, there are some exceptions. Seafood soup in Provence, for example, often contains linguine or vermicelli, and this type of soup is the model for Saffron-Scented Seafood Soup. Angel-hair pasta, although long, is thin and delicate, and nicely complements Rich Garlic Soup.

For most soups, use any small attractive shape you like. Many of us grew up with chicken alphabet soup, and this is just one example of the many imaginative pasta shapes there are—try stars, bow ties, squares, wheels, ditali and tiny shells. Stuffed pastas are sensational in soups, as in Chicken Soup with Agnolotti &

From left to right: Salmon Chowder with Pasta & Herbs, page 166; Chicken Soup with Agnolotti & Asparagus, page 160; Mediterranean Tomato Soup with Pasta, page 162

159

Asparagus, because the flavor and texture of the stuffing shines through. Of course, in clear broth the shapes will show better than in thick creamy soups.

In much of the Far East, soup with noodles is the custom for lunch every day. Oriental noodles, from bean threads to rice noodles to wheat noodles, are perfect in soup. (For more about Oriental noodles, see Exotic Pasta, page 144.)

Chicken Soup with Agnolotti & Asparagus

By using fresh or frozen packaged agnolotti, ravioli or tortellini with any stuffing— meat, vegetables or delicate cheeses like ricotta—together with fresh vegetables and good broth, it is easy to prepare delicious soups like this one.

◆ *Photo on page 158.*

5 cups Chicken Stock, page 187
12 thin asparagus spears (about 7 oz. total), fresh or thawed frozen
Salt and freshly ground pepper to taste
1 small carrot, diced (about ½" x ¼" x ¼" pieces)

½ cup frozen corn kernels, if desired
16 to 20 homemade white or green agnolotti, ravioli or tortellini, page 121, or fresh or frozen packaged
2 teaspoons snipped fresh chives

Skim fat thoroughly from stock. Peel fresh asparagus and cut off white bases. Cut stalks of fresh or frozen asparagus in 1-inch pieces and leave tips whole. Pour stock into a medium saucepan and add a pinch of salt and pepper. Add carrot dice and bring to a simmer. Cover and cook over medium-low heat about 6 minutes or until tender. Transfer carrot to a bowl with a slotted spoon.

Add asparagus and corn, if desired, to soup. Cover and simmer over low heat about 4 minutes or until tender. Transfer asparagus and corn to bowl.

Add pasta to soup. Cover and cook over medium heat, stirring occasionally, about 8 minutes or until tender but firm to the bite; cut off a piece of pasta to check. Return carrots, asparagus and corn to soup and heat a few seconds. Add chives. Taste and adjust seasoning. Serve hot.
Makes 4 first-course servings.

Broccoli Cream Soup with Pasta Shells

Pasta shells and broccoli flowerets contribute texture to the smooth light-green soup of intense broccoli flavor. A spoonful of sour cream provides an attractive topping.

3 pounds broccoli, cut in medium flowerets, stalks reserved
3 tablespoons butter
2 medium shallots, minced
1 large garlic clove, minced
2 tablespoons all-purpose flour
3½ cups chicken stock or broth, homemade, page 187, or good-quality packaged
1 bay leaf

Salt and freshly ground pepper to taste
Freshly grated nutmeg to taste
⅔ cup whipping cream
1 cup small pasta shells
2 to 3 tablespoons chicken stock or milk, if desired
Red (cayenne) pepper to taste
About ½ to ¾ cup sour cream (for serving)

Peel broccoli stalks with a paring knife; slice stalks. Add to a large saucepan of enough boiling salted water to cover generously; return to a boil. Drain immediately, rinse under cold water and drain well.

Melt butter in a heavy medium saucepan over low heat. Add shallots and garlic. Cook 1 minute, stirring. Whisk in flour. Cook over low heat, whisking constantly, 2 minutes. Remove from heat. Gradually whisk in 3 cups stock. Cook over medium-high heat, whisking constantly, until mixture thickens and comes to a boil. Add bay leaf and a pinch of salt, pepper and nutmeg.

Reserve 2 cups small flowerets. Add remaining broccoli flowerets and stalks to stock mixture. Bring to a boil, stirring. Reduce heat to low. Cover and simmer over low heat, stirring often. As broccoli becomes more tender, crush slightly with a spoon while stirring. Simmer about 20 minutes or until broccoli is very tender. Discard bay leaf.

With a slotted spoon, transfer cooked broccoli to a food processor or blender (in batches if necessary) and puree. With blades turning, gradually add rest of soup to puree. Puree until very smooth. Return soup to saucepan and bring to a boil, stirring.

Add enough of remaining stock to bring soup to desired consistency. Bring to a boil, stirring. Set aside 6 tiny broccoli flowerets. Add remaining flowerets to soup and cook 2 minutes, uncovered. Add cream and bring again to a boil, stirring. If necessary, simmer 1 or 2 minutes until soup reaches desired consistency. (Soup can be kept, covered, 2 days in refrigerator.)

Bring a medium saucepan of water to a boil and add salt. Just before serving, add pasta and cook uncovered over high heat, stirring occasionally, about 5 minutes or until tender but firm to the bite. Drain well.

Reheat over medium-low heat, stirring. If soup is too thick, add a little stock or milk. Remove soup from heat and stir in pasta and red pepper. Taste and adjust seasoning. Serve each bowl garnished with a dollop of sour cream and a reserved broccoli floweret.

Makes 6 first-course servings.

Garlic Soup with Angel-Hair Pasta

Plenty of garlic is used in this soup, but its flavor is mellow because the garlic cooks in chicken stock until it is tender.

1 quart chicken stock or broth, homemade, page 187, or unsalted packaged
25 medium garlic cloves, peeled, lightly crushed
1 bay leaf
10 fresh sage leaves or ½ teaspoon dried leaf, crumbled
¼ teaspoon hot red-pepper flakes or pinch of red (cayenne) pepper

Salt and freshly ground pepper to taste
2 ounces dried angel-hair pasta or capellini
2 tablespoons chopped fresh parsley leaves, preferably Italian (flat-leaf)
Bowl of freshly grated provolone, Gruyère or Parmesan cheese (for serving)

Combine stock with garlic, bay leaf, sage, pepper flakes or red pepper, salt and pepper in a medium saucepan. Bring to a boil. Cover and simmer over low heat about 15 minutes or until garlic is very tender. Discard bay leaf. Remove garlic and fresh sage leaves. Chop both coarsely with a knife.

Return garlic mixture to soup; bring to a boil. Add pasta and cook over medium heat, separating strands occasionally with a fork, about 4 minutes or until just tender but firm to the bite. Stir in parsley.

Taste and adjust seasoning. Serve with grated cheese. Use a ladle and slotted spoon or tongs to serve broth and pasta.

Makes 4 first-course servings.

VARIATION
Rich Garlic Soup: Beat 1 large egg yolk and ¼ cup whipping cream in a small bowl. After cooking pasta, gradually beat ½ cup soup liquid into yolk mixture. Stir yolk mixture quickly into remaining soup. Stir in parsley.

161

Delicate Chicken Soup with Bean Threads

This light soup is low in calories and makes a pleasing appetizer before a rich or spicy main dish. It can easily be made more substantial for a lunch or supper soup by the addition of canned baby corn and straw mushrooms or soaked dried Chinese or Japanese mushrooms.

5 cups Chicken Stock, page 187
Piece of gingerroot about ¼ inch thick, peeled
¼ teaspoon hot red-pepper flakes
1 (4- or 5-oz.) boneless chicken breast half or boneless chicken thigh, skin removed, cut in about ¾-inch cubes
Salt to taste

14 ounces bean curd (tofu)
3 ounces very thin bean threads, broken in about 5-inch lengths
1 (8-oz.) can water chestnuts, drained, rinsed, sliced
⅓ cup thinly sliced green onions
¼ cup cilantro (fresh coriander) leaves

In a medium saucepan, bring chicken stock to a simmer with gingerroot and pepper flakes. Add chicken and a pinch of salt. Cover and cook over low heat about 5 minutes or until chicken is just tender. Remove chicken to a plate with a slotted spoon. Discard gingerroot.

Drain bean curd in a colander and cut in ¾-inch cubes; you will need about 2 cups. Add bean curd and bean threads to soup. Cook over low heat about 2 minutes or until bean threads are just translucent. Stir in water chestnuts, green onions, cilantro and chicken. Taste and adjust seasoning.
Makes 4 first-course servings.

Note: If several types of bean curd are available, choose the firm type.

Mediterranean Tomato Soup with Pasta

Make this only when you have very ripe tomatoes—they are the soul of this soup while the ditali, or pasta thimbles, give it body. The soup is relatively easy to prepare because there is no need to peel or seed the tomatoes. After cooking, they are pureed in either a food mill or food processor. A garnish of tomato slices and basil sprigs looks very attractive.

✦ *Photo on page 158.*

4 to 5 tablespoons olive oil
1 large onion, minced
2½ pounds ripe tomatoes, cut in large dice
4 large garlic cloves, chopped
2 cups chicken stock or broth, homemade, page 187, or packaged
1¼ cups water
1¼ teaspoons dried leaf oregano, crumbled

Salt and freshly ground pepper to taste
1 cup small pasta, such as thimble-shaped ditali (salad macaroni)
2 tablespoons coarsely chopped fresh basil leaves
Bowl of freshly grated Parmesan cheese (for serving), if desired

Heat olive oil in a large saucepan over medium-low heat. Add onion and cook, stirring occasionally, about 12 minutes or until soft but not brown. Add tomatoes, garlic, stock, water, oregano, salt and pepper; bring to a boil. Cover and cook over low heat 45 minutes.

Puree soup in a food mill; or puree in a food processor and strain, pressing so pulp goes through strainer. (Soup can be kept, covered, 2 days in refrigerator.) Return soup to saucepan and reheat. If soup appears thin, simmer uncovered 2 to 3 minutes to thicken slightly.

Bring a medium saucepan of water to a boil and add salt. Just before serving, add pasta and cook uncovered over high heat, stirring occasionally, 5 to 8 minutes or until tender but firm to the bite. Drain well. Add to soup.

Stir in 1 tablespoon basil. Taste and adjust seasoning. Sprinkle with remaining 1 tablespoon basil. Serve with Parmesan cheese, if desired.
Makes 4 first-course servings.

Chicken Soup with Rice Noodles, Spinach & Chinese Mushrooms

1 ounce dried black Chinese mushrooms or shiitake mushrooms (about 10)
2 quarts chicken stock or broth, homemade, page 187, or good-quality packaged
3 green onions, quartered crosswise
3 slices (about ¼ inch thick) peeled gingerroot
Salt and freshly ground pepper
6 ounces thin rice noodles or rice vermicelli
¼ cup thinly sliced green onions
10 ounces spinach, stems removed, leaves rinsed, torn in bite-size pieces (about 6 cups leaves)
1 to 2 tablespoons rice wine or 2 tablespoons dry sherry

Chinese flavorings quickly turn simple chicken stock into a refreshing first course. Asparagus or thin strips of leeks, celery or zucchini can be cooked in this light soup instead of spinach.

In a medium bowl, soak mushrooms in hot water to cover 30 minutes. Remove from water. Rinse and squeeze gently to remove excess water. Cut off and discard stems; quarter caps.

Skim any fat from surface of stock. Combine stock, quartered green onions, gingerroot and a pinch of salt and pepper in a large saucepan. Bring to a boil and simmer uncovered over low heat 30 minutes. Add mushrooms and simmer 15 minutes. (Soup can be kept, covered, 2 days in refrigerator.)

Put noodles in a large bowl. Cover generously with hot water and soak 10 minutes. Drain well.

Reheat soup if necessary. Remove and discard quartered green onions and gingerroot, using a slotted spoon. Add noodles and simmer about 4 minutes or until tender but firm to the bite. Remove from heat. Add sliced green onions and spinach. Stir until spinach is wilted. Stir in wine. Taste and adjust seasoning. Ladle into bowls and serve.

Makes 6 first-course servings.

Rich Chicken Soup with Pasta & Dill

4 to 4½ cups homemade chicken stock or broth, page 187, or unsalted packaged
Salt and freshly ground pepper to taste
1¼ cups fresh or dried pasta wheels or other small pasta shapes
2 large egg yolks
¼ cup whipping cream
2½ tablespoons snipped fresh dill
2 tablespoons freshly grated Parmesan cheese
Bowl of freshly grated Parmesan cheese (for serving)

Delicately flavored with Parmesan cheese and fresh dill, this elegant appetizer soup is rich yet not thick.

Skim fat thoroughly from stock. Pour 4 cups stock into a medium saucepan and add a pinch of salt and pepper. Bring to a boil. Add pasta and cook, stirring occasionally, until tender but firm to the bite, about 5 minutes for fresh wheels and up to 8 minutes for other shapes. If stock appears to have reduced, add remaining ½ cup stock and bring to a simmer.

Meanwhile, whisk egg yolks and cream in a small bowl. Gradually beat in ¼ cup soup liquid, without including pasta. Stir in 2 tablespoons dill and 2 tablespoons Parmesan cheese.

Remove soup from heat. Stir in egg-yolk mixture. Heat over low heat, stirring constantly, 4 minutes or until slightly thickened; do not boil. Remove from heat. Taste and adjust seasoning. Sprinkle with remaining dill and serve immediately with more Parmesan.

Makes 3 or 4 first-course servings.

Like many versions of traditional minestrone, this soup is flavored with pesto and has plenty of vegetables. The addition of chicken makes it satisfying enough to be a main course and gives the broth greater depth of flavor.

Chicken & Green-Vegetable Minestrone with Parmesan

1 pound chicken drumsticks or thighs
7 cups water
Salt and freshly ground pepper to taste
¼ cup olive oil
1 large onion, chopped
2 celery stalks, cut in thin slices
1 large boiling potato
2 large Swiss chard leaves, cut in about 2" x ½" strips
½ teaspoon dried leaf thyme, crumbled

Pesto, see below
4 small zucchini, cut in cubes
1½ cups small tri-colored pasta shells
8 ounces fresh peas, shelled, or ½ cup frozen peas
½ cup canned garbanzo beans, rinsed
Bowl of freshly grated Parmesan cheese (for serving)

Put chicken in a medium saucepan and add water. Add salt and pepper; bring to a simmer over high heat. Cover and poach over medium-low heat about 30 minutes or until chicken is no longer pink when cut. Remove from liquid. Discard skin; remove meat from bones and dice.

Heat olive oil in a large saucepan over low heat. Add onion and cook, stirring often, 15 minutes or until very soft but not brown. Add celery and cook over medium heat, stirring, 7 minutes.

Peel potato. Cut potato in ½-inch dice and add to saucepan of onion mixture. Add chard, chicken cooking liquid, thyme and a pinch of salt and pepper; bring to a boil. Cover and simmer over low heat 25 minutes. (Soup can be kept, covered, up to 2 days in refrigerator; refrigerate chicken separately.)

Prepare Pesto; set aside. Bring soup to a simmer if necessary. Add zucchini and simmer 10 minutes. Add pasta and simmer about 5 minutes or until nearly tender. Add peas, garbanzos and chicken; simmer about 3 minutes or until peas are tender.

Remove from heat. Ladle into a heated tureen, if desired. Stir in Pesto. Taste and adjust seasoning. Serve immediately with Parmesan cheese.
Makes 6 main-course servings.

Pesto

4 medium garlic cloves, peeled
1 cup fresh basil leaves (1½-oz. bunch)
½ cup freshly grated Parmesan cheese (1½ oz.)

2 tablespoons pine nuts
⅓ cup extra-virgin olive oil

Chop garlic in a food processor by dropping cloves down feed tube 1 at a time, with blade turning. Add basil, Parmesan cheese, pine nuts and olive oil. Process, scraping down sides of container a few times, until mixture is well blended. Reserve at room temperature. (Pesto can be kept, covered, 2 days in refrigerator.)
Makes ¾ cup.

Saffron-Scented Seafood Soup

Soup Base, see below
4 ounces fresh or dried linguine
8 ounces sea-bass fillet, cut in ¾-inch dice
4 ounces scallops, rinsed, halved
4 ounces medium shrimp, shelled, deveined if desired
2 tablespoons chopped fresh parsley leaves

1½ teaspoons chopped fresh thyme leaves or ½ teaspoon dried leaf, crumbled
Bowl of freshly grated Gruyère or Parmesan cheese (for serving), if desired

A simple fish stock adds depth of flavor to this festive soup, a cousin of the Provençal bouillabaisse and the ciuppin of the Italian Riviera. The shrimp, scallops and linguine in the wonderful Mediterranean-style broth make a light but elegant main course.

Prepare Soup Base; set aside. Bring a large saucepan of water to a boil; add salt, then pasta. Cook uncovered over high heat, separating strands occasionally with a fork, about 2 minutes for fresh or 8 minutes for dried or until tender but firm to the bite. Drain, rinse with cold water and drain well.

Bring Soup Base to a simmer. Discard cheesecloth bag. Add sea bass and scallops to soup. Simmer 2 minutes. Add shrimp and simmer 2 minutes or until seafood is just tender. Add linguine, parsley and thyme. Taste and adjust seasoning. Pour into a heated tureen. Serve with cheese, if desired.
Makes 4 main-course or 6 first-course servings.

Soup Base

1 pound fish bones or fish pieces for chowder
6 cups water
¼ cup olive oil
1 large onion, halved, sliced thin
2 medium leeks, white part only, split, rinsed well, sliced
2 celery stalks, sliced
1 fresh thyme sprig or ¼ teaspoon dried leaf, crumbled
1 bay leaf
5 parsley sprigs without leaves

1¼ pounds ripe tomatoes, peeled, seeded, chopped, or 1 (28-oz.) can plus 1 (14-oz.) can whole plum tomatoes, drained, chopped
3 medium garlic cloves, chopped
¼ teaspoon lightly crushed saffron threads
Salt and freshly ground pepper to taste
1 tablespoon tomato paste

Rinse fish bones or pieces for chowder. Put in a large saucepan. Add water; bring to a boil and skim off foam. Simmer uncovered over low heat, skimming occasionally, 15 minutes. Strain into a large bowl, reserving stock.

Heat oil in a large wide casserole over medium-low heat. Add onion, leeks and celery. Cook, stirring often, about 10 minutes or until soft but not brown. Tie thyme, bay leaf and parsley in a piece of cheesecloth; add to casserole. Add tomatoes and garlic; heat 1 minute. Add reserved stock, saffron, salt and pepper; bring to a boil. Cook uncovered over low heat 30 minutes. Add tomato paste and cook 1 minute. (Soup Base can be prepared ahead to this point and kept, covered, 1 day in refrigerator.)

Note: If sea-bass fillets are not available, substitute haddock, cod or halibut.

In this creamy soup of diced fresh salmon accented by tarragon or chives, I like to use tri-colored pasta spirals when they are available.

◆ *Photo on page 158.*

Salmon Chowder with Pasta & Herbs

Chowder Base, see below
1¼ cups fresh or dried tri-colored spirals or other small pasta
12 ounces salmon fillet, cut in 1" x 1" x ½" cubes
¼ cup additional milk or whipping cream, if desired
1 teaspoon fresh thyme leaves or ¼ teaspoon dried, crumbled
2 teaspoons minced fresh parsley leaves

2 teaspoons snipped fresh chives or chopped fresh tarragon leaves, or a mixture of both
Salt and freshly ground pepper to taste
Red (cayenne) pepper to taste
Oyster crackers or other crackers or French or Italian bread (for serving)

Prepare Chowder Base; set aside. Bring a medium saucepan of water to a boil; add salt, then pasta. Cook uncovered over high heat, stirring occasionally, about 5 minutes for fresh spirals or up to 8 minutes for other shapes or until tender but firm to the bite. Drain, rinse with cold water and drain well.

Bring Chowder Base to a simmer. Add salmon cubes. Simmer, uncovered over low heat, about 2 minutes or until salmon is barely tender. (Chowder can be kept, covered, up to 1 day in refrigerator; refrigerate vegetables and pasta separately.)

Reheat chowder, if necessary, over low heat. Remove from heat and stir in pasta and vegetables. If chowder is too thick, stir in up to ¼ cup milk or cream and heat a few seconds, stirring. Stir in thyme, parsley and chives, tarragon or herb mixture. Season to taste with salt if needed, freshly ground pepper and red pepper. Serve hot with crackers or bread.

Makes 6 first-course or 4 main-course servings.

Chowder Base

1½ cups bottled clam juice
½ cup water
½ cup diced carrots (about ⅜-inch dice)
3 small zucchini, quartered lengthwise, cut in ¼-inch slices

2 tablespoons butter
1 medium onion, minced
2 tablespoons all-purpose flour
1 cup milk
½ cup whipping cream

Combine clam juice, water and carrots in a medium saucepan; bring to a boil. Simmer uncovered over low heat about 6 minutes or until carrots are tender. Transfer carrots to a bowl with a slotted spoon. Bring cooking liquid to a boil. Add zucchini and bring to boil. Cook uncovered over medium-high heat about 2 minutes or until barely tender. Drain thoroughly, reserving cooking liquid. Transfer zucchini to bowl of carrots; set aside. Measure 1½ cups cooking liquid.

Melt butter in a heavy medium saucepan over medium-low heat. Add onion and cook, stirring often, about 10 minutes or until very soft but not brown. Sprinkle with flour and cook over low heat, stirring constantly, 2 minutes. Add 1½ cups cooking liquid and stir. Increase heat to medium-high and bring to a simmer. Simmer over low heat 5 minutes. Stir in milk and cream; bring to a boil. Remove from heat.

Turkey-Wing Soup with Pasta & Peas

This satisfying soup is colorful, full of vegetables and very chunky. It can be served as a main-dish soup for a light meal and is perfect for a cold winter day.

4½ to 5 pounds turkey wings, patted dry
4 tablespoons vegetable oil
2 medium onions, chopped
4 medium carrots, diced
2 large garlic cloves, chopped
1 pound ripe tomatoes, peeled, seeded, chopped, or 1 (28-oz.) can whole plum tomatoes, drained, chopped
¼ cup brandy
1 quart chicken stock or broth, homemade, page 187, or packaged
1 quart water
2 bay leaves

1 tablespoon chopped fresh thyme leaves or 1 teaspoon dried leaf, crumbled
2 teaspoons chopped fresh rosemary or ¾ teaspoon dried, crumbled
Salt and freshly ground pepper to taste
1⅓ cups small pasta shells
8 ounces green beans, cut diagonally in 1-inch pieces
1½ pounds fresh peas, shelled, or 1½ cups frozen peas
Bowl of freshly grated Parmesan or romano cheese (for serving), if desired

Cut each turkey wing in 2 pieces at joints, or in 3 pieces if wing tips are attached. Heat 3 tablespoons oil in a large saucepan or enameled casserole over medium-high heat. Add turkey wings in batches; brown. Transfer to a plate.

Add 1 tablespoon oil to pan; heat over medium-low heat. Add onions and carrots. Cook, stirring often, about 10 minutes or until onions are soft but not brown. Add garlic and cook 30 seconds, stirring. Add tomatoes and bring to a boil. Return wings to pan. Pour brandy over them; bring to a boil. Add stock, water, bay leaves, thyme, rosemary, salt and pepper; bring to a boil. Cover and simmer, turning turkey pieces over once or twice, about 2 hours or until very tender.

Discard bay leaves and any wing tips. Remove other wing sections. Skim fat from broth. Remove meat from bones and tear or cut meat in thin strips about 1 inch long. (Soup can be kept, covered, 2 days in refrigerator; refrigerate turkey separately.)

Bring broth to a boil. Add pasta and green beans. Cook uncovered over medium heat 5 minutes. Add peas and cook about 8 minutes or until pasta shells are tender but firm to the bite. Return turkey to broth and heat briefly. Taste and adjust seasoning. Serve soup with cheese, if desired.
Makes 6 to 8 main-course servings.

Note: When browning turkey wings and other poultry, use a frying screen to prevent splatters.

To peel and seed tomatoes, cut out the cores then turn the tomatoes over and slit the skin in an *X*-shaped cut. Put the tomatoes in a saucepan of enough boiling water to cover them generously and boil about 10 seconds. Remove them with a slotted spoon and put them in a bowl of cold water. Leave for a few seconds. Remove them and pull off the skins with the aid of a paring knife. Halve the tomatoes horizontally with a chopping knife. Hold each half over a bowl, cut side down, and squeeze to remove the seeds.

COOKING TIP

PASTA DESSERTS

Pasta, like rice, can be used to make a number of tasty desserts when paired with whipping cream, sour cream or butter and with fresh or dried fruit. For example, couscous with dried fruit is a traditional North African dish that makes a good winter dessert or an unusual treat for breakfast or brunch. Folding whipped cream and fruit into couscous turns it into a dessert that resembles a creamy rice pudding, as in Couscous with Strawberries & Cream.

Delicious baked puddings can be made from pasta. The best-known type, often called *noodle kugel,* has long been part of Jewish and Eastern European culinary tradition. For the most basic sweet kugel, cooks combine cooked egg noodles with a little sugar, melted butter or margarine and eggs. Generally, fresh fruit is added, especially apples, or dried fruit. Kugel can be enriched with chopped nuts and flavored with cinnamon or citrus zest. Some versions have sour cream, cottage cheese or both, as in Noodle & Apple Kugel with Sour Cream. Kugels are usually baked in and served from a casserole but they can also be baked in individual cupcake tins and unmolded. Hazelnut

Canneloni Cheese Blintzes, page 171

Noodle Pudding, served with a delicious hazelnut-liqueur sauce, is an intriguing cross between a kugel and a soufflé. Other noodle puddings, such as Creamy Pasta Pudding à l'Orange, do not require baking.

Canneloni and manicotti tubes can be used like quick crepes, as in Canneloni Cheese Blintzes. They make blintzes and baked crepe desserts easier to prepare because there is no need to make a batter and fry crepes one by one.

The contrast of hot cocoa pasta, cold vanilla ice cream and warm glossy chocolate-Grand Marnier sauce makes this dessert enormously appealing. It is fun to serve for a casual meal. You can use homemade or purchased chocolate noodles. If you like, make a double recipe of Chocolate Sauce and keep the extra for serving again with your favorite ice cream.

Chocolate Pasta with Ice Cream & Chocolate Sauce

Chocolate Sauce, see below
Pinch of salt
8 ounces dried cocoa noodles or orange noodles or 9 to 10 ounces fresh, homemade, page 181 or 182, or packaged

2 tablespoons unsalted butter, room temperature
4 scoops vanilla ice cream

Prepare Chocolate Sauce; keep warm. Bring a large pot of water to a boil; add salt, then pasta. Cook uncovered over high heat, separating strands occasionally with a fork, 30 seconds to 2 minutes for fresh or 2 to 5 minutes for dried or until tender but firm to the bite. Drain well. Transfer to a medium bowl. Add soft butter and toss.

Gently spoon some of pasta onto each plate. Make a hollow in center. Put a scoop of vanilla ice cream in hollow. Pour Chocolate Sauce over ice cream. Drizzle a little sauce over pasta.
Makes 4 servings.

Chocolate Sauce

4 ounces semisweet chocolate, chopped
2 tablespoons water

3 tablespoons Grand Marnier
1 tablespoon unsalted butter

Combine chocolate, water and Grand Marnier in a medium bowl. Set above a saucepan of hot water over low heat. Let stand until chocolate is melted, stirring occasionally. Remove from heat. If serving soon, leave bowl above hot water. Stir in butter a few minutes before serving. (Sauce can be kept, covered, 1 week in refrigerator. Reheat in bowl above hot water before serving.)

Canneloni Cheese Blintzes

Strawberry Sauce, see below
Cheese Filling, see below
12 dried canneloni tubes
6 tablespoons unsalted butter,
   cut in 24 pieces

2 tablespoons powdered sugar
4 fresh strawberries (for
   garnish), if desired
Sour cream (for serving)

For these quick delicious blintzes there is no need to make crepes because the filling is enclosed in canneloni. They contain a sweet cottage- and cream-cheese filling and are served with both strawberry sauce and sour cream. They're good for dessert, or for brunch with champagne.

◆ *Photo on page 168.*

Prepare Strawberry Sauce and Cheese Filling; refrigerate. Bring a large pot of water to a boil; add salt, then pasta. Cook uncovered over high heat, stirring occasionally, about 6 minutes or until just tender but firm to the bite. Drain well. Transfer to a large bowl of cold water.

Butter a 13" x 9" x 2" baking dish. Remove 1 canneloni from water and put on a work surface. Slit lengthwise with a knife, open flat and pat dry. Put 3 tablespoons Cheese Filling along 1 long end. Roll up in cigar shape. Put in buttered baking dish seam side down. Continue filling canneloni and arranging in baking dish in 1 layer touching each other. (Canneloni can be prepared 1 day ahead to this point and kept, covered, in refrigerator. Bring to room temperature before continuing.)

Preheat oven to 400F (205C). Dot each canneloni with 2 small pieces of butter. Cover with foil. Bake 15 to 20 minutes or until heated through. (There will be a generous amount of butter in baking dish to keep them moist.) Use a spoon or brush to baste canneloni with butter in dish. Sprinkle with powdered sugar. Return to oven and bake uncovered 3 minutes longer.

If desired, prepare strawberry fans for garnish. Leave green tops on strawberries. Cut each berry in 4 or 5 slices lengthwise from bottom but not all the way through to top, so they remain attached to berry.

Remove canneloni from dish, leaving excess butter behind. Serve hot, with Strawberry Sauce and sour cream. Garnish each serving, if desired, with a strawberry, spreading out slices in fan shape.
Makes 4 servings.

Strawberry Sauce

1½ cups fresh or thawed frozen
   strawberries
2 to 2½ tablespoons powdered
   sugar, sifted

Few drops of fresh lemon juice, if
   desired

Puree strawberries in a food processor or blender until very smooth. Whisk in 2 tablespoons powdered sugar. Taste and add more sugar if desired. Add lemon juice if desired. Refrigerate until ready to use. (Sauce can be kept, covered, 2 days in refrigerator.)

Cheese Filling

8 ounces cream cheese, softened
½ cup cottage cheese, drained in
   a strainer
¼ cup ricotta cheese
2 large egg yolks

3 tablespoons sugar
½ teaspoon finely grated lemon
   zest
½ teaspoon strained fresh lemon
   juice

In a medium bowl, mash cream cheese with a fork until smooth. Beat in remaining ingredients. Refrigerate 15 minutes.

Always cook several more canneloni than you need because a few will probably tear.

COOKING TIP

Couscous with Strawberries & Cream

2½ cups fresh strawberries, halved lengthwise, sliced crosswise
6 tablespoons sugar
1⅓ cups milk
Pinch of salt

⅔ cup couscous
1¾ cups whipping cream, well chilled
2½ teaspoons pure vanilla extract
6 to 8 medium strawberries, halved lengthwise, for garnish

Put strawberries in a medium bowl. Sprinkle with 2 tablespoons sugar; toss gently. Refrigerate 20 minutes.

Bring milk, 1 tablespoon sugar and a pinch of salt to a simmer in a medium saucepan, stirring until sugar is dissolved. Stir in couscous; cover pan immediately and remove from heat. Let stand 15 minutes or until milk is absorbed. Transfer couscous to a large bowl. Fluff with a fork, tossing grains to separate them. Cool to room temperature. Chill a large bowl for whipping cream.

Whip 1 cup cream in chilled bowl until it holds soft peaks. Add 2 tablespoons sugar and 2 teaspoons vanilla. Whip cream until just stiff. Gently fold whipped cream into couscous, followed by sliced strawberries and their liquid. Spoon mixture into 6 to 8 dessert dishes; smooth tops. Cover and refrigerate at least 2 hours or overnight.

Chill a medium bowl. Whip remaining cream in chilled bowl until it holds soft peaks. Add remaining 1 tablespoon sugar and remaining ½ teaspoon vanilla. Whip cream until stiff. Transfer to a pastry bag fitted with a decorative tip. Garnish center of each serving with 2 strawberry halves, pushed lightly into dessert and pointing upward and outward. On edge of each dish pipe a ring of whipped-cream rosettes. Serve cold.
Makes 6 to 8 servings.

Couscous with Raisins & Dried Apricots

½ cup plus 1 tablespoon sugar
2 cups water
10 thin slices peeled gingerroot, each about 1 inch across
1 cup dried apricots (about 4 oz.)
½ cup (4 oz.) unsalted butter

⅔ cup dark raisins
1½ cups couscous (about 10½ oz.)
Pinch of salt
1½ cups milk
1 cup hot milk (for serving)

Combine sugar, water and gingerroot in a medium saucepan. Bring to a boil, stirring. Remove syrup from heat. Cover and let stand 20 minutes. Add apricots to syrup; bring to a simmer. Cover and poach over low heat about 15 minutes or until tender. Let cool in syrup. Transfer apricots in syrup to a bowl or container. Cover and refrigerate 4 hours or overnight.

Cut butter in 16 pieces and let come to room temperature.

Transfer apricots in syrup to a medium saucepan. Cover and heat until warm. Add raisins and shake pan to submerge them. Cover and let stand 10 minutes.

Combine couscous with a small pinch of salt in a medium saucepan. Shake pan to spread couscous in an even layer. Scatter 6 pieces (3 tablespoons) butter

172

over couscous. Bring 1½ cups milk to a boil in a medium saucepan. Pour it evenly over couscous; immediately cover saucepan of couscous tightly and let stand 5 minutes. Scatter remaining butter pieces on top; cover and let couscous stand 1 minute. Fluff mixture with a fork to break up any lumps in couscous, tossing until mixture is blended.

To serve, mound couscous on a platter and arrange apricots and raisins on top with a slotted spoon. Serve couscous in heated bowls. Serve hot milk separately in a pitcher.

Makes 4 servings.

Creamy Pasta Pudding à l'Orange

2½ cups milk	**4 tablespoons sugar**
1 cup very fine short noodles	**2 oranges**
Pinch of salt	**½ cup whipping cream, well**
3 large egg yolks	**chilled**

Bring milk to a simmer in a heavy medium saucepan. Add noodles and salt. Cook over low heat, stirring occasionally, 20 minutes or until noodles are tender and absorb most of milk. Remove from heat.

Beat egg yolks with 3 tablespoons sugar in a small bowl. Stir mixture into noodles. Return to low heat. Cook, stirring, about 6 minutes or until thick; do not overcook or boil, or egg yolks may curdle. Transfer immediately to a medium bowl. Finely grate 1 teaspoon zest from orange; stir into noodle mixture. Let cool to room temperature. Chill a small bowl for whipping cream.

Use a sharp or serrated knife to cut skin and pith from 1 orange. Separate sections by cutting on each side of membrane between them, inward to center; fold back membrane and cut to remove segment. Continue until all segments have been removed; discard membranes. Cut segments in dice.

Whip cream in chilled bowl with remaining 1 tablespoon sugar until soft peaks form. Fold into noodle mixture in 2 portions. Gently fold in diced orange segments.

Spoon into 4 (⅔-cup) ramekins. Cover and refrigerate about 2 hours or until thickened. (Dessert can be kept, covered, up to 1 day.) Serve garnished with more orange segments cut from second orange.

Makes 4 servings.

Cooking noodles in milk gives them a richness so they can be made into creamy desserts like this pudding, flavored with fresh orange zest and topped by orange segments.

Use a sharp or serrated knife to cut skin and pith from 1 orange.

Separate sections by cutting inward to center on each side of membrane between sections. Fold back membrane and cut gently to remove segment. Continue until all segments have been removed; discard membranes.

Hazelnut Noodle Pudding

*This noodle dessert resembles
a light bread pudding in
texture. The hazelnut-liqueur
custard sauce gives it special
elegance.*

Custard Sauce, see below
1/3 cup hazelnuts (filberts)
2 1/2 cups milk
4 ounces very fine noodles or
    vermicelli, broken in 2-inch
    pieces (about 2 cups)
Pinch of salt
1 1/2 teaspoons finely grated
    lemon zest

Sugar for coating baking dish
6 tablespoons sugar
4 large eggs, separated, room
    temperature
2 tablespoons Frangelico
    (hazelnut liqueur)

Prepare Custard Sauce; set aside. Preheat oven to 350F (175C). Toast hazelnuts on a small baking sheet in oven about 7 minutes or until skins begin to split. Transfer to a strainer. Rub hot nuts against strainer with a terry-cloth towel to remove most of skins. Cool nuts; chop coarsely. Increase oven temperature to 400F (205C).

Bring milk to a boil in a heavy medium saucepan. Add noodles and salt. Cook over low heat, stirring often with a fork to keep strands separate, about 20 minutes or until noodles are soft and absorb most of milk. Stir in lemon zest.

Butter a 6- to 7-cup soufflé dish or deep baking dish; coat sides lightly with sugar. Add 3 tablespoons sugar to noodles; mix over low heat until dissolved. Transfer to a bowl; cool 3 minutes. Add hazelnuts and egg yolks; mix well.

Beat egg whites in a large bowl until soft peaks form. Beat in remaining 3 tablespoons sugar. Continue beating at high speed about 30 seconds or until whites are stiff and shiny but not dry. Fold into noodle mixture in 2 batches. Transfer to prepared baking dish. Bake in preheated oven 25 to 30 minutes or until slightly puffed and firm on top.

Just before serving, stir liqueur into Custard Sauce. Serve pudding as soon as it is ready. To serve, spoon pudding onto plates and pour sauce over and around it. Makes 4 or 5 servings.

Custard Sauce

3/4 cup milk
3/4 cup whipping cream
6 large egg yolks, room
    temperature

1/4 cup sugar

Combine milk and cream in a heavy medium saucepan; bring to a boil.

Whisk egg yolks lightly in a large heatproof bowl. Add sugar and whisk until thick and smooth. Gradually whisk in hot milk. Return mixture to saucepan, whisking. Cook over medium-low heat, stirring sauce and scraping bottom of pan constantly with a wooden spoon, until sauce thickens slightly and reaches 170F to 175F (75C to 80C) on an instant-read thermometer; after 5 minutes of cooking sauce, remove it from heat and check its temperature. To check whether it is thick enough without a thermometer, remove sauce from heat, dip a metal spoon in sauce and draw your finger across back of spoon—your finger should leave a clear trail in sauce that clings to spoon. If it does not, continue cooking 30 seconds and check again. Do not overcook sauce or it will curdle.

Strain immediately into a bowl and stir about 30 seconds to cool. Cool to room temperature. (Sauce can be kept, covered, 2 days in refrigerator. Bring to room temperature before serving.)

Mango Sauce

2 pounds ripe mangoes
About ½ cup powdered sugar,
  sifted

2 to 3 teaspoons strained fresh
  lemon or lime juice, if desired

When mangoes are in season, serve this colorful sauce with Hazelnut Noodle Pudding, opposite, or, for an exotic touch, with Canneloni Cheese Blintzes, page 171.

Peel mangoes using a paring knife. Cut flesh away from pits. Puree mango flesh in a food processor or blender. Add ½ cup powdered sugar and process until very smooth. Taste, and add a little more powdered sugar, if desired. Strain mixture into medium bowl, pressing on pulp in strainer. Use a rubber spatula to scrape mixture from underside of strainer. Stir in lemon or lime juice, if desired. Cover and refrigerate 30 minutes. (Sauce can be kept, covered, 1 day in refrigerator.) Stir before serving. Serve cold or at room temperature.

Makes about 1⅓ cups, 4 to 5 servings.

Noodle & Apple Kugel with Sour Cream

1 medium Golden Delicious
  apple
6 tablespoons butter
8 ounces wide egg noodles
1 cup creamy cottage cheese
1½ cups sour cream
4 large eggs, separated

5 tablespoons plus 2 teaspoons
  sugar
1½ teaspoons ground cinnamon
Pinch of salt
¼ cup raisins
Sour cream (for serving), if
  desired

Kugel is sometimes known as noodle soufflé. Besides apples, it is good with sliced pears or diced pineapple.

Butter a deep 8- to 10-cup baking dish. Preheat oven to 350F (175C). Peel, halve and core apple. Halve again and cut in very thin slices. Melt 4 tablespoons butter.

Bring a large pot of water to a boil; add salt, then pasta. Cook uncovered over high heat, stirring occasionally, about 5 minutes or until tender but firm to the bite. Drain, rinse with cold water and drain well. Transfer to a large bowl. Toss with melted butter. Stir in cottage cheese, 1½ cups sour cream, egg yolks, 4 tablespoons sugar, 1 teaspoon cinnamon, a pinch of salt, apple slices and raisins. Mix 2 teaspoons sugar and remaining ½ teaspoon cinnamon in a small bowl; set aside.

Beat egg whites in a large bowl until soft peaks form. Add remaining 1 tablespoon sugar and continue beating 30 seconds or until stiff and glossy. Gently fold ¼ of whites into noodle mixture; fold in remaining whites.

Transfer noodle mixture to buttered baking dish. Sprinkle cinnamon and sugar mixture evenly on top. Dot with remaining 2 tablespoons butter.

Bake in preheated oven about 50 minutes or until puffed and golden brown. Serve hot or warm. If desired, serve with additional sour cream.

Makes 4 to 6 servings.

PASTA BASICS

COOKING PASTA

In a book called "Cooking in 10 Minutes" written in France in the 19th century, before there were many time-saving conveniences, the author, Edouard de Pomiane, gave a very helpful hint. As soon as you enter your home, he instructed, before you even take off your coat, put a large pot of water on to boil. He explained that one would always need it for something. This is a great rule to remember when cooking pasta.

Although the cooking time of most pasta is only a few minutes, bringing a large pot of water to a boil takes a little while. So the first thing to do when you start a pasta recipe is to bring the water to a boil in a covered pot over high heat. Generally there is no need to measure; you just fill a pasta pot or other large pot about $2/3$ or $3/4$ full of water. When the water is boiling rapidly, you add salt. Some cooks also add a tablespoon of oil to prevent sticking but this is not necessary if you are using plenty of water.

If you wish to measure, here are the amounts to use:

For 8 to 12 ounces pasta: 3 to 4 quarts water, 1 tablespoon salt

For 12 ounces to 1 pound pasta: 5 quarts water, $1^1/2$ tablespoons salt

The pasta is added to the boiling salted water. It should be stirred from time to time, or the strands of long thin pasta should be lifted occasionally with a fork or with tongs to prevent sticking. The pasta should be cooked uncovered over high heat until tender but firm to the bite, what is often referred to as *al dente.* The way to check is by tasting often, especially when cooking fresh pasta, which is sometimes ready in as little as 30 seconds and overcooks easily. Use tongs to remove long strands of pasta from the water for checking and a slotted spoon for small pastas.

If the sauce requires rather long cooking, it should be prepared before the pasta is cooked, then reheated gently when the pasta is nearly done. The sauce should be hot when it is tossed with the pasta.

Although some cooks rinse pasta immediately after cooking, this is not necessary except if you want to cool the pasta quickly for a salad or if you must cook it ahead. Indeed, some producers, especially of flavored pastas, instruct not to rinse their pasta because it will lose flavor.

EQUIPMENT

For cooking pasta, a large pot is necessary so the pasta can boil in plenty of water and a large colander or large strainer is needed to drain it. A special pasta pot with a draining insert is useful because you can drain the pasta and toss it with the sauce immediately, rather than losing time going to the sink and pouring the pasta into a colander. See photo page 179.

For making pasta, a hand-crank or electric pasta-rolling machine is a very useful piece of equipment. See photos pages 178 and 179.

A few other types of equipment are useful and will make cooking easier:
- A scale is important for weighing pasta, especially the long types that cannot be measured accurately in cups.
- Tongs are good for removing long pasta from the water and are convenient for serving it too.
- Large wooden pasta forks are ideal for stirring pasta as it cooks without bruising it and for tossing pasta with sauce. If wooden ones are not available, other large forks can be used. A pair of chopsticks is also efficient for stirring pasta as it cooks.
- Pasta spoons with prongs are useful for serving pasta.
- Special pasta serving bowls can be found in some shops. Their wide shallow form makes tossing and serving pasta easy because the sauce gets evenly distributed.

ESTIMATING PASTA WEIGHT WITHOUT A SCALE

For long thin pastas such as spaghetti, vermicelli, capellini and linguine, some pasta companies suggest this way of estimating the weight of the pasta: Hold a bunch of pasta $1/2$ inch from the end. Measure the diameter of the bunch at the end you are holding. If its diameter is $3/4$ inch, you have 2 ounces of pasta.

If its diameter is 1 inch, you have 4 ounces. For 8 ounces, simply use half a 1-pound package. You can also buy a gadget that measures portions of long pastas by a similar principle, although a scale is much more useful.

MAKING FRESH PASTA
Watching professional pasta makers display their skill is fascinating. I enjoyed seeing a Chinese pasta-maker "throw noodles" in Hong Kong, and was impressed by a woman in a small restaurant kitchen in Bologna who mixed large quantities of noodle dough made with 60 eggs by hand and rolled it out with a very long rolling pin.

Students in my pasta cooking classes, however, are delighted to discover that fine-quality pasta dough can be made in a minute with the aid of a food processor. And it does not take long to roll it out in a hand-crank or an electric rolling machine. This method is easy and fairly quick when small quantities are involved. Although some pasta experts insist that pasta dough mixed by hand and rolled out with a rolling pin is best, I find this is too much work and requires too much practice for most people.

Most pasta machines cut the dough in two widths: medium noodles or fettuccine, and very thin noodles called *tagliarini* or *tagliolini,* although some have attachments for other shapes. All the dough recipes in this chapter can be cut either way.

If you have an extrusion pasta machine which pushes the pasta dough through discs to shape it, the dough required is stiffer and so it is best to follow the dough recipes that come with your machine.

If you make pasta often, you may want to invest in a pasta rack, a convenient item for hanging homemade noodles or other long pasta shapes so they dry evenly. See photo page 179.

If semolina flour is available, it will make wonderful homemade pasta that holds together well and can be easily cooked so it is al dente. All-purpose flour, especially unbleached, also gives very good results and is the type generally used by cooks in Italy. Pasta made with all-purpose flour softens quickly during cooking and must be watched carefully or it will overcook. Bread flour can also be used.

FLAVORED PASTAS
Pasta can be flavored with a great variety of vegetables, herbs and spices. The greatest effect these additions have is to color the pasta. The additonal flavor is usually not very pronounced. Strong spices work better for flavoring pasta than most fresh herbs because they are more concentrated. Generally the taste of herbs and some spices is very subtle in the pasta itself and often it is pleasantly reinforced by putting more of the flavoring in the accompanying pasta sauce.

These pastas, although fun to make, are not economical—the flavorings lose much of their strength from being combined with flour and being boiled, whereas the same amount of flavoring would do much more for the dish if it were added to the sauce. But these colorful pastas do look attractive on the plate and are becoming more and more popular and increasingly available at fine stores and restaurants. They make possible some interesting combinations, even when just a few simple ingredients are added. I like to toss curry or cumin pasta, for example, with a little butter, small cooked cauliflowerets and coarsely chopped cilantro leaves, for a quick lunch. Chili pasta is wonderful with smoked chicken or turkey, diced tomatoes and a little butter or olive oil.

BASIC PASTA SIDE DISHES
There are many pasta side dishes throughout the book but in this chapter you will find a few of the simplest ones that are suitable for almost any shape of pasta. Here you will find the quickest and easiest "sauces" for pasta—olive oil, softened butter and heated cream—as well as tomato sauce.

When you are trying a new type of pasta, especially a flavored one, you can simply toss it with butter or fine olive oil, salt and pepper. All pasta is delicious like this and its flavor comes through. An endless variety of ingredients can be added to the basic recipes: fresh herbs, grated cheese, sautéed garlic, vegetables, seafood and meats.

TOMATO SAUCES AND STOCKS
Tomato sauces are the most popular sauces for pasta. They can be light or rich, smooth or chunky, delicate or robust.

Stocks add depth of flavor to the sauces for many pasta dishes and can make the difference between an acceptable sauce and a delicious one. Although it is easy to buy canned or frozen stocks, the taste of homemade stock is much better. Stocks are economical to make. They can simmer virtually unattended and thus involve little work, and they keep well in the freezer.

Basic Egg Pasta

This dough is used for making noodles of all sizes and for stuffed pastas, page 118. Pasta made with semolina flour has a brighter yellow color than pasta made with regular flour.

1½ cups all-purpose flour, preferably unbleached	**2 teaspoons vegetable oil or olive oil**
2 large eggs	**1 to 5 teaspoons water, if needed**
¼ teaspoon salt	**Additional flour, if needed**

To make dough in food processor: Combine all-purpose flour, eggs, salt and oil in food processor fitted with the metal blade. Process until ingredients are well blended and dough just holds together in sticky crumbs that can be easily pressed together, about 10 seconds. If dough is dry, sprinkle in enough water, about 1 teaspoon at a time, processing about 5 seconds after each addition, until it is moist. Press dough together to a ball. Transfer to a work surface and knead a few seconds until it is a fairly smooth ball, flouring lightly if dough sticks to surface.

To make dough by hand: Mound flour on work surface or in a large bowl. Make a well in center. Add eggs, salt and oil to well; blend with a fork. Gradually draw flour from inner edge of well into center, first with fork, then with your fingers, until all flour is incorporated. Add water by teaspoons if flour cannot be incorporated; dough will be very stiff and dry but will soften during kneading as moisture becomes more evenly distributed. Clean your hands. Knead dough on a clean work surface about 5 minutes or until fairly smooth and pliable, flouring only if dough is sticky.

Wrap dough in plastic wrap; or set it on a plate and cover with an inverted bowl. Let stand 30 minutes if it was made in a food processor or 1 hour if it was made by hand. (Dough can be kept up to 4 hours in refrigerator; let stand about 30 minutes to come back to room temperature before using.)

Prepare a pasta rack; or generously flour 2 or 3 trays or baking sheets. Turn smooth rollers of a pasta machine to widest setting. Cut pasta dough in 4 pieces; leave 3 pieces wrapped or covered. Flatten 1 piece of dough in about a 4-inch square and lightly flour it. Run through rollers of machine at widest setting. Fold from each end so ends just meet in center, press seams together and flatten again slightly. Run dough through rollers again. Repeat folding and rolling, lightly flouring only when necessary to prevent it from sticking, until smooth and velvety, about 7 more times. Turn dial of pasta machine 1 notch to adjust to next narrower setting. Without folding piece of dough, run it through machine. Continue to

If using a food processor, process flour mixture until well blended and dough just holds together in sticky crumbs that can be easily pressed together; this takes about 10 seconds.

Press dough together into a ball. Transfer to a work surface and knead for a few seconds until it is a fairly smooth ball, flouring lightly if dough sticks to surface.

Flatten 1 piece of rested dough in about a 4-inch square and lightly flour it. Run through rollers of pasta machine at widest setting. Fold from each end so ends just meet in center, press seams together and flatten again slightly. Run dough through rollers again.

feed dough through rollers without folding, turning dial 1 notch lower each time; dust with flour as necessary and cut dough in half crosswise if it gets too long to handle. Stop when dough is ¹⁄₁₆ inch thick (generally this is on next to narrowest setting of machine).

Hang dough sheet to dry on a pasta rack or on the back of a towel-lined chair. Repeat with remaining pieces of dough. If preparing bow ties, shape them (see page 180). For noodles of any width, dry dough sheets about 10 minutes or until they are firmer and have a leathery texture but not until they are brittle; if brittle they will fall apart when cut.

Cut pasta dough as desired (see page 180). Let noodles dry on pasta rack or on floured tray or baking sheet. Dry short pasta shapes on trays or baking sheets. Dry pasta at least 10 minutes, if using immediately, or up to several hours. If noodles are on tray or baking sheet, gently toss occasionally to prevent sticking. (Pasta can be refrigerated, covered loosely, on tray; or can be gently put in plastic bags. It will keep up to 5 days in refrigerator; it can also be frozen.)

Makes about 9 or 10 ounces fresh pasta.

VARIATIONS

For 12 ounces pasta dough, use 3 eggs, 2¼ cups flour, ½ teaspoon salt and 1 tablespoon oil. For about 1 pound pasta, double ingredients of basic recipe.

Basic Egg Pasta with Semolina Flour: Substitute 1½ cups very finely ground semolina flour for all-purpose flour. Make dough in food processor, adding 1 tablespoon water along with other ingredients. Process until mixture forms a ball, gradually adding more water if dough is dry. Continue with directions for Basic Egg Pasta. Do not use this dough for pasta that requires rolling to the narrowest setting because the dough may tear.

Tips for Making Fresh Pasta

- Hold the dough straight while running it through the pasta machine, especially when it becomes thin. Catch the dough as soon as it comes out and drape it over your hand so it will not stick together. Handle the dough carefully when it becomes thin; it tears easily.
- Do not feed the dough into the pasta machine too fast; do not pull on it, or it may stretch and tear.
- To keep homemade pasta longer, you can let it dry on baking sheets until it is quite brittle, then gently put it in plastic bags and refrigerate. Weight of pasta decreases as it dries.

Repeat folding and rolling, lightly flouring only when necessary to prevent dough from sticking, until smooth and velvety, about 7 more times. Continue rolling and adjusting machine settings according to recipe instructions. Dry dough sheets.

To cut medium noodles or fettuccine, move handle of pasta machine to wider noodle setting and put each sheet of dough through machine. Let noodles dry on a pasta rack or over the back of a chair. Herb, tomato, curry and spinach pasta dough are seen here.

A pasta pot fitted with a drainer is useful for cooking pasta.

179

Medium Noodles or Fettuccine

Move handle of pasta machine to wider noodle setting. Put each sheet of dough through machine, holding it with 1 hand and catching pasta with other hand. If strands stick together while being cut, dough is too wet; dry remaining dough sheets a little longer before cutting them. Separate strands.

Thin Noodles or Tagliarini, Tagliolini

Move handle of machine to narrow noodle setting. Proceed as for fettuccine.

Wide Ribbons or Pappardelle

After drying dough sheets, place 1 sheet of dough on a lightly floured work surface. Using a knife or fluted pastry wheel, cut dough in strips slightly over ½ inch wide. Continue with remaining sheets.

Bow Ties, Butterflies or Farfalle

Make dough sheet; do not dry. Using fluted pastry wheel, trim uneven edges all around dough sheet. With fluted wheel, cut dough in 2" x 1½" rectangles. Bring the 2 long sides of each rectangle together in center, folding in 4 lengthwise to make a lengthwise crease in center. Pinch tightly to seal in bow-tie or butterfly shapes.

FLAVORED PASTA DOUGH

The use of flavored pasta doughs in restaurant and home cooking has proved to be one of the most exciting culinary developments of recent years for pasta lovers.

The chart on page 183 will give you suggestions for mixing and matching complementary flavors and recipes.

PASTA FLAVORED WITH VEGETABLES, CITRUS FRUIT AND SEAFOOD

Vegetables are added to pasta dough mainly for color, but the color of vegetable pasta is a pastel version of the original vegetable color. The color of the dough becomes paler when cooked. Beet pasta dough, for example, is purple but the cooked noodles are pink; they should be served simply, with butter, page 184, or with garlic oil, page 185, so the color of the pasta shows well. These pasta doughs, especially those containing vegetable puree, often need to be floured more than usual during rolling because they tend to be sticky.

Black pasta is made with squid ink, which can now be purchased in small packages that each contain about ½ teaspoon. Although they are expensive, they are easy to use. The pasta comes out midnight black and makes possible many beautiful dishes, such as Salmon & Black-Pasta Salad with Caviar, page 27.

During my most recent visit to Italy, a new type of fresh pasta caught my eye at the fresh-pasta shops—smoked-salmon pasta. This pasta has a delicate salmon color and good flavor. A simple way to serve it is to toss the cooked pasta with 2 or 3 tablespoons butter, then to sprinkle each serving with diced smoked salmon or lox and, for a finishing touch, add a dollop of sour cream and sprinkle it with chives.

The following recipes use the quantities given in Basic Egg Pasta, page 178.

Spinach Pasta Made with Fresh Spinach

Use only 1 egg. Remove stems of 8 ounces fresh spinach and rinse leaves well. Cook uncovered in a medium saucepan of boiling salted water to generously cover over high heat about 2 minutes or until wilted. Rinse until cool and squeeze dry. Puree in food processor. Add egg and process until blended. Add remaining ingredients and proceed as in Basic Egg Pasta, page 178.

Spinach Pasta Made with Frozen Spinach

Use only 1 egg. Cook 1 (10-ounce) package frozen leaf spinach uncovered in a medium saucepan of boiling salted water over high heat about 3 minutes or until thawed. Rinse until cool and squeeze dry. Puree in food processor. Measure puree; return ½ cup to processor. Add egg and process until blended. Add remaining ingredients and proceed as in Basic Egg Pasta, page 178.

Beet Pasta

Use only 1 egg. Preheat oven to 375F (190C). Rinse 8 ounces small or medium beets and trim roots and tops, leaving beets whole and skin intact. Wrap beets tightly in foil and put in a heavy shallow baking dish. Bake about 1 hour for small beets or 1¼ hours for medium ones or until tender when pierced with a knife. Remove skins. Transfer beets to food processor and puree. Measure puree; return ⅓ cup to processor. Add egg and process until blended. Add remaining ingredients and proceed as in Basic Egg Pasta, page 178. This dough tends to be wet; if extra flour is needed, remove dough from processor and lightly knead in flour by hand. Cut dough in 6 pieces before rolling out and flour it often during rolling.

If you would like additional beets for salad, bake an extra 8 ounces together with beets above.

Carrot Pasta

Use only 1 egg. Peel and thinly slice 6 ounces carrots (about 1⅓ cups slices). Cook carrots in a medium saucepan of boiling salted water to cover over medium heat about 10 minutes or until very tender. Drain well and puree as fine as possible in food processor. Return puree to saucepan and cook over medium heat, stirring constantly, to dry puree as much as possible without scorching, about 3 minutes. Measure puree; return ½ cup to processor. Add egg and process until blended. Add remaining ingredients and proceed as in Basic Egg Pasta, page 178.

Tomato Pasta

Use only 1 egg. Process ⅓ cup tomato paste with egg until blended. Add remaining ingredients and proceed as in Basic Egg Pasta, page 178. When rolling and cutting noodles, flour generously because dough tends to be sticky.

Tri-Colored Pasta

Use equal amounts Basic Egg Pasta, Spinach Pasta and Tomato Pasta.

Lemon Pasta

Instead of 2 eggs, use 1 egg and 1 egg yolk. Process with 2 tablespoons strained fresh lemon juice and 3 tablespoons finely grated lemon zest. Add remaining ingredients and proceed as in Basic Egg Pasta, page 178.

Orange Pasta

Use only 1 egg. Process egg with ¼ cup thawed frozen orange-juice concentrate and 3 tablespoons finely grated orange zest (from about 4 small oranges). Add remaining ingredients and proceed as in Basic Egg Pasta, page 178. If any more liquid is needed to moisten dough, use orange juice instead of water.

Note: For 12 to 15 ounces Orange Pasta (needed for Roast-Duck Salad with Orange Fettuccine, page 24), use 2 eggs, ¼ cup plus 1 teaspoon orange-juice concentrate, ¼ cup finely grated orange zest, 2¼ cups flour, ½ teaspoon salt and 1 tablespoon oil. Divide dough in 6 portions before rolling.

Black Pasta

Use only 1 egg. Omit salt. Mix about 2 tablespoons squid ink (from 9 (4-gram) packages) with ¼ cup water. Combine squid ink mixture with remaining ingredients and proceed as in Basic Egg Pasta, page 178. Omit step of kneading by hand; instead put dough in a plastic bag and press to a ball.

Smoked-Salmon Pasta

Use only 1 egg. Omit salt. Finely chop 4 ounces smoked salmon or lox in food processor. Add remaining ingredients and proceed as in Basic Egg Pasta, page 178.

PASTA FLAVORED WITH HERBS AND SPICES

Herb pastas have a subtle herb flavor and a color ranging from pale green to olive green, depending on the herb used. I have made pasta with large amounts of fresh basil leaves but the fresh taste is lost; I find that dried basil works better. Although cilantro is an assertive herb, the taste of cilantro pasta is delicate. Garlic pasta, on the other hand, has plenty of flavor.

Saffron pasta has a light-yellow color flecked with saffron strands and a subtle flavor. Chili and curry pastas are both flavorful and colorful.

For whole-wheat pasta it is possible to use all whole-wheat flour if more egg or liquid is added, but a dough made with equal parts all-purpose and whole-wheat flours still has good whole-wheat flavor and is much easier to handle. Even people who try to use mainly whole-wheat flour in their cooking usually mix it with white flour for pasta.

The following recipes use the quantities given in Basic Egg Pasta, page 178.

Herb Pasta

Mince ½ cup small parsley sprigs in food processor. Add eggs, salt, 2 teaspoons dried rosemary, 1 tablespoon *each* dried leaf thyme, dried leaf basil and dried leaf oregano and process until well blended. Add remaining ingredients and proceed as in Basic Egg Pasta, page 178.

Basil Pasta

Add ¼ cup dried leaf basil to dough along with flour. Add remaining ingredients and proceed as in Basic Egg Pasta, page 178.

Chili Pasta

Peel 4 medium garlic cloves and mince in food processor. Add 1 tablespoon ground cumin, ½ teaspoon red (cayenne) pepper, 1 tablespoon plus 1 teaspoon paprika, 1 tablespoon dried leaf oregano, eggs and salt and process until blended and garlic is minced finely. Add remaining ingredients and proceed as in Basic Egg Pasta, page 178.

Cilantro Pasta

Measure 2 cups medium-packed cilantro (fresh coriander) leaves. Rinse and dry well. Chop cilantro briefly in food processor. Add remaining ingredients and proceed as in Basic Egg Pasta, page 178.

Cocoa Pasta

Reduce flour to 1⅓ cups. Mix 3 tablespoons unsweetened cocoa with flour. Add remaining ingredients and proceed as in Basic Egg Pasta, page 178.

Cumin Pasta

Add 4 teaspoons ground cumin to processor along with eggs. Add remaining ingredients and proceed as in Basic Egg Pasta, page 178.

Curry Pasta

Combine eggs with 1 tablespoon ground cumin, 2 teaspoons ground turmeric, 1 teaspoon ground ginger, ½ teaspoon red (cayenne) pepper and 2 teaspoons ground coriander in food processor; process to blend. Add remaining ingredients and proceed as in Basic Egg Pasta, page 178.

Garlic Pasta

Peel 6 medium garlic cloves and mince in food processor. Add eggs and salt and process until blended and garlic is minced finely. Add remaining ingredients and proceed as in Basic Egg Pasta, page 178.

Saffron Pasta

Omit oil. Put ½ teaspoon slightly crushed saffron threads in a small cup. Add 1½ teaspoons hot water and let stand 20 minutes to soften. Put in food processor and puree with eggs. Add remaining ingredients and proceed as in Basic Egg Pasta, page 178.

Whole-Wheat Pasta

Replace flour in Basic Egg Pasta, page 178, by ¾ cup whole-wheat flour mixed with ¾ cup all-purpose flour.

Guide to Using Flavored Pastas

All flavored pastas can be tossed with olive oil or soft butter to make quick, simple dishes or used as the basis for more elaborate preparations. Following are ideas for ingredients to combine with or serve alongside flavored pasta. The flavored pastas in this chart are either available commercially, or, when there is an asterisk, a recipe for making them is found in the book. If you come across a flavored pasta that does not appear here, follow the suggestions for the pasta that is closest in flavor, color and character.

Pasta Flavor	Good with	Suggested Recipe
beet*	seafood, meat, poultry, salads	Goat Cheese, Spinach & Whole-Wheat Pasta Salad
bell pepper	poultry, meat, vegetables	Tomato Noodles with Chicken & 40 Cloves of Garlic
carrot*	meat, poultry	Linguine with Steak & Double-Mushroom Madeira Sauce
confetti, tri-color*	seafood, meat, poultry, salads	Vermicelli with Veal & Lemon Sauce
mushroom, wild mushroom	veal, poultry, mushrooms	Green & White Fettuccine with Veal, Spinach & Morel Sauce
spinach-nutmeg	vegetables, cheese	Fettuccine Alfredo with Vegetable Julienne
tomato-basil	poultry, seafood, vegetables	Tomato Fettuccine with Sole Fillets & Lemon Butter
black* (squid ink or olive)	seafood, vegetables	Black Pasta with Crab Newburg Sauce
lobster, seafood	seafood	Lobster & Angel-Hair Pasta Salad with Fines Herbes
seaweed	seafood, vegetables	Vermicelli with Mediterranean Sea-Bass Sauce
smoked salmon*	fresh or smoked seafood	Salmon & Black-Pasta Salad with Caviar
basil*	seafood, poultry, cheese, vegetables	Creamy Fettuccine with Porcini, Prosciutto & Peas
Cajun	seafood, poultry, meats, sausages, vegetables	Shrimp with Chili Pasta
chili*	seafood, poultry, meat, vegetables	Chili Pasta with Smoked Turkey
cilantro*	seafood, poultry, meat, vegetables	Chili-Topped Spaghetti
cocoa*	poultry, desserts	Spicy Southwestern Turkey with Cocoa Pasta
cumin*	poultry, meat, sausages	Tri-Colored Pasta-Pepper Medley with Chicken
curry*	seafood, poultry, meat, vegetables	Fettuccine with Creamy Clam Sauce
garlic*, garlic-parsley	vegetables, mushrooms, seafood	Spaghettini with Japanese Eggplant & Sweet Peppers
herb*	seafood, poultry, mushrooms, vegetables	Herb Fettuccine with Wild Mushrooms
lemon*	seafood, poultry, vegetables	Linguine with Shrimp Scampi & Broccoli
orange*	poultry, desserts	Roast-Duck Salad with Orange Fettuccine
saffron*	seafood, poultry, veal	Scallops with Saffron Butter Sauce on a Bed of Pasta
tarragon-chives	seafood, poultry	Shrimp & Spinach-Fettuccine Salad with Tarragon
whole-wheat*	vegetables, cheese	Linguine with Broccoli, Sun-Dried Tomatoes & Pecorino Cheese

To find suggested recipes, see index.

BASIC PASTA SIDE DISHES

The following recipes explain how to flavor pasta in the most basic and quickest ways. It can be simply tossed with butter, as in Buttered Pasta, gently heated with cream, as in Pasta à la Crème, enriched with a flavored olive oil, as in Pasta with Garlic Oil, or moistened with one of the many types of tomato sauce. All these recipes contain a small number of ingredients.

Buttered Pasta

This is probably the simplest pasta recipe yet one of the best, especially for sampling fresh and fine-quality, dried, flavored pastas that may have a subtle taste. Olive oil, either plain or extra virgin, and flavored oils such as herb oil, can be substituted for the butter. The amount of oil or butter to use depends on how rich a dish you would like. Serve this pasta with any fish, meat or poultry.

9 to 10 ounces fresh fettuccine, noodles or other pasta shapes of any flavor, homemade, page 178, or packaged, or 8 ounces dried
3 to 6 tablespoons butter, room temperature

Salt and freshly ground pepper to taste
2 tablespoons chopped fresh parsley leaves or other fresh herbs, if desired

Bring a large pot of water to a boil; add salt, then pasta. Cook uncovered over high heat, separating strands occasionally with a fork, 30 seconds to 2 minutes for fresh fettuccine or 2 to 5 minutes for dried or until tender but firm to the bite. Drain well. Transfer to a heated serving bowl or return to pot. Add butter and toss thoroughly but gently. Season with salt and pepper. Add parsley or herbs if desired, and toss again. Serve immediately on heated plates.
Makes 4 side-dish servings.

Pasta à la Crème

This recipe involves a somewhat unusual technique that is popular in France: the pasta is cooked slightly less than usual, then finishes cooking in the cream, so it absorbs plenty of cream and has a very rich flavor. Freshly grated nutmeg complements the delicate taste. This is good with subtly flavored main courses.

8 ounces dried noodles, spaghetti, macaroni, linguine, vermicelli or fettuccine
¾ cup whipping cream or crème fraîche

2 tablespoons butter
Freshly grated nutmeg to taste
Salt and freshly ground pepper to taste
Bowl of freshly grated Parmesan cheese (for serving), if desired

Bring a large pot of water to a boil; add salt, then pasta. Cook uncovered over high heat, separating strands occasionally with a fork, until nearly tender but still very firm to the bite; it should be slightly underdone. Drain well.
Bring cream to a simmer in a sauté pan or deep skillet. Add pasta and cook over medium heat, tossing, until cream is absorbed. Remove from heat and add butter, nutmeg, salt and pepper. Toss until butter is absorbed. Taste and adjust seasoning. Serve immediately on heated plates. Serve with Parmesan cheese, if desired.
Makes 4 side-dish servings.

Pasta with Garlic Oil

This pasta is served as a first course or late-night snack in Italy. In America it would be served as a simple side dish to accompany roast chicken or beef. The garlic is cooked gently in oil until the oil absorbs its flavor, so it is subtle. Some people use chopped garlic, but I like the delicate flavor achieved this way.

8 large garlic cloves, peeled
6 tablespoons olive oil
1 or 2 dried hot red peppers, if desired
Salt and freshly ground pepper to taste

8 ounces dried linguine, perciatelli (long macaroni), spaghetti or vermicelli
3 tablespoons chopped fresh parsley leaves

Crush garlic cloves but keep whole so they can be removed from oil. Heat oil, garlic, hot peppers, if desired, and a pinch of salt in a very small saucepan over low heat. Cook, stirring often and pressing occasionally on garlic, about 12 minutes or until garlic is deep golden brown. Keep warm over very low heat.

Bring a large pot of water to a boil; add salt, then pasta. Cook uncovered over high heat, separating strands occasionally with a fork, 6 to 9 minutes or until tender but firm to the bite. Drain well. Transfer to a heated serving bowl.

Remove garlic from oil and discard; reserve hot peppers. Pour oil over pasta and toss. Add parsley, salt and ground pepper; toss. Garnish with hot peppers, if desired.
Makes 4 side-dish servings.

Pasta with Fresh Tomato Sauce & Cheese

This is probably the most frequently prepared pasta dish. It is good with all shapes of pasta and with many flavored pastas, especially garlic pasta and herb pasta. Parmesan is the most popular cheese for the dish but a variety of other cheeses are good too, from the assertive pecorino-romano, plain romano, asiago, provolone, Gruyère, Swiss, Greek kefalotiri, ricotta salata and sharp cheddar to mild cheeses like mozzarella and Monterey Jack.

2 cups Fresh Tomato Sauce, page 186
8 ounces dried linguine, spaghetti, noodles, fettuccine, tagliarini, or herb, basil or garlic pasta or 9 to 10 ounces fresh
1 to 2 tablespoons olive oil, preferably extra virgin, or soft butter, if desired
2 tablespoons minced fresh herbs (parsley, basil, chives, tarragon or cilantro), if desired

½ cup freshly grated Parmesan or kefalotiri cheese, or ¼ cup pecorino-romano, or ⅓ cup mixed grated Parmesan and romano, or ¾ cup grated Gruyère or Swiss cheese
Salt and freshly ground pepper to taste
Bowl of grated cheese (for serving)

Heat Fresh Tomato Sauce in a medium saucepan; keep warm over low heat.

Bring a large pot of water to a boil; add salt, then pasta. Cook uncovered over high heat, separating strands occasionally with a fork, 30 seconds to 2 minutes for fresh or 2 to 8 minutes for dried, depending on shape, or until tender but firm to the bite. Drain well. Transfer to a large heated serving bowl.

Toss with oil or butter if desired, then with 1⅓ cups sauce, herbs if desired, cheese, salt and pepper. Taste and adjust seasoning. Serve remaining sauce and more cheese separately.
Makes 4 first-course or side-dish servings.

Pasta with Tomato-Cream Sauce

This delicate sauce is also wonderful with tortellini, ravioli and other stuffed pastas.

2 cups Fresh Tomato Sauce, below
1 cup whipping cream
1 to 2 teaspoons tomato paste
Salt and freshly ground pepper to taste
9 to 10 ounces fresh basil, cilantro, herb or egg fettuccine, homemade, pages 182 or 178, or packaged, or 8 ounces dried fettuccine, linguine, vermicelli or medium shells

1 or 2 tablespoons butter, room temperature
2 to 3 tablespoons chopped fresh basil, cilantro (fresh coriander) or parsley leaves, if desired

Bring Fresh Tomato Sauce to a boil in a medium saucepan over medium heat. Whisk in cream and bring to a boil, stirring with whisk. Simmer over medium heat about 5 minutes or until slightly thickened. Strain sauce through a fine strainer set over a small saucepan, pressing on sauce with the back of a spoon to extract all of liquid and scraping puree from underside of strainer with a rubber spatula. Reheat sauce. Whisk in tomato paste. Add salt and pepper.

Bring a large pot of water to a boil; add salt, then pasta. Cook uncovered over high heat, stirring occasionally, 30 seconds to 2 minutes for fresh or 2 to 8 minutes for dried, depending on shape, or until tender but firm to the bite. Drain well. Transfer to a large heated serving bowl. Reheat sauce just to a simmer. Add enough sauce to pasta to moisten, and toss. Add butter and herbs, if desired. Taste and adjust seasoning. Serve any remaining sauce separately.

Makes 4 first-course or side-dish servings.

TOMATO SAUCES & BASIC STOCKS

Flavorful tomato sauces and stocks are the building blocks of good pasta sauces. Tomatoes have a unique ability to cook into a sauce that is naturally thick and of the perfect consistency for tossing with pasta. Fresh Tomato Sauce is wonderful on its own, or as part of other sauces. It can be flavored with many different herbs, as in the variations opposite, or with cream, as in Pasta with Tomato-Cream Sauce, above.

Stocks, also called broths, are basically soups that take advantage of the flavors in bones and meats. During cooking, they gradually turn the water into a tasty liquid and thicken it so the stock adds taste and body to any sauce or soup in which it is used.

Fresh Tomato Sauce

This is sometimes called "marinara sauce" in America as well as in southern Italy, although in other parts of Italy *marinara* refers to a seafood sauce. Any ripe tomatoes can be used. I prefer plum tomatoes; they are often the ripest and least expensive type and have the most pulp to give good body to the sauce. This is a slightly chunky sauce, but it can be pureed into a smooth one.

3 tablespoons olive oil, vegetable oil or butter
½ cup minced onion
2 medium garlic cloves, minced
2 pounds ripe tomatoes, preferably plum tomatoes, peeled, seeded, finely chopped

1½ teaspoons fresh thyme leaves or ½ teaspoon dried leaf, crumbled
1 bay leaf
Salt and freshly ground pepper to taste

Heat oil or butter in a large heavy skillet over medium-low heat. Add onion and cook, stirring, until very soft but not browned, about 10 minutes. Add garlic and cook 30 seconds.

Add tomatoes, thyme, bay leaf, salt and pepper. Bring to a boil. Cook uncovered over medium-high heat, stirring often, 10 to 15 minutes or until tomatoes are very soft and sauce is fairly thick; reduce heat if necessary as sauce begins to thicken because it burns easily. Discard bay leaf. Taste and adjust seasoning. (Sauce can be kept, covered, up to 3 days in refrigerator; or it can be frozen.)
Makes about 2 cups.

Note: For recipes that call for 3 cups sauce, follow recipe opposite but use ⅔ cup minced onion, 3 to 3¼ pounds tomatoes and a little more garlic and thyme, if desired. Tomatoes will require about 20 minutes to cook.

Tomato Sauce with Herbs: Add 1 tablespoon chopped fresh rosemary to sauce at same time as garlic. Or stir one of the following herbs into finished sauce:
2 to 3 tablespoons chopped fresh parsley leaves
3 to 4 tablespoons chopped fresh basil leaves
3 to 4 tablespoons chopped fresh tarragon leaves
3 to 4 tablespoons chopped fresh oregano leaves
2 tablespoons chopped cilantro (fresh coriander) leaves
Tomato Sauce Made with Canned Tomatoes: Substitute 2 (28-ounce) cans whole plum tomatoes for fresh tomatoes. Drain in a strainer. Cook as above, using a wooden spoon to crush and break tomatoes in little pieces as they cook.
Smooth Tomato Sauce: For a relatively smooth thick sauce, that flows instead of being chunky, puree finished sauce in a food processor.

Large-Quantity Fresh Tomato Sauce

When tomatoes are inexpensive and at their peak, make this sauce and freeze it in 1- or 2-cup quantities. Its flavor is like that of Fresh Tomato Sauce, opposite. Because of the large quantity, the tomatoes are not spread out as much in the pan and their cooking time is longer.

¼ cup olive oil, vegetable oil or butter
1 large onion, minced
6 to 8 garlic cloves, minced
8 pounds ripe tomatoes, peeled, seeded, finely chopped
2 teaspoons dried leaf thyme, crumbled
1 bay leaf
Salt and freshly ground pepper to taste

Heat oil or butter in a heavy 4- to 5-quart casserole over medium heat. Add onion and cook 10 minutes or until soft but not brown. Add garlic and cook 30 seconds. Add tomatoes, thyme, bay leaf, salt and pepper. Bring to a boil. Cook uncovered over high heat, stirring often, 10 minutes. Reduce heat to medium. Cook 45 minutes or until thick. Discard bay leaf. Taste and adjust seasoning. (Sauce can be kept, covered, up to 3 days in refrigerator; or it can be frozen.)
Makes about 7 cups.

Chicken Stock

With the addition of a little salt, this makes a delicious chicken soup.

3 pounds chicken wings, or a mixture of wings, backs, necks and giblets (except livers)
2 onions, quartered
2 carrots, quartered
2 bay leaves
12 parsley stems
10 black peppercorns
About 4 quarts water
2 fresh thyme sprigs or ½ teaspoon dried leaf, crumbled

Combine chicken, onions, carrots, bay leaves, parsley and peppercorns in a stock pot or other large pot. Add enough water to cover ingredients. Bring to a boil, skimming foam. Add thyme. Reduce heat to low so stock bubbles very gently. Partially cover and cook 3 hours, skimming foam and fat occasionally. Strain stock into large bowls. If not using immediately, cool to lukewarm. Refrigerate until cold and skim solidified fat off top. (Stock can be kept 3 days in refrigerator; or it can be frozen.)
Makes about 2½ quarts.

Beef Stock

This stock adds a good meaty flavor to sauces and soups.

4 to 5 pounds meaty beef soup bones, chopped in pieces by butcher if possible
2 onions, rinsed but not peeled, root end cut off, quartered
2 carrots, scrubbed but not peeled, quartered crosswise
2 celery stalks, cut in 3-inch pieces

2 bay leaves
12 parsley stems
3 large garlic cloves, unpeeled
10 black peppercorns
$3^1/2$ to $4^1/2$ quarts water
2 fresh thyme sprigs or $^1/2$ teaspoon dried leaf, crumbled

Preheat oven to 450F (230C). Roast bones in a large roasting pan in oven, turning them over once, about 30 minutes or until they begin to brown. Add onions and carrots. Roast about 30 minutes or until browned.

With a slotted metal spatula, transfer bones and vegetables to a stockpot or other large pot. Add celery, bay leaves, parsley, garlic, peppercorns and enough water to cover ingredients. Bring to a boil, skimming foam. Add thyme.

Partially cover and cook over very low heat, so stock bubbles very gently, skimming foam and fat occasionally. During first 2 hours of cooking, add hot water occasionally, if necessary, to keep ingredients covered. Cook stock for total of 6 hours. Strain stock. Skim off fat if using stock immediately; or cool stock, refrigerate until cold and skim solidified fat off top. (Stock can be kept 3 days in refrigerator; or it can be frozen.)
Makes $1^1/2$ to 2 quarts.

VARIATION
Brown Veal Stock: Substitute veal bones, preferably knuckle bones, for beef bones.

Fish Stock

This is the quickest of stocks, requiring only twenty minutes of simmering.

2 pounds fish bones, tails and heads, or $1^1/2$ pounds fish pieces for chowder
1 tablespoon butter
1 medium onion, sliced

2 quarts water
1 bay leaf
12 parsley stems
2 fresh thyme sprigs or $^1/2$ teaspoon dried leaf, crumbled

Put fish bones or pieces in a sieve in the sink. Let cold water run over bones 5 minutes.

Melt butter in a stockpot or large saucepan over low heat. Add onion and cook, stirring often, about 7 minutes or until softened. Add fish bones or pieces, water, bay leaf and parsley. Bring to a boil, skimming foam. Add thyme. Simmer uncovered over medium-low heat, skimming occasionally, 20 minutes.

Strain through a fine strainer into a large bowl. If not using immediately, cool to lukewarm. Refrigerate or freeze. (Stock can be kept 2 days in refrigerator; or it can be frozen.)
Makes about 1½ quarts.

INDEX

Metric Chart

Fahrenheit to Celsius

F	C
200—205	95
220—225	105
245—250	120
275	135
300—305	150
325—330	165
345—350	175
370—375	190
400—405	205
425—430	220
445—450	230
470—475	245
500	260

Comparison to Metric Measure

When You Know	Symbol	Multiply By	To Find	Symbol
teaspoons	tsp	5.0	milliliters	ml
tablespoons	tbsp	15.0	milliliters	ml
fluid ounces	fl. oz.	30.0	milliliters	ml
cups	c	0.24	liters	l
pints	pt.	0.47	liters	l

When You Know	Symbol	Multiply By	To Find	Symbol
quarts	qt.	0.95	liters	l
ounces	oz.	28.0	grams	g
pounds	lb.	0.45	kilograms	kg
Fahrenheit	F	5/9 (after subtracting 32)	Celsius	C

Liquid Measure to Liters

1/4 cup	=	0.06 liters
1/2 cup	=	0.12 liters
3/4 cup	=	0.18 liters
1 cup	=	0.24 liters
1-1/4 cups	=	0.3 liters
1-1/2 cups	=	0.36 liters
2 cups	=	0.48 liters
2-1/2 cups	=	0.6 liters
3 cups	=	0.72 liters
3-1/2 cups	=	0.84 liters
4 cups	=	0.96 liters
4-1/2 cups	=	1.08 liters
5 cups	=	1.2 liters
5-1/2 cups	=	1.32 liters

Liquid Measure to Milliliters

1/4 teaspoon	=	1.25 milliliters	1-1/2 teaspoons	=	7.5 milliliters
1/2 teaspoon	=	2.5 milliliters	1-3/4 teaspoons	=	8.75 milliliters
3/4 teaspoon	=	3.75 milliliters	2 teaspoons	=	10.0 milliliters
1 teaspoon	=	5.0 milliliters	1 tablespoon	=	15.0 milliliters
1-1/4 teaspoons	=	6.25 milliliters	2 tablespoons	=	30.0 milliliters